# EMPIRE OF WORDS

# EMPIRE OF WORDS

## THE REIGN OF THE OED

*John Willinsky*

PRINCETON UNIVERSITY PRESS    PRINCETON, NEW JERSEY

Copyright © 1994 by Princeton University Press
Published by Princeton University Press, 41 William Street,
Princeton, New Jersey 08540
In the United Kingdom: Princeton University Press,
Chichester, West Sussex
All Rights Reserved

*Library of Congress Cataloging-in-Publication Data*
Willinsky, John, 1950–
Empire of words : the reign of the OED / John Willinsky.
p.   cm.
Includes bibliographical references and index.
ISBN 0-691-03719-1 (CL)
1. Oxford English dictionary.
2. English language—Lexicography.
3. English language—Etymology.
I. Title.
PE1617.094W55   1994
423′.028—dc20   94-11247

This book has been composed in Sabon

Princeton University Press books are printed
on acid-free paper and meet the guidelines
for permanence and durability of the Committee
on Production Guidelines for Book Longevity
of the Council on Library Resources

Printed in the United States of America

1   3   5   7   9   10   8   6   4   2

# Contents

_____ *Preface and Acknowledgments* _____

THIS BOOK began, if books can be said to have known beginnings, with a simple question that was occasionally asked in my years as a schoolteacher, when my students and I would turn to the dictionary for information on origins and nuances, for linguistic authority and language games: Where exactly did the meanings in these word-books come from? The work that follows, as it addresses that question specifically in the case of the Oxford English Dictionary, is my way of repaying the hours these students spent with me in good faith; I trust I have a better answer for them now than I did then.

The result of this inquiry into the origins of meaning in the OED is perhaps best prefaced by two statements made during the final stages of the work, one broadcast publicly to the world and the other spoken to me at my desk. In the first, Queen Elizabeth was given to reflect, at the end of a particularly difficult year for the British crown, on the vulnerability of great institutions: "No institution—city, monarchy, whatever—should expect to be free from the scrutiny of those who give it their loyalty and support, not to mention those who don't. But we are all part of the same fabric of our national society, and that scrutiny, by one part or another, can be just as effective if it is made with a touch of gentleness, good humor, and understanding." A week after the queen's pronouncement, Arron, my youngest son, taking the full measure of my struggles over this book, asked me, "The dictionary is kind of a last resort, don't you think?" There seems to be just the right play of meaning in both comments to qualify them as ideal citations for opening this extended analysis of the OED.

As a second prefatory point to this project, I wish to acknowledge those who have greatly contributed over the years to its development and to my pleasure in working on it. Without listing the particular forms of their support and assistance—for they know well enough the parts they played in this project, if not the full extent of my appreciation for their help—I want to express my gratitude to Andrea Allingham, Donna Lee Berg, Tim Bray, Sylvia Brendel, Robert Brown, Alice Calaprice, Peter Chin, Oliva Dela Cruz, Allan Garshowitz, Robert Graham, Jack Gray, Jim Greenlaw, Rienhard Hartmann, Anne Hawson, William Hunter, Pamela Johnson, Linda Jones, Sidney Landau, Ranjini Mendis, Margareet Moerland, Thomas Paikeday, Darrel Raymond, Roger Simon, John Simpson, Tim Snider, Sara Tulloch, Edmund Weiner, and Pamela Willinsky. I am also indebted to both Oxford University Press and the

Centre for the New Oxford English Dictionary at the University of Waterloo for graciously facilitating the research that has gone into this project. Finally, I am happy to note that this work was made possible by the generous support of the Social Sciences and Humanities Research Council of Canada and the University of British Columbia.

# Abbreviations

CWW  *Caught in the Web of Words: James Murray and the Oxford English Dictionary* by Elisabeth Murray (New Haven: Yale University Press), 1977

OED  *The Oxford English Dictionary*, 1st ed., 10 vols., edited by James A. H. Murray, Henry Bradley, W. A. Craigie, and C. T. Onions (Oxford: Oxford University Press), 1933; 2d ed., 20 vols., prepared by John Simpson and Edmund Weiner, 1989

TLS  *The Times Literary Supplement*, 1917–

TPS  *Transactions of the Philological Society* (London: Trübner), 1854–; *Proceedings of the Philological Society* (London: George Bell), 1842–1853

# EMPIRE OF WORDS

--------------------- CHAPTER 1 ---------------------

# Introduction

IN JANUARY of 1884, the Clarendon Press at Oxford proudly offered the
public a new and rather unusual serial magazine. The first issue consisted
of an alphabetical listing of roughly seven thousand English words, beginning with *a* and ending with *antyteme*, with each word followed by a
definition and by supporting citations from a wide range of literature.
The serial was entitled *A New English Dictionary on Historical Principles; Founded Mainly on the Materials Collected by the Philological
Society*. The title page noted that the work was "Edited by James A. H.
Murray, LL.D., President of the Philological Society, with the Assistance
of Many Scholars and Men of Science." The paperbound fascicles of this
new dictionary then appeared at irregular intervals, anywhere from one
to seven times a year (with bound volumes of the fascicles published every
few years). It was only in 1928, forty-four years after the first fascicle was
issued, that the most patient students of the language were able to purchase the 125th and final number of this initially serialized dictionary. A
complete, twelve-volume edition of the work was published in 1933, at
which point it was renamed the *Oxford English Dictionary*, giving rise to
the familiar acronym *OED*. The first complete edition included a "Supplement," largely of words that had been missed over the long course of
serialization. This was followed by a little more than two decades of in-
activity in the editing of the *OED*, after which the Press went to work on
a full-scale supplement that eventually ran to four volumes, issued between 1972 and 1986 under the direction of Robert Burchfield. In 1989,
through the use of advanced computer technology, Oxford University
Press merged all of the earlier texts and, adding a small number of new
words and meanings, published a second edition of the dictionary in
twenty volumes. This dictionary represents well over a century of editorial activity committed to assembling what the Press rightly claims is
"the most authoritative and comprehensive dictionary of English in the
world."[1]

The aspect of this history that I explore in this book is the selection of
citations and the particular contribution of that process to the comprehensive authority of the *OED*. Decades before that first fascicle appeared,
the Philological Society of London, which initiated the project, began to
invite its members, as well as the public at large, to gather citation slips

for every word in the English language by tapping its enormous published resources. The slips were no more than "a half-sheet of notepaper" on which readers copied a quotation that illustrated the use of a given word, along with details of the quotation's precise location in the work, as well as when and in what edition it was published. The Society's various appeals for quotations during the latter half of the nineteenth century resulted in an amazing collection of over five million citation slips. The resulting *OED* includes a third of these citations which serve to authorize this dictionary's definitions. By attending to who and what the citations represent, I am proposing, we can better understand the sources of linguistic authority that have, from Victorian to modern times, given shape to the English language in this particular form.

As orderly and ordinary a procedure as this editorial process sounds, in the course of this study I have found that the citations in the *OED* often misbehave. They can very easily testify against the dictionary's definition, thereby disturbing the very resolution of meaning that is at the heart of the dictionary. They can make apparent how skewed the dictionary's coverage of the language is. They can leave one wondering how it is that words and meanings have moved across great periods of time. Citations, it turns out, raise as many questions as they are supposed to settle about the basis of authority and the determination of sense. A ready instance of this citational equivocation is found in the relevant sense of *cite* from the *OED*:

> cite, *v.*
> 3. To quote (a passage, book, or author); gen. with implication of adducing as an authority.
> 1535 JOYE *Apol. Tindale* (Arb.) II As Rabbi Kimhy cyted of Bucere vpon that same vearse taketh Judicium. 1576 FLEMING *Panoplie Ep.* 47 This verse cited by Cicero, is not to bee founde in Euripides. 1596 SHAKS. *Merch. V.* I. iii. 99 The diuell can cite Scripture for his purpose. 1611 BIBLE *Transl. Pref.* 3 Wee omit to cite to the same effect S. Cyrill. 1728 POPE *Dunc.* I. 1 *note*, I cite the whole three verses. 1856 EMERSON *Eng. Traits, Lit. Wks.* (Bohn) II. 105, I could cite from the seventeenth century sentences and phrases of edge not to be matched in the nineteenth. 1867 FREEMAN *Norm. Conq.* I. App. 757 The authority cited for the statement.

To review the guiding principles of an *OED* entry, we can say that, according to the best efforts of the readers for the dictionary, *cite* was first used in this authoritative sense by George Joye on page 11 of his 1535 pamphlet, *An Apology Made To Satisfy, If It May Be, William Tindale*, as edited by Edward Arber ("Arb.") in 1883. Working from the last remaining copy of the pamphlet, Arber republished Joye's work, as part of a Victorian revival of interest in old English texts that fed the results of its

selective recovery of the past into the record of the new English dictionary. Further emphasizing the partial history of the language available for
citation is the fact that in 1546, the authorities had ordered that Joye's
works be burned. Although copies, or at least a copy, of his work obviously escaped, that would not always have been the case with such not-
infrequent orders. Further to the point, Joye's polemic is about the questionable reliability of what turned out to be, centuries later, frequently
cited material in the *OED*. Joye takes issue with William Tindale (also
spelled Tyndale), whose translation of the New Testament Joye indemni-
fies: "So shal he translate it falsely corruppe the text and bringe the reder
in to no small errour." While Tindale's supposedly false translations, as
they act as an influence on the language, are thus worthy of citation, Joye
has introduced the word *cite* in the act of calling the process into question. Tindale's contested Bible is the source of some 2,000 citations in the
*OED*, not to count its substantial contribution to the very well cited King
James Bible. But then Tindale lost his life over the controversy in 1536, as
yet another reminder of how textual authority forms an important and
often troubled chapter in English history. The citations for *cite* that follow Joye suggest that, in truth, not only do rabbis and devils, Cicero and
Emerson, cite for their own purposes, but that they are, in turn, cited in
a circulation of meanings on which this book seeks to throw some light.

In what follows, I consider this immense project's place in the construction of a usable past, a selective tradition, that is by all means made
up of the literary heritage of Shakespeare and the Bible, but is filled out
with broad representation from the British book trade and working press,
running from Grub Street and Drury Lane to Fleet Street. The first edition
of the *OED*, in its particular patterns of favored and neglected sources,
represents Victorian interests in the integration of theology and science,
nation and empire. Here was the culmination of a cultural investment in
the worth of the book, an emerging middle class's privileging of the art
and commerce of print. The authority of the citation grows out of the
impact of this new technology on Renaissance and Reformation Europe.
"By the incomprehensible prouidence of Almightie God," Walter Haddon wrote in a sixteenth-century attack on Catholicism, "the worthy Arte
of Emprintyng was erected, by meanes whereof good Letters and Bookes
came to Marte: and Printers shoppes discouered the soggy and darkened
cloudes of this olde motheaten barbarousnes" (cited by Jones, 1953,
p. 32). Print, the public broadcasting system of Protestantism, capitalism, and the middle class, lent itself to the creation of a standard for governing public discourse. Biblical translations and vernacular dictionaries
were but two instruments that promulgated this textual realm, both of
which were to become, I would note, best-selling works for Oxford University Press. Samuel Johnson and his sponsoring booksellers had met the

call for an ordering of the language in the eighteenth century, and the *OED* was to bring the project through the Victorian era and into the twentieth century, seeking once again a commercially viable, rather than court-appointed, authority over the English language. What began life as *A New English Dictionary* in 1884 was to testify at every turn to the merits of not only the language's rich vocabulary, but through its citations the wealth of prose, poetry, narrative, and exposition of those who, for the most part, lived by working the language. It was part of that particularly English claim on science and civilization, merit and accomplishment, that would take its proud stand amid what Haddon identifies as the "barbarousnes" of the world.

This book deals with somewhat more than a century's worth of editorial work on the *OED*. I examine the process of selecting citations over this period of time not only out of historical interest in the who-and-what of English publishing, but as the *OED* continues to reflect and shape our understanding of the language. It may seem all too obvious that the language's great dictionary would, in finding warrant for its words and definitions, have little choice but to consult the published record of the language. For that reason, it is worthwhile considering how the *OED* might have otherwise authorized its definitions. The citations might, for example, have been restricted to sizable excerpts from the "best writers" of literary and sacred works, as in, for the most part, Johnson's *Dictionary*. The citations might have been confined to those expository texts in which the language can be said to be more prosaically at work, as the editors at Merriam-Webster have been known to insist (Willinsky, 1988a). In yet other variations on this authorization scheme, *The Dictionary of American Regional English* relies on the living memory of native speakers to bring to life older senses and expressions of the nation's language, while the *American Heritage Dictionary* deploys panels of notables to advise its readers of preferred usage and meaning. Finally, there have been guides to the language that have located the true meaning of words solely through the etymology of their origins, such as John Tooke's *Diversions of Purley* from the end of the eighteenth century.

The members of the Philological Society, however, decided to put the entirety of their faith in the printed record of the language, relying upon, in effect, the great imaginary library often thought to encompass, as it inscribes, the English character. Their dictionary was to be written, in the first instance, by the nation's writers. It meant assembling the works of poets, playwrights, historians, essayists, journalists, sermonizers, translators, editors, diarists, pamphleteers, and letter-writers, as if these word-workers had for a thousand years been engaged in the common project of giving meaning and form to this one language. It is the editorial process of culling citation, and the language it constructs with the writer at its center, that I wish to consider in some detail in this book, beginning, by way of completing this introduction to the project, with a book review and a computer.

I

On the publication of the third volume of *A Supplement to the Oxford English Dictionary* in 1982, Roy Harris, a professor of linguistics at Oxford at the time, wrote a long and critical review of the work for *The Times Literary Supplement*. As one might expect, bad notices are a relatively rare event in the life of this dictionary. Harris does not hesitate to take exception to the entire project for what he terms a "black and white lexicography" that perpetuates "that eminently Victorian ideal" of a staid literary standard (1982, p. 935). While Harris allows that James Murray, as principal editor of the first edition, possessed a liberal concept of the English language, he feels it was lost to the process of producing the dictionary: "Like all British radical initiatives, however, Murray's lexicography succumbed to compromise and Establishment assimilation" (ibid.). A number of Harris's criticisms—such as the dictionary's privileging of literary writers and its shortcomings in "founding an impartial descriptive 'science' of words"—are further substantiated in the course of this book. Yet Harris concludes his review with a recommendation that misses the accomplishment of the dictionary, by suggesting that "a serious start must be made on treating the recording of English vocabulary as part of the systematic structures of communication in modern society" (p. 936). I think it can be argued that whatever its gaps and inconsistencies, at the very least, the *OED* represents more than "a serious start . . . on treating the English vocabulary as part of the systematic structures of communication." This dictionary finds a good part of its authority in grounding its definitions in those brief citations drawn from the history it has constructed of the published language. More than that, I think it fair to say that this dictionary's substantial record of the language has played a formative role in the systematic structuring of communication. The *OED*, after all, does more than provide a catalog of some 300,000 English words. It defines the scope of the English language, attesting to both its historical reach and global currency; it establishes the possibility of fixed points of meaning, definite senses, located in the publishing activity of a number of writers. Through its use of supporting quotations for each entry, this dictionary defines who has given this language shape and meaning, then and now.

Roy Harris's critical review of this national enterprise, as you might imagine, did not go without challenge. A rebuttal by Robert Burchfield, editor of the *Supplement*, appeared in the next issue of the *TLS* taking issue with this Oxford don's effrontery in attacking the dictionary. Burchfield launched his counterassault on two fronts, the first dismissing the "chilly semi-scientific works of professors of linguistics" who have generally ignored the *OED*, and the second noting that Harris "nowhere in his two *TLS* pages gives an inkling of what kind of work his substitute for a dictionary would be" (1982, p. 1233).[2] That my sometimes critical book perpetuates both of Burchfield's complaints should, I think, be understood from the outset. My work does not represent the fully scientific use of the dictionary by a professor of linguistics. My academic background, rather, is in the study of educational practices and institutions, especially as these entail the teaching of language, literacy, and literature. Out of these interests, I have been drawn to question what this authoritative dictionary has made of the English language, discovering in the process that the details of its making invoke a number of relevant educational issues in the history of writing, nation, and empire. That both Samuel Johnson and James Murray began their careers in schoolrooms, rather than in the academic study of language, may be worth noting in thinking about the import of English lexicography, and certainly the academic tensions to which Burchfield is alluding will be revisited below.

On the critic's failure to propose a substitute for the criticized dictionary, I, too, fall short. While I do consider areas of underrepresentation in citation and the introduction of new technologies in covering the language, my primary concern is not with describing how the *OED* might have been or should be. I do not presume anything more than to advocate that readers turn to the dictionary with a greater awareness of the *OED*'s citation program, and that editors continue to show an openness toward new sources and about the limitations of the existing program. This final point seems especially important in light of Oxford University Press promotional materials that, in referring to how "the language continues to develop throughout the world, so the English of today is truly international," insist that "the *Oxford English Dictionary* records all these influences minutely."[3] We need a far more realistic and accurate sense of the dictionary's limitations and its opportunities for improving its systematic, if not minute, coverage of the language.

In concluding his rebuttal of Harris's critique, Burchfield laments modern scholarship's lack of stature, stating that, at best, professors of linguistics might end up building a "barn" for language compared to "the castle of *OED*, *kraut geweorc* (the work of giants) as the Anglo-Saxons would have called it" (1982, p. 1233). There is something apt to this image of a neogothic, archly Victorian fortress, but something anachronistic about it as well, as if it were a relic imitating an age of imitations, bolstered with modern additions meant to blend with the original. In contrast to most surviving castles, the dictionary is largely serving its original purpose; it is practical and functional, assisting readers and writers on a daily basis while defending the glory of the language. And as to whether it was built by giants or built out of giants—and Burchfield is typically more modest about his work—it does seem to reflect the work of diligent and devoted people who knew the value of perseverance and delighted in attention to detail.

As one might imagine, Burchfield was not alone in leaping to the defense of the *OED*, after Harris's review in the *TLS*. Among the other letters was one from John Chandos that spells out the gratefully acknowledged authority which this dictionary brings to the language: "What is important is that 'ordinary people' (meaning most of us) shall have the opportunity of learning from the practice and example of educated teachers the meaning of words they use and the nature of the language they have inherited. Then the changes they may project will be wrought from a state of competence and not of insufficiency" (1982, p. 1010). The spirit which Chandos evokes, of a dictionary guiding ordinary people to the language of their educated teachers, has remained intact since the project's inception among the membership of the Philological Society of London in 1857. This faith in the inheritance of a disciplined language can be felt in the uncritical reliance on reference works such as the *OED*. Chandos's letter suggests the authoritative role a dictionary plays in people's understanding of language, with all that implies for their thinking about schooling and public discourse in general. If there is a philosophical distinction to be made on behalf of the dictionary between being *an* authority and being *in* authority, it is thoroughly collapsed through the commonsense acquiescence *to* the authority of the *OED*, as represented by Chandos's letter. I am proposing that this widespread faith in this dictionary of dictionaries deserves to be informed by a better grasp of who has been called upon to authorize and underwrite the definition of the language in the first instance.

II

My efforts at uncovering how the English language has been imagined and assembled for this dictionary have been made possible by recent developments in what computers can do with texts. Since 1984, *The Oxford English Dictionary* has been the particular focus of research on "text-dominated databases," leading to a number of breakthroughs in the ability of machines to manipulate the extremely complex and "dynamic" body of this dictionary (Tompa and Raymond, 1989). During this time, teams of lexicographers and computer scientists from Oxford University Press, IBM, and the University of Waterloo joined forces to design and build a database that could properly house both the mass and intricate structure of this dictionary. The roughly $1.7 million database-development project was located at the University of Waterloo Centre for the New Oxford English Dictionary in Canada, while the entire text of the *OED* was rendered "machine-readable" by International Computaprint Corporation at two locations in the United States. With the electronic text of both the first edition and the *Supplement* housed within the newly developed database, the dictionary was capable of being opened to inquiry in a way that no book had been before. For Oxford University Press, it made possible the electronic integration of all of the text that had been published from 1884 to 1986 in a second edition of the *OED*. It also created the conditions for a continual updating and revising of the dictionary without physically having to reset the text in type; and it prepared the way for the marketing of an electronic version of the dictionary for use on personal computers. For reader and researcher, the computerized version of the *OED* means that one can gather detailed information on the development of the English language, as represented in the dictionary, while, at the same time, one could also critically examine the making of the dictionary itself. This second option proved the starting point for my book.

In assembling an electronic version of the *OED*, each of the elements of the dictionary entry, from sense to citation, was flagged so that the dictionary that was accessible alphabetically by headword could now be organized by authors cited, date of first citation, language of origin, and any combination thereof. This means one can search all instances of a given author or a series of leading book titles in the dictionary; one can also work with specific periods of word origins, or certain sets of authors, or a single poem or language of origin, and from there the possibilities multiply. Given Burchfield's concern that linguists were not using the riches represented by the *OED*, the electronic version of the dictionary offers researchers the opportunity to make large definitive gains on, for example, earlier studies such as Otto Jespersen's *Growth and Structure of the English Language*, which is still widely used in university courses nearly ninety years after its original publication. Where Jespersen had lightly sampled the dictionary in approaching a number of historical questions about the English language, it is now possible to conduct exhaustive measures on topics that Jespersen raised, such as the period of greatest influx of French loan words (1251–1400) after the Norman invasion (1982, p. 87).

But electronic access to this dictionary also invites queries about the historical formation of the dictionary itself, questions about the writers and works selected by the editors of the *OED* to constitute the history of the language. This second course, of looking at the dictionary rather than through it to the language itself, was the one I followed, like Alice through the computer screen, behind which lay the superstructure of the dictionary as it had developed between 1858 and 1989 (see table 1.1 in the Appendix). In the course of developing a computerized version of the dictionary, leading up to the production of the second edition in 1989, Oxford University Press and the University of Waterloo allowed me access to the citations and entries that defined four aspects in the history of this dictionary:

1. The first edition of the *OED*, with the first volume appearing in 1888 and ending with the tenth and final volume of the dictionary published in 1928.

2. *A Supplement to the Oxford English Dictionary*, issued in four volumes between 1972 and 1986 and incorporating the earlier "Supplement" that had been appended to the *OED* in 1933.

3. The five thousand items assembled between 1984 and 1988 for addition to the second edition of the dictionary.

4. The second edition, itself, published in 1989, integrating the earlier supplements with the original dictionary.

The specific periods of time covered by the Press's reading program have altered considerably over the years, beginning with the considerable goal of covering six centuries of published work in the language, while more recent times have been concerned with the language of the last few decades. Comparisons between Victorian and current practices also need to be tempered in light of the great difference between the 1.8 million citations involved in the first edition and 15,000 citations that support the 5,000 new items that were added to the second edition. And yet common to the different editorial periods under examination is the combination of a systematic reading program directed by the editors, the consultation of supporting reference words, and the unsolicited submissions of interested readers and language hounds. This analysis of the *OED*'s documentation reveals not only a consistently mixed record of creative and prosaic elements, but also areas of less-than-adequate coverage, most notably of women, Commonwealth, and working-class writers from all levels of literate activity otherwise covered by the citations. The *OED* will always represent something of the times in which it is being edited, as it absorbs common concerns about the state of the language. The century's worth of figures for who and what have been most heavily cited, forming the *data*, in turn, for this book, reveal both constants of intertextual regard and a shift among cultural centers, from the literary to the journalistic, from the humanities to the sciences, from Great Britain to the United States.

The delegates of Oxford University Press who watched the work on the first edition of the dictionary stretch over six decades must have asked themselves many times if such a dictionary were not as doomed as the various proposals for an English-language academy had been. They saw their investment in the project gradually rise to £300,000, in the face of sales which for the initial parts of the dictionary did little better than 4,000 copies (CWW, p. 252). It must have seemed both a project and a language that was better left to find its own way in the world. However, the delegates' long-standing faith in this work and its schoolmaster editor, down from the border country by way of London, was destined, after this shaky start, to reward the Press here on earth. Today, the Oxford family of dictionaries, made up of close to 150 titles with the OED at its head, enjoys worldwide sales of five million books a year.[4] It is the largest employer of lexicographers in the language, with "over 80 inhouse authors working on dictionaries," dictionaries that extend from English, through dozens of specialized disciplines, to sixty-five foreign languages (Shenker, 1989, p. 86). This aspect of the Oxford University Press's hold on the English language is felt around the globe, whether one looks at the fifty countries that currently form the Commonwealth of former British colonies, or the 28 percent of the world's 160 nations in which English is currently an official language (Mackey, 1991). But then, too, the OED has no less of a market in countries such as Japan. English does have a claim on the title of world language, although we must not mistakenly assume the extent of its universality. At this point, it is estimated that only 15 percent of the world's population use English on a regular basis. In many parts of the globe, it primarily serves commercial, professional, and administrative interests, giving a particular take to its title as a world language and a reminder of its colonial legacy (Bailey, 1991, p. vii).

Today, the current co-editor of the OED, Edmund Weiner, speaks of the Press's commitment to covering the complete common core of "all the major world Englishes"; he describes the vocabulary of English as "federated rather than centralized" (1990, p. 501). Given this expanded recognition of an imperial legacy that the Press must find ways of moving beyond, Weiner still calls for lexicographers to "do their job with sufficient thoroughness" in ways that do not prove any less discerning than the practices of their Victorian ancestors: "The vocabulary that receives immediate attention must be that which is perceived to have the greatest cultural 'importance'"(ibid.). There is no escaping the need for selection, for limiting by some process the extent of the language that comes to be defined as the English language. Weiner does observe a certain collapse of the boundary between spoken and published language—"any variety of English is permitted to appear in print"—which means that in many ways "the language is no longer prefiltered" for the lexicographer, as it was in James Murray's day (p. 496).

This study of the *OED* is concerned with tempering such idealizations, informing them in light of persistent and inevitable filtering processes, finding out the patterns of this dictionary's cultural interests and selective representation in its Victorian origins and its late twentieth-century manifestations. My principal concern is that, as we continue to consult this nineteenth-century artifact, we appreciate its editorial origins. This dictionary, in all of its magnificence, could reasonably be considered as the last powerful outreach of an imperial age; it is an icon of learnedness that continues to shape the modern understanding of the word on a global scale. We need to appreciate how the *OED* has fashioned the English language out of classical allusion and poetic metaphor, scientific discovery and scholarly research, while filling it out with the prose of a working press and publishing trade. Rather than seeing its inscription of the language fading with the passing of all things Victorian, the *OED* has found the means to expand its market and authority around the world long after the empire of its origins has deflated.

It is still easy to mistake what we find in the dictionary for the entirety of the English language, to imagine that the definitions provided in its pages are carefully lifted, via the citation, directly out of the language. To consider the idea is to realize that we know better, not only as print is only one code in the use of an English language that has a long history of authority and resistance, but as the print record of the *OED* forms its own record of the language's past and present. My aim with this book is not to spoil the pleasures of visiting this fascinating castle of the English language. It is meant to give greater pause over the work, over what has gone into the making of the most comprehensive dictionary of English in the world, so that *The Oxford English Dictionary* can reveal more of what it has made of the language, which in turn will leave its interested readers in a better position to play a substantial role, as they have since the beginning, in its evolution as the English language's great dictionary.

## CHAPTER 2

# At Trench's Suggestion,
# 1858–1878

"THE SCHEME originated," James Murray explains in the preface to the first fascicle of *A New English Dictionary*, "in a resolution of the Philological Society, passed in 1857, at the suggestion of the present Archbishop of Dublin (Dr. Trench)." While little else is said of the parenthetical Dr. Trench in Murray's 1884 introduction to this new dictionary, no one did more to set the project in motion than the dean of Westminster at the time. While readers now turn to the *OED* for an authority that is largely secular, scholarly, and institutional—Oxonian, in a word—Richard Chevenix Trench's philological interests were inspired by new levels of rigor in continental scholarship even as he was intent on doing God's work with the English language and nation. Trench first laid out the ideals of a scientific lexicography to which Murray would, beginning some two decades later, devote the remainder of his life, refining it and bringing it to fruition, if not entirely in the form that Trench had in mind. Taken together, their work represents its own form of a shifting authorization across the century's continuum of spiritual and scientific interests in language. The project was made possible in the first instance by Trench's vision of an English philology that through his learning could maintain distinct connections with these two poles. Out of his vision of a new English dictionary that would systematically capture the history and character of a people, the Society was eventually able to mobilize well over a thousand contributing readers in a project supervised by six senior editors over a period of seventy years.

When Richard Trench put forward his suggestion in 1857, he had belonged to the Philological Society for less than a year. He was fifty years of age and had established himself as that sort of Victorian cleric who was both scholar and poet, with a wide variety of books to his name. He had originally been, his biographer notes, the sort of retiring and learned churchman favored by the era, a "man of scholarly tastes and habits who was quite willing to serve for long periods in a country parish, perfecting his knowledge and engaging in literary pursuits" (Bromley, 1959, p. 133). But having proven his intellectual mettle from within this pastoral retreat, Trench decided to cut a more public figure by taking up the post of professor of theology at King's College, London, in 1847. Within a decade of moving to London, he assumed the deanship of Westminster and joined the Philological Society. He had begun to lecture on how God's word was inscribed in the moral tenor of the English language. Trench's passionate reconciliation of faith and philology, forming its own version of a natural theology, offered the Philological Society, attended in good part by clerics, a renewed source of faith in an age when many were setting science against religion. His well-publicized beliefs in the ability of the English language to serve as a sure moral guide, if approached through philology, may well have inspired not only the membership of the Society but that far larger group of readers who were to collect citations for this project with such dedication. However, his actual time with the Society was brief. Six years after first addressing the Philological Society, he moved on to the challenging archbishopric of Dublin. It proved to be the end of his published work on language, and he appears to have lost touch with the Philological Society and what was still in those early years the struggling project for which he provided a good deal more than just an initiating suggestion. He lived to see the first fascicle of *A New English Dictionary* published in 1884, dying two years later in London, where he was buried in the nave of Westminster Abbey.

The actual resolution Trench put before the Philological Society in 1857 called for a far more modest venture than the editing of an entirely new dictionary. It proposed "a Committee to collect unregistered words in English" which was to be composed of, as it turned out, Richard Trench, Herbert Coleridge, and Frederick Furnivall (*TPS*, 1857, p. 141). Its mission, in effect, was to sweep up overlooked bits of the lexicon for the publication of an addendum to existing dictionaries. However, it was destined for more than supplementary work, with each of the members coming to play a significant role in seeing the *OED* underway. While Trench inspired the work to come, Coleridge, grandson of the great poet, and Furnivall would both hold important editorial positions in the project.

As the committee began to consider just what had been left out of the language's great dictionaries, Trench found himself drawn into a critical reappraisal of the repeated failures of these works to provide a reliable guide to the language. He felt compelled to mount the first sustained and thorough critique of English lexicography, and out of this bold critique emerged a proposal for a new English dictionary on historical principles. For the November 1857 meeting, Dean Trench decided that instead of presenting to the Philological Society a list of words missing from the language's leading dictionaries, he would deliver part 1 of his paper, "On Some Deficiencies in our English Dictionaries" (*TPS*, 1857). By the next meeting and the conclusion of the lecture, it had become obvious to members of the Society that, given the systemic faults of English lexicography, it would not do to simply supplement what was already grossly inadequate.

The catalog of deficiencies which Trench presented to the Society cleared a wide swath for the Society to begin afresh on a new English dictionary that would, in effect, place the language on a firm philological footing. Trench explained to the membership, with numerous illustrations, that in at least six areas of philological concern (three of which touch on the importance of citations), English dictionaries often came up short: (1) existing dictionaries, as a rule, omitted obsolete words "necessary to enable the student to read his English classics with comfort and with profit"; (2) they failed to represent the full extent of word families, with "some members inserted, while others are omitted"; (3) they "do not always take sufficient care to mark the period of the rise of words, and, where they have set"; (4) they do not record "and illustrate by suitable quotations, the earlier uses which words have now left behind"; (5) they do not use "all the best and aptest passages which serve to distinguish a word from its synonyms"; and (6) they omit passages "by which might be usefully adduced in illustration of the first introduction, etymology, and meaning of words" (*TPS*, 1857, pp. 8–70). And, as if these shortcomings did not add up to a serious enough problem, Trench also felt that many English dictionaries were far too encyclopedic in their coverage of the language and in their definition of English vocabulary. His identification of these many failings spoke to a vision of a superior dictionary, broad in its historical reach and painstaking in its documentation of the history of meaning.

It is true that Trench's spirit of *marshal the facts* was fast becoming the touchstone of the scientific and enterprising age, but this was also a backward-looking project for the dean. "The Dictionary is an historical monument," Trench emphasized, "the history of a nation contemplated from one point of view" (p. 6). The dictionary is indeed a history of the language, as well as a commentary on the era of its editing. Trench envisioned the ideal dictionary telling of the English language's greatness. Among the instances of this greatness cited in his lecture, he pointed to the lack of success which the seventeenth-century philosopher Henry More had experienced in promoting the adoption into English of such Latinisms as *coaxation* and *mirificent* (pp. 6–7). Here, then, is the proud, untold history of an English, Trench declared in effect, judicious even in its classicism. At another point on this same theme, Trench recalls "a remark of [Samuel Taylor] Coleridge, that you might often learn more from the history of a word than from the history of a campaign; and this is true" (p. 44). So true, in fact, that one might well mistake the history of the language, as told by Trench, for a campaign to establish the place of English against earlier and current pretenders to the throne of the world's sovereign tongue—Latin, French, and German.[1]

As part of its celebration of a proud linguistic history, this scholarly dictionary of the English language was to eschew prescription that presumed to tamper with this development. Trench's faith in the core of truth that lies within each word meant that the dictionary should amount to no more than "an inventory of the language," with the lexicographer serving as "an historian of [the language], not a critic" (pp. 4, 5). Here was a faith in the fact that words spoke for themselves as witnesses to the history of the language. He remained adamant that a proper dictionary was no more than an inventory of the language, as opposed to a guide to proper usage, and he did not hesitate to belittle those who turn to the dictionary for that sort of assurance: "There is a constant confusion here in men's minds. There are many who conceive of a Dictionary as though it had this function, to be a standard of the language; and the pretensions to be this which the French *Dictionary of the Academy* sets up, may have helped on this confusion. It is nothing of the kind" (*TPS*, 1857, p. 5). It may seem odd to say that the dictionary is "nothing of the kind" when it comes to setting standards, for this not only misrepresents the necessarily selective processes of lexicography, but the freedom of readers to use a book as they see fit. Nor does this call of Trench's for an impartial and comprehensive inventory of the language, to be profusely illustrated with excerpts from English literature, really diminish the dictionary's claim on setting a standard for the language.

If his dictionary was not about to dictate good usage, it would *illustrate* such usage, with the historical and literary authority of the citation serving ostensibly as a proper and far more democratic foil to the forty dignitaries of the Academy across the channel. Following up on the national chauvinism of his remarks, Trench makes an appeal to British traditions of individual liberty that called for each Englishman to determine his own linguistic course: "Those who desire, are welcome to such a book: but for myself I will only say that I cannot understand how any writer with the smallest confidence in himself, the least measure of that vigour and vitality which would justify him in addressing his countrymen in written or spoken discourse at all, should consent in this matter to let one self-made dictator, or forty, determine for him what words he should use, and what he should forbear from using" (*TPS*, 1857, p. 5). This strongly assumed freedom of expression, as a right to address the nation, needs to be placed within the political context of mid-nineteenth-century Great Britain, especially as the dictionary can as easily serve those in need of rhetorical confidence as provide grounds for dismissing their language. The Stamp Act, which for many years had been directed at the publication of working-class newspapers, had only recently been repealed. Efforts for a universal right to vote, if only universally among *men*, were still being successfully resisted by the propertied classes, as was the fight for a state-supported education system. There were questions to be asked in those days about whose language, whose nation, whose right in addressing his countrymen? It might seem that Trench, in calling for linguistic liberty, was addressing an enfranchised and educated public. He was confident that the truth of the word will win out, with the writer in the lead and the philologist following close behind, with his assignment "to collect and arrange all the words, whether good or bad" (p. 5). It might seem that the dictionary was born of scholarship's happy association with English liberty. But that was not the whole of it for Trench.

Trench rejects the French model of linguistic dictatorship in favor of a representative and vigorous democracy, governed by the collecting and arranging of the lexicographer who attends to the enfranchised, that is, the published writer for the most part. There were, then, liberal and conservative elements to Trench's lexicographical vision. The language was constituted by those who used it, while the sense of *use* was restricted, with few exceptions, to published instances of the language. What was to be a scientific inventory, from Trench's point of view, described the exclusiveness, in effect, of a powerful print community of publishers, writers, and readers in Great Britain that was dominated by a rising middle class. The poignancy of this exclusiveness is found in the struggle of the industrial classes during the Victorian era to find a hearing for themselves. There were official commissions established by the government to examine aspects of what Disraeli and others described as a country taking the form of two nations. Trench's inventory of the written language did hold out the promise, however faint, of enabling all who could open this work to find the means of addressing their countrymen and women in what would be a common language. The dictionary could well contain instances of published language from every sector of society, especially as a working-class press began to emerge. The dictionary possesses a double function: reinforcing the house of language while opening the door that much wider to the public converse of the pen for all to consult, in principle if not in practice. The argument has always been that out of such liberties, opportunity arises.

But for all of the political implications of Trench's philology, his far more explicit interest, not surprisingly, was in striking an accord between philology and theology. Although his critique of English dictionaries is little concerned with his religious interests in language, by the time he joined the Philological Society his views on linguistic forms of divine intervention were well known. God had set, he declared in his popular lectures on the study of words, "such a seal of truth upon language, that men are continually uttering deeper things than they know" (1859, p. iv). The historical dictionary proposed by Trench would gently open that seal, exposing the deeper truth that lies within the unfolding history of the word. The deeper meaning that most interested Trench was the moral imperative that lay buried beneath the surface, a point he made especially clear in his lectures to the pupils of the Diocesan Training School, Winchester: "Seeing then that the language contains so faithful a record of the good and of the evil which in time past have been working in the minds and hearts of men, we shall not err, regarding it as a moral barometer, which indicates and permanently marks the rise or fall of a nation's life" (1856, p. 59). These popular lectures, first published in 1851 as *The Study of Words*, thundered against instances of "moral contagion" that could lead to such abuses as had been enacted against the word "religion" by the "Papal domination in Europe" (p. 12). On a gentler note, he pointed to Adam's naming of the animals as "the clearest intimation of the origin, at once divine and human, of speech; while yet neither is so brought forward as to exclude the other" (p. 17).[2] Philology served Trench, above all, in bringing forward "attestations for God's truth." He pointed out, as one of the primary examples, how "the word 'pain' . . . is derived from 'poena,' " which surely bore witness to the truth, "Pain *is* punishment; so does the word itself, no less than the conscience of every one that is suffering it, declare" (1856, p. 39). He then went on to point out that " 'plague' means properly and according to its derivation, 'blow,' or 'stroke' " (ibid.).

Trench's later thinking about the dictionary suggests how he saw this word-book carrying forward its own adamic task, its own "intimation of the origin, at once divine and human," for the English language. The biblical analogy, as the dictionary is the other text bearing, in effect, the seal of God, seems all the more appropriate, as Trench had earlier lent the weight of his scholarship to the revision of the New Testament.[3] His historical philology promised a further realization of a spiritual authorization for the English language through the Philological Society's dictionary. The word-histories that were finally assembled for *A New English Dictionary* did substantiate Trench's etymologies in many cases, as *pain* is derived from the Latin *poena* (penalty, punishment) and was used in this associated sense, with citations dating from 1279, but then this first sense of the term is marked "*Obs.*" (obsolete). That is, the dictionary that he inspired did not go out of its way to serve as a special witness "to God's truth, the fallings in of our words with his unchangeable word"; it did not mark the "true uses of the word" or "its abuses" (p. 39). The *OED* lends little support for a *return to* the origins of sense and meaning.

However, there is a distinction to be made, much to the dean's credit, between his classroom lessons in philology and what he called for in a proper historical dictionary. He did not insist on a dictionary explicitly devoted to pulling back the "flimsy veil of sentiment over sin," as he put it in *On the Study of Words*; he did not call for definitions that would point out such acts of linguistic malpractice as "calling a child out of wedlock a 'love-child' instead of a bastard" (p. 56). Nonetheless, the *OED* can be said to serve Trench with citational histories that form, if one wishes, a moral record of the good and evil of a people, "where they present themselves to us under the fewest disguises" (p. 59). As he called on the dictionary to represent "an inventory of the language," constructed by historians rather than by critics of the language, it would seem that Trench trusted history to speak for itself.

The "moral imperative" that the intellectual historian Hans Aarsleff (1988, p. 37) identifies as underlying Trench's quest for a complete record of the English language was vested in its potential as a foundational document on which to anchor his faith, to bolster his argument, and to serve generally as the guiding light that he and others could provide for the people during an era of troubled faiths. With something of the holiness that had once marked the monastic study of natural history, Trench came to propound a science of language that, in its capacity to provoke the wonder and truth of language, was a testimony to God and a warrant for empire. He brought to the project a moral and spiritual regard for language which he subordinated to the philological principles that had emerged out of classical scholarship. The part that Trench's particular meeting of theological and philological interests played in the devotion to the project experienced by a considerable number of people who volunteered their service for this project, I cannot say. At the very least, we might imagine that an accord between High Churchman Trench to Dissenter Murray on the level of the spiritual comfort and insight afforded by studying this divine instrument of language.[4] If the *OED* failed to support Trench's faith in the word, the dictionary still manages to provide for many readers a decided point of reverence for the language's accomplished history. If it did not fulfill Trench's sense of the moral benefits of returning to the roots of the language the full burden of his faith in the word, there remains for many a moral sensibility to this great dictionary's constitution of the English language out of a history of instances for, as Trench would have it, good and evil.

Although broadly focused, Trench's spiritual philological crusade was clearly directed at the century's great language debate set off by the materialist and amoral linguistic theory of John Horne Tooke. Aarsleff points out that Tooke had turned language away from God's seal, opening words instead to their earthly material origins, revealing the *thing*-edness in *thinking*, the *heaven* that is "some place, any place *heav*-en or *heav*-ed" (cited in Aarsleff, 1988, p. 40). Lexicographically, Tooke's rooting of words in their original and singular material sense was to inspire Charles Richardson's *A New Dictionary of the English Language,* first been published in 1836. Richardson's *Dictionary* featured the historical arrangement of citations, principally of a literary nature, that brought to light what he described as, after Tooke, the "one radical meaning" of each word.[5] None of this would do for Trench, and not simply because it was mostly bad philology. Such a godless end to language's mystery could not simply be supplemented by an additional word-list of overlooked items, as the Philological Society had originally planned. An entirely new English dictionary was necessary to put an end to this sort of materialism. As Aarsleff describes it, "This tampering with the moral barometer, was precisely what the new dictionary was designed to make impossible" (1988, p. 41). He goes on to speculate that Trench's "plan for the new dictionary was conceived and quickly advanced precisely to prevent Richardson's work from becoming what it called itself, 'a new dictionary'" (p. 42).

As a complement to the spiritual themes, Trench also placed the moral disposition of English in direct contrast to the decadence of "savage" tongues. He cites missionary reports from South Africa on the "loss" of any linguistic concept of the divine among local inhabitants, and the absence of "any word in the least corresponding to our 'thanks'" in "two of the principal tribes of Brazil" (1856, p. 20). His philology contributed to the careful positioning of the English language against the *otherness* of far-off jungle and savanna, an otherness that was created in the face of the increasing moral responsibility of sustaining a wide-ranging British imperialism. In this introductory lecture on language and thought, he concludes that "there is no such witness to the degradation of the savage as the brutal poverty of his language, so there is nothing that so effectually tends to keep him in the depths to which he has fallen" (p. 20). Trench was bringing to a wide and interested audience the racial and theological dimensions of the new sciences of philology and anthropology. His efforts to "remove the veil which custom and familiarity have thrown over" the English language were meant to incite his Winchester pupils, as well as his larger audience, to a greater Anglicization of the world: "There is nothing that will more help than will this to form an English heart in ourselves and in others. We could scarcely have a single lesson on the growth of our English tongue, we could scarcely follow up one of its significant words, without having unawares a lesson in English history as well, without not merely falling on some curious fact illustrative of our national life, but learning also how the great heart which is beating at the centre of that life was gradually shaped and molded" (1856, p. 27).

At work here are elements of what has been termed a "muscular Christianity." *On the Study of Words* has as its epigraph a line from the poet Coleridge that speaks all too well of a certain missionary zeal: "Language is the armoury of the human mind, and at once contains the trophies of its past, and the weapons of its future, conquests." Language, no less than other elements in English life, was brought to bear in Christianity's last great flowering on a global scale, in hand with English colonial expansion. It was the sort of talk that might equally inspire the missionary spirit among his pupils as well as, perhaps, the creation of a dictionary that established the vast, bottomless riches of the English language, that fortified the larger mission of transporting abroad the moral superiority of the English and their language. As English Bibles had been sent abroad by the boat-load, in editions that had benefited by Trench's biblical scholarship, the way was being prepared for a new English dictionary to follow. That Oxford University Press, principal publisher of the Authorized Version of the Bible, would see fit to acquire the Trench-inspired *OED* some two decades later only adds to this particular conjunction of corresponding texts in the cultural extensions of the empire (Howsam, 1991).

Years before turning his attention to the dictionary, Trench had supported the prophetic speculations of another Philological Society member, Thomas Watts, on the promise of English as a world language—"the world is circled by the accents of Shakespeare and Milton"—a concept whose day is now upon us as the legacy of imperialism and the future of multinationals. "At present the prospects of the English language," Watts claimed in an address to the Philological Society in 1850, "are the most splendid that the world has ever seen. It is spreading in each of the quarters of the globe by fashion, by emigration, and by conquest" (*TPS*, 1850, p. 212). To Watts's vision, Trench could not resist adding the hope that through such linguistic largesse, "the English Church . . . may yet in the providence of God have an important part to play for the reconciling of a divided Christendom" (cited in Aarsleff, 1983, p. 223). The intricate weave of missionary and linguistic zeal was part of the moral imperative carried in on the shoulders of British imperialism. An imperial frame of mind also allowed certain democratic elements to take root at home through, for example, competitive examinations that were introduced for positions in the Indian civil service in 1853 featuring a major section on English language and literature. Dr. Trench was sensitive to the expansive needs of his educated class in its desire to conquer the world's mysteries. His remarks on the deficiencies of English dictionaries spoke to a deeper urge in the British psyche for a record of the accomplishment of the English language.

On the home front, Trench's philology also had a way of fitting in with the struggle for national unity, addressing what Tony Crowley argues were prevailing "anxieties about the status of British scholarship [in relation to German and French accomplishments] in its study of the native language, combined with an increased sense of the 'patriotic' importance of such work" (1989, p. 37). A common language and unified vision was indeed an issue during a time when the industrial classes in England, for example, were increasingly making themselves heard in their fight for universal enfranchisement, a time in which talk was of a nation increasingly divided by social-class disparities. This project of creating a history of the English language, with citations running back to the heroic days of *Beowulf* and *The Pearl*, needs to be understood as one of many cultural contributions to state formation during this age. The period was busy with civic-minded gentlemen keen to assemble cultural cathedrals celebrating the British accomplishment.

In 1837, the year Queen Victoria ascended the throne, Sir Anthony Panizzi became Keeper of Printed Books at the British Museum, devoting his efforts to overcoming previous neglect of Great Britain's literary heritage: "This emphatically *British* library ought to be directed," Panizzi recommended, "most particularly to British works and to works relating to the British Empire, its religious, political and literary as well as scientific history, its laws, institutions, commerce, art, etc." (cited in Miller, 1973, p. 160). Panizzi assembled the makings of a great British library over the next two decades, by which point the Philological Society was prepared to undertake its awesome lexicographical project committed to putting on display, out of similarly scholarly, pedagogical, and ideological purposes, not only the finest artifacts of English culture in print, but the very history of the English language. In 1856, only a few years before the Philological Society began work on a *New English Dictionary*, Lord Stanhope was granted his long-held wish with the founding of a National Portrait Gallery, and its first acquisition, as if to emphasize its foreshadowing of the dictionary, was the "Chandos" portrait of William Shakespeare, donated by the earl of Ellesmere (Hake, 1932).

The governing proposition of this Victorian age, historian John Vincent has recently observed, "was that proper nation states had properly unified and continuous cultures" (1992, p. 7). In England's case, this unity is to be found, in Vincent's opinion, not only by the *OED* but also by the *Golden Treasury* assembled already in 1861 by Francis Turner Palgrave, "the Jewish founder of English pastoral nationalism"; Stopford Brooke's *Primer of English Literature*, "which sold 500,000 copies by 1916, corner[ing] the educational market, while leaving little doubt about English supremacy"; and Leslie Stephen's *Dictionary of National Biography*, "that triumph of muscular atheism" (ibid.). It does seem to affirm the point that all the oldest English traditions were invented in the last quarter of the nineteenth century, which Richard Shannon notes in his book on the crisis of British imperialism (1974, pp. 12–13).

The importance of history to fostering a sense of national identity was also stressed by John Stuart Mill, who in *Representative Government*, from 1861, points to the importance of language, religion, geography, and race, while allowing that "the strongest of all is identity of political antecedents; the possession of a national history, and consequent community of recollections; collective pride and humiliation, pleasure and regret, connected with the same incidents in the past" (1940, p. 360). As if to meet Mill's call, Thomas Macaulay, who had earlier succeeded in having English made the language of instruction in British India, completed his definitive four-volume *History of England* in that same year. Equally so, 1861 saw the distribution of a circular to Philological Society members containing a statement by Frederick Furnivall that did not miss the opportunity of capitalizing on this interest in building self-assuring monuments to the English race, even as he, ever the ardent democrat, tried to keep the language open to all:

> We have set ourselves to form a National Portrait Gallery, not only of the worthies, but of all the members, of the race of English words which is to form the dominant speech of the world. No winged messenger who bears to us the thoughts and aspirations, the weakness and littleness, of our forefathers; who is to carry ours to our descendants: is to be absent,—
>
> Fling our doors wide! all, all, not one, but all, must enter. (CWW, p. 137)

The dictionary that arose from Trench's suggestion took its place with these nation-building monuments, coming out virtually in tandem with *The Dictionary of National Biography*, which first began to appear in 1882. *A New English Dictionary* would do its part to establish the quality of the English people. The dictionary proposed a national language that reaffirmed all of those elements of culture, religion, geography, and race that had long figured in the thinking of the English, but had not been realized on such a scale in earlier periods. Here, then, was a record of Englishness, set out for display in the British Museum and National Gallery, *A New English Dictionary* and *The Dictionary of National Biography*, giving proof of an advanced and advancing civilization. Yet what had become increasingly apparent at the time was that the ideology of conquest and development had also to be carried on at home among the industrial classes living in their own urban colonies just outside the gates of the factories. The public museum movement seemed to grow with the British discovery of "cultures" and "artifacts" abroad that came with each extension of the Union Jack. The museum turned these exotic and occasionally pillaged objects, many of them bequeathed by the English aristocracy, into a public utility that promised to act as a civilizing force, an attractive alternative to the pervasive gin palaces. The Victoria and Albert Museum, which developed out of the Great Exhibition, was, as Donald Horne describes it, home to many hopes of the age: "These South Kensington buildings represent the voice of nineteenth century capitalism at its most enlightened, buoyant with optimism and reason and belief in improvement. Education, science, art and technology would bring light. Free enterprise would bring abundance to the world and this abundance facilitate eternal progress" (1984, pp. 121–122). These themes of education, science, art and technology were no less present in the minds of those who were to begin work on the Philological Society's dictionary later in that same decade of the 1850s.

Equally relevant to this lexicographical project and other nation-building measures was the gradual elevation of English language and literature. The English-language dictionary had begun as a hard-word glossary in the service of the nation's literature in Elizabethan times. Samuel Johnson had collected on the favor by drawing openly on the status of the best writers to warrant his definitions, while in the process promoting individual works by citation and affirming literature's central role in the language. Johnson's *Dictionary* was the first to suggest the possibilities of an English literary canon as its own source of authority, distinguishable from the prevailing Greek and Roman pantheon shared by all of Europe. A few years later, he began work on what became the *Lives of the Poets*, originally dispersed throughout a ten-volume collection of English literature. Its publication, in conjunction with Thomas Wharton's three-volume *History of English Poetry*, brought to the British marketplace the attractive notion of a national literary heritage. Lawrence Lipking has described how the works of Johnson and Wharton were happily met by an eighteenth-century reading public eager to bask in this "glorious national poetic pantheon . . . shaped by a need for a definition of the superiority of the national character" (1970, pp. 328–329).

By the 1830s, English literature was introduced at the University of London. The Reverend Thomas Dale, as professor of English language and literature at London, advised his students in those early days that, "when touching upon that glorious and inexhaustible subject, the LITERATURE of our country—I shall esteem it my duty—and I trust I shall find it my delight—to inculcate lessons of virtue through the medium of the masters of our language" (cited in Palmer, 1965, p. 20). So, too, was it with Trench. His wide-ranging investigations into etymology led him, he held, to the actual and authentic aspects of words as sources of meaning and thought at the very heart of the nation. Certainly, his lectures on the deficiencies of English dictionaries displayed prodigious learning. Aarsleff holds that he "deserves to be remembered for the truly Faradayan

saintliness he brought to the enterprise" (1983, p. 230). There was indeed
that mix of science, religion, and populism to the lectures, as Trench
dipped with seeming ease into the roots and far reaches of English vocabulary working from the obscurest reaches of the island's literature. This
was a science of the language that had little trouble singing the praises of
English as "a strong, an harmonious, a noble language" (1859, p. 8). Yet
it meant a special burden to be borne by Richard Trench and other like-
minded British citizens: "The case of national language I consider at all
times a sacred trust and a most important privilege of the higher orders of
society" (p. 9). The higher orders, as Trench was all too aware, had been
thoroughly imbued with the view that the sacred trust of learning was
kept to the noble realm of the classical languages. In allowing that "the
inestimable advantages mental and moral" afforded by the study of Latin
and Greek were reaching fewer students with the rise of education especially among the commercial classes, he offered the next best thing for
ensuring a well-wrought nation: "For that formation of discipline which
these languages would, better than any other have afforded . . . our own
language and literature will furnish the best substitutes" (p. iv). Trench's
new linguistic order was based on the recovered nobility of the English
language against, one might say, the decline of the English nobility. With
the passing of each Reform Bill during the nineteenth century, the British
middle classes, bolstered by a rising periodical press, advanced its political enfranchisement, its purchase on public discourse, and the nation as
a whole. It was only fitting that it equip itself with a great national dictionary testifying to its historical claim on language, culture, and nation,
as an encoding of its sacred trust.

Thus, when at Richard Trench's suggestion a proposal for a new dictionary was put before the Philological Society in 1857, both the Society
and the nation at large were ripe for a major undertaking. The Society
had formed in London in 1842 for "the investigation of the structure, the
Affinities and the History of Languages; and the Philological Illustration
of the Classical Writers of Greece and Rome." A good proportion of the
members were Oxbridge-educated and a number of them were dignitaries
in the Church of England. There were a few women members, although
for the most part they seem absent from the lists of officials of the Society.
In matters of language, the Society represented a gathering of amateur
and professional interests in language, committed to a modern scientific
approach to philology, that brought together lawyers, priests, professors,
and other interested parties (Aarsleff, 1983, p. 215). The Society paid
homage to the classics, while demonstrating an equally Romantic fond-
ness for the Saxon roots of the country's native language. It drew connections between the ancient civilizations and the language of their native
land. While the universities had a strong academic hold on the classical

languages, the study of English was a relatively unexplored territory. The Philological Society was, as James Murray later put it, "the only body in England then interesting itself in the language" (1970, p. 46).

At the Society's January 7, 1858, meeting, two months after Trench's lectures, it was resolved "that instead of the Supplement to the Standard English Dictionaries now in course of preparation by the order of the Society, a New English Dictionary should be prepared under the Authority of the Philological Society" (*TPS*, 1858, p. 198). The Supplement, assembled by Coleridge's 150 or so volunteers, was eventually published as *A Dictionary of the First or Oldest Words in the English Language*. But it was clear by this point that the membership of the Society had been moved by both Dean Trench's vision of a superior lexicography and, as had often been the case in matters philological in Great Britain, the German development of the great *Deutsches Wörterbuch*, the first volume of which the Grimm brothers had published in 1854. The following January, the Philological Society issued a "Proposal for the Publication of a New English Dictionary by the Philological Society" (*TPS*, 1857).

Given Trench's point that the project could no longer fall within the compass of one individual's lifetime of even the most devoted work, the new dictionary set out in the Society's proposal was to be based on a bold, but not unprecedented, call to the educated public to take hold of their heritage as freemen, that is, as writers and readers, and *write their own dictionary*: "We do but follow the example of the Grimms, when we call upon Englishmen to come forward and write their own Dictionary for themselves, and we trust that our invitation may be responded to still more effectually than theirs has been" (*TPS*, 1857, p. 8). This was a call to participate in the republic of words, a democratic appeal to the nation. The regulations pointed out that six hundred sheets of notepaper sold for 2*s.*, "thus admitting of the registration of 1200 words at a trifling expense" (p. 10). And large quantities were at issue. "The first requirement of every lexicon is," the Philological Society boldly proposed, "that it should contain *every word occurring in the literature of the language it professes to illustrate* (p. 2, original emphasis). This dictionary was to capture the very lettered soul of this proud nation preparing to define itself by its history, literature, and scientific spirit. The Society's proposal for a historical dictionary was "to show more clearly and fully than has hitherto been done, or even attempted, the development of the sense or various senses of each word" (*TPS*, 1857, p. 4).

Although turning to "the best writers" as a guide was already a commonplace among those who would direct others in their writing, the Philological Society was determined to improve on Johnson's idiosyncratic manners of citation. While Johnson rejected the pattern of the French Academy whose members had taken it upon themselves to create their own examples for their dictionary, he was following a continental tradition. Voltaire had complained that a dictionary without quotations was a skeleton, while French readers widely respected the renegade Academician Antoine Furetière's *Dictionnaire universal* of 1690, which was amply illustrated by French literature (Lyons, 1900, p. 182). In his *Plan* for the dictionary, Johnson had fearlessly raised the question of how one presumes to select these authorities who will dictate meaning. He cleverly deferred to the judgment of his presumed patron, Lord Chesterfield, by described himself "as the delegate of your Lordship" (Lyons, p. 137), while also crediting the selection previously undertaken by the revered poet, Alexander Pope: "It has been asked, on some occasions, who shall judge the judges? And since with regard to this design, a question may arise by what authority the authorities are selected, it is necessary to obviate it, by declaring that many of the writers whose testimonies will be alleged, were selected by Mr. Pope, of whom I may be justified in affirming, that were he still alive, solicitous as he was for the success of this work, he would not be displeased that I have undertaken it."[6]

By the time his *Dictionary* was published in 1755, Johnson had dispensed with his patron (a term he defined as "commonly a wretch who supports with insolence, and is paid with flattery") and fully thrown in his lot with the republic of letters. In the *Dictionary*, no less than over the course of his career, Johnson was to stand for the authority of the author in the marketplace, for those who wrote for a *living*, who proved their worth by wit and pen. In speaking to and for the "common reader," he was part of a new era in the published life of the language. Johnson claimed in the preface to have selected citations that represented "all that was pleasing or useful in *English* literature," while paying little mind to the historical development of meaning that was to so engage the Philological Society. In the actual editing of the *Dictionary*, Johnson took liberties with those citations that did not quite fit his purpose, liberties that the Philological Society, governed by the scientific spirit of a new age, did not think of allowing itself.[7] The *Dictionary*, richly arrayed with citations, also spoke for Johnson, a point that was not long in drawing critical comment from his contemporaries, such as Thomas Edwards, who declared it was "a vehicle for Jacobite and High-flying tenets by giving many examples from the party pamphlets of Swift, from South's Sermons and other authors in that way of thinking" (cited in DeMaria, 1989, p. 65). An editor's choice of citations is of lexicographical consequence.

Johnson's literary labors contributed to a new sense of modern nationhood in which the educated classes were happy to have English writers take charge of the language, with the freeborn William Shakespeare at their head, just as Shakespeare's histories had earlier celebrated the achievement of "the world's best garden" at the hand and sword of its kings. For Johnson, the authority of poetic genius was complemented by an equally compelling faith in an English liberty that resisted efforts to fix the language, to enclose it as the village commons had been enclosed. This tension between authority and liberty in the English language was posed by Johnson in terms of the question, "By what authority are the authorities selected?" It was enough to position the lexicographical project within the long, ongoing struggle for liberal democracy in a Great Britain that was asking much the same question on a somewhat more political front. More specifically, Robert DeMaria has described the democratic aspects of Johnson's *Dictionary* as both ideological (in bringing the timeless truths of English literature to the common reader) and material (in its signaling of the independence of writer and reader represented by the book in the marketplace) (1989, p. 72). But the essential point remains that, with language no less than with people, politics is principally a matter of representation. Johnson's *Dictionary* brought to the marketplace those English voices that he felt needed to be heard in the contest of spiritual and secular values, in the assertion of English nationhood. But once the authorities are selected and begin to assert themselves, there is this other side to the coin. The idea of a language "fixed by lexicographic authority" was something that Johnson, by the time he came to write the preface for his completed work, was not prepared to endorse. Yet this disavowal made little difference to the fact that his *Dictionary* was soon treated by many people as a stand-in for an English-language academy that admitted little dissent. Johnson's citations were meant to offer readers only an exemplary instance, rather than a permanent model. But readers will have their way with books.

Closer to the Philological Society's project in date and the use of citations was Charles Richardson's *New Dictionary of the English Language . . . Illustrated by Quotations from the Best Authors*, published in 1835–1836, which was the first English dictionary to turn the citations into a literary history of the lexicon, although with only 16,500 entries, compared to Johnson's 39,000, his dictionary failed to represent a substantial advancement in lexicography. The Society went a step further, in putting the emphasis on historical completeness, rather than literary merit, in its efforts to assemble quotations for "the epoch of the appearance of each word" (*TPS*, 1857, p. 4). The request was for readers to carry on a "careful analysis of the works of the principal writers, extracting all remarkable words, and all passages which contain definitions or explanations, or which, by reason of their intrinsic merit, are specially eligible as illustrative quotations" (p. 6). The proposal describes the "regulations" governing the general collecting of citations, from the dimensions and cost of paper for citations to the epochs of the English language's history to be searched, finally arriving at this rule of thumb for selecting a cite: "*each quotation must be extensive enough to carry a complete sense by itself"* (p. 10, original emphasis).

But perhaps the boldest of the lexicographical aims of the Society, working under the spell of Trench's new philology, was to declare that its members, in assembling this new English dictionary, were not about to serve as "an arbiter of style" (*TPS*, 1857, p. 2). The disinterested Society declared that "we cannot refuse to admit words into the Dictionary which may not be sanctioned by the usage of more than one writer, or be comfortable in their structure to ideas of taste" (p. 3). Yet the Society did have a hand in admitting words through, at least on a few occasions, a strikingly democratic process. On November 8, 1860, Herbert Coleridge read the paper, "On the Exclusion of Certain Words from A Dictionary," before the Society in which he argued that a mock word such as *devilship* should not be accepted, as "it never was intended even by its author for general circulation or adoption" (*TPS*, 1860, p. 39). After patiently hearing him out, the members, affirming the principle that "*all* words should be admitted," voted to include "Mr. Coleridge's instance *devilship*, and its class"; they agreed, however, that "word-puns, such as *hepistle*, *shepistle*, should be excluded" (p. 43).

Once the proposal had been accepted, the first years of the project were marked by the committed earnestness of its initial editor, Herbert Coleridge, a lawyer of independent means given to the study of Icelandic. Coleridge had published his plans for the work in an open letter to Trench that was appended to later editions of Trench's lectures on the deficiencies of English dictionaries. In the letter, Coleridge affirmed that the dictionary was to be "the voluntary and independent labors of numerous individuals, all working on a common plan" (*TPS*, 1857, pp. 71–72). To that end, Coleridge estimated rather optimistically that the first installment would be out in two years' time. He did hold that such a work should not be forced into print with "undue precipitation," given that this was "a book which is to serve as a general interpreter and a standard of the noblest and most copious language now spoken by man" (p. 78). Coleridge, taking his lead from Trench, adopted as his first principle the credo of the German classical philologist, Franz Passow, which he cited as "'that every word should be made to tell its own story'" (*TPS*, 1857–58, p. 124). Here was the call to a thoroughly descriptive linguistics, a science bent on unlocking the etymological secrets contained in the natural history of language.

During 1859 and 1860, Coleridge produced the *Canones Lexicographici or Rules To Be Observed in Editing the New English Dictionary of the Philological Society* while working with Trench and Furnivall. What is perhaps most interesting about Coleridge's *Canones* is the degree to which they describe a rather different dictionary than the one Murray was to begin producing some two decades later through the Philological Society's auspices. It begins with the *Canones*' crucial identification of the source of meaning. In this document, Passow's prescription that words be left to tell their own story is interpreted as locating the meaning of each word through its history. The *Canones* called for "*Meanings*, deduced logically from the Etymology" which had the basis of Trench's philological stance (*TPS*, 1857, p. 6). This was certainly Samuel Johnson's ostensible position, judging from the extended title, *Dictionary of the English Language in which the Words are Deduced from their Originals and Illustrated in their Different Significations by Examples from the Best Writers. . . .* Johnson's definitions, needless to say, were not always so deduced in practice. To get ahead of myself somewhat, Murray's rather different tack, at least in principle, was consistently to separate meaning from etymology. In effect turning Passow's principle around, Murray states in the preface to the first volume of the *OED* that he worked with "the development of form and meaning," which was illustrated by "a series of quotations ranging from the first known occurrence of the word to the latest, or down to the present day; *the word being thus made to exhibit its own history and meaning*" (emphasis added).[8] The citation was to be the principal guide to the meaning of each word, superseding its etymology. It is a point to which I will return in the next chapter.

A second feature of the dictionary proposed by the *Canones*, and later discarded, was its division into three parts. The first part was to include the words common to the language as well as, interestingly enough, "provincial and local words," "slang words and phrases," and "Americanisms and colonialisms" (*TPS*, 1857, p. 4). The second part was to deal with "technical and scientific terms," as well as "proper names of persons and places," while the third part consisted of "An Etymological Appendix" (pp. 3–4). This awkward arrangement was determined by notions of different classes of readers, popular and scholarly, without offending either, an idea that was eventually and fortunately deemed threatening to the general integrity of the project.

The third point at which the *Canones* promised a different sort of *OED* is in the regard paid to the spoken life of the language: "This Dictionary shall record, under certain limitations, the existence of every word in the language for which sufficient authority, whether printed or oral, can be adduced" (*TPS*, 1857, p. 3). It went so far as to allow that "provincialisms" were admissible to the main dictionary "whether furnished or not with the otherwise indispensable passport of a quotation" (p. 11). In supporting the *Canones* through a series of revisions, the Society took a stand against what it felt was "theoretical propriety" in favor of "a large class of readers, whom it is most desirable to interest in its success" (ibid.). The expression that Coleridge uses more than once in calling for the sanctioning of oral language is "where the fact of their existence can be vouched for by some credible authority." This radical if short-lived principle appears to have been the result of arguments forcibly put to the Society in May 1860 by the noted linguist the Reverend Derwent Coleridge, son of Samuel Taylor and uncle to Herbert. The Reverend Coleridge accused the Society of trying to sidestep the prescriptive functions of a dictionary, as it inevitably is "regulative in effect, though declarative in form." He rebuked the Society for treating English in the manner of a "so-called dead language," as if all that was left of it was its surviving texts, to which he countered, "In the living language, we have the living instinct of those who speak it, to which we can apply" (*TPS*, 1860, pp. 156, 158). That is, while the Society appeared to deny any responsibility for being a "self-constituted authority," it was shoring up that authority by borrowing from the tradition of classical studies. Although the footnotes of the Society's *Transactions* indicate that Derwent Coleridge's suggestions "have been partially adopted," it turned out that forms of oral authority, based on the word of "those who speak it," were not to be enough when it came to the actual editing of the dictionary. His criticism makes it clear, however, that in following Passow's classicist model and the lead of German philology, as the dictionary eventually did, the Society's *New English Dictionary* was taking its impress from the study of classical Greek and Latin more fully than is typically realized. One effect of this, one might argue, is the way it elevates, by analogy, the dictionary's citations to the status of the treasured "extant remains" of English civilization.

Amid all of his best-laid plans for this new dictionary, Herbert Coleridge's tenure as editor ended tragically in 1861 when he died of consumption at the age of thirty-one. The plans for the technical and etymological parts of the dictionary were eventually dropped, while restrictions were placed on words considered to lie outside the common core of the vocabulary, from the provincial to the scientific. The project had to be contained in its breadth, in favor of achieving through the citations a greater degree of historical depth. As it was, Murray expanded the chronological reach of the dictionary to the gathering of words and citations from before the year 1000, back to the early vernacular translations of Alfred, king of the West Saxons. The original starting year of 1250, around which the original reading program was organized, had been accepted by the Society as "the commencement of English," as opposed to "the preceding semi-Saxon" era (*TPS*, 1857, p. 3).[9] As for local, slang, colonial, and scientific terms, they were only to qualify for inclusion in the dictionary a century later, with the editing of the *Supplement*. On the other hand, sufficient and credible *oral* authority for the use of a word has yet to be found acceptable by the editors of the *OED*. This is not simply the enforcement of a scholarly principle. By the nineteenth century, despite the best intentions of the *Canones*, a certain distance had sprung up in people's minds between dictionary English and the spoken word. The *OED*'s entry for *dictionary* records a number of derisive instances that play on this popular distinction:

> **1632** J. HAYWARD tr *Biondi s Eromena* A iv, I would not . . . be taken (or rather mistaken) for a Dictionary-tutred Linguist. . . . **1830** GALT *Lawrie T.* VII. iii (1849) 318 Miss Beeny was an endless woman with her dictionary phraseology. **1831** CARLYLE *Sart. Res.* I. iv, He . . . calls many things by their mere dictionary names. **1858** R. S. SURTEES *Ask Mamma* i. I His fine dictionary words and laboured expletives.

After Coleridge's unexpected death and Richard Trench's departure for Dublin two years later in 1863, Furnivall alone remained to carry the editorial torch forward. It proved to be another false start for the dictionary. Furnivall, for all his keenness in initiating new societies and projects, was not suited to the painstaking task of editing the dictionary. James Murray's biographer and granddaughter, Elisabeth Murray, suggests that Furnivall "lacked the accuracy and the patience essential, but his sustained enthusiasm—however misdirected—was impressive" (*CWW*, p. 137). He is said to have served his friend, Kenneth Grahame, as the model for the always-keen Water Rat in the children's classic, *Wind in the Willows*, a book written at Furnivall's urging (Carpenter, 1985, p. 192). Furnivall had originally made an impressive start in contributing to the project by securing publishing agreements, first with Trübner & Co. in 1858 and then with John Murray in 1862. If these contracts had not lapsed in the face of the repeatedly unfulfilled promises of Furnivall, it would obviously have meant a very different dictionary than the one produced by Oxford University. Undeterred by these failures, Furnivall turned his energies to founding the still-extant Early English Text Society (EETS) in 1864. He shaped this organization along the principles of the cooperative movement; it was to be the first of some seven literary societies he set in motion, along with the Working Men's College in London and a ladies' rowing team. With the EETS, and to a lesser degree the other societies, Furnivall was attempting to extend the historical reach of this national project by securing a reliable source of improved raw materials. His intention was to recruit Philological Society members and other interested parties in producing reliable editions of the language's initial literary works, many of which had fallen into neglect, if not utter oblivion. Under Furnivall's sometimes tactless and abrasive hand, the EETS was soon publishing five to eight editions annually, many of which became significant sources of citations for the *OED* in what amounted to a double process of selection of a suitable past for the English language.

In the 1872–73 EETS series, a certain James A. H. Murray made his editorial debut with the publication of the sixteenth-century *Complaynt of Scotlande*. The work features an introduction that runs to more than one hundred pages, featuring Murray's typically astute and somewhat subversive discovery about the Scottish dialect of his own heritage: "I have everywhere found the language of the *Complaynt* familiar as the tones of childhood, and ever and anon have been surprised at the sanction which it gives to forms or idioms which I had thought to be modern 'vulgarisms' of the local patois, but which are thus shown to have a pedigree of three and a half centuries to plead" (*CWW*, p. 92). The establishment of long-lost pedigrees was eventually to consume Murray's life as the editor of the language's greatest dictionary. It was work that could, on occasion, act as a check on English tendencies to sneer at dialects other than their own; it served equally well as a historical record that affirmed an English claim to a continuous literary heritage of great depth and artfulness. The dictionary that finally emerged as a result of Trench's suggestion may not have satisfied him in its demonstration that God's seal had been unequivocally set on the English language. Nearly three decades separated suggestion and publication, at a time when people were turning to the rising scientific spirit for salvation. For those concerned with the special responsibilities borne by English as one of the world's great civilizing languages, however, it can still be said that *A New English Dictionary* was to be very much the work that Trench had in mind.

## CHAPTER 3

# Murray's Editorship, 1879–1915

FOLLOWING the untimely death of the project's first editor, Herbert Coleridge, the Philological Society engaged in a protracted search for a publisher who would not only agree to take on the *New English Dictionary*, but to support the considerable editorial labor required to bring it to completion. The project of amassing the necessary base of citations struggled along, as it became increasingly apparent that Frederick Furnivall, who was now in charge of the work, was not the one to see a project of this magnitude through. In 1877, during what began to seem like promising negotiations with the delegates of Oxford University Press, James Murray, then president of the Philological Society, became involved in the preparation of specimen pages for the proposed dictionary. While Furnivall continued to negotiate with the Press in his typically feisty manner, Murray quietly developed prototype entries for the dictionary that amounted to miniature masterpieces in information management through typography. While crediting "the great French Dictionary of M. Littré" for some of *A New English Dictionary*'s features, including its page size, Murray would later take credit, in the preface to the first volume, for "the typographical distinctions." The specimen pages provided convincing instances of a new level of system and detail in English lexicography as part of a Victorian passion for bringing order and design to seeming chaos, and the better part of Murray's original design is still in use in both the published and electronic versions of the *OED*. Although Murray had not yet expressed an interest in editing the new dictionary at this point, he was quick to defend the specimen pages against criticisms raised by Friedrick Max Müller, Oxford's first professor of comparative philology and one of the Delegates of the University Press. Professor Müller initially objected to the lack of expertise among readers for the project and took exception to certain etymologies that Murray had submitted (*CWW*, pp. 151–154). It was not long, however, before Müller proved himself an advocate of the project, especially after Murray deferred to the professor on a number of small points—"We must humor the Dons," Furnivall had advised him—although Murray insisted that Müller was anything but his equal in matters of English philology.

As it turned out, Müller kept his direct influence on the editing of the dictionary, as well as his association with its principal editor, to a minimum, even after the project was moved from London to Oxford some years later. However, given Müller's undisputed eminence as the country's leading professor of philology in those early years of the dictionary, it is still worth pausing for a moment over the intellectual impact of this Leipzig-trained scholar, who arrived in England on a commission by the East India Company to translate the sacred *Rigveda* from Sanskrit. As Richard Trench had set the fervent tone for the dedicated amateur philologist, Professor Müller began in the 1860s to capture the English imagination with his inquiries into "the science of language" (1864), although by the end of the century his work was in thorough disrepute (Dowling, 1986, pp. 72–77). Among those who attended Müller's popular lectures on language were Alfred Tennyson, J. S. Mill, Michael Faraday, and Queen Victoria. Müller's interests were in establishing a science of language that could arrive at the ultimate roots or "phonetic cells" underlying the words we speak. If he was careful to distinguish his work from the more theological efforts of such figures as Richard Trench, he did not rule out the language's religious element. The idea of God, he felt, could be found in every mother tongue (Olender, 1992, p. 88). Yet Müller explicitly rejected the treatment of philology "as a key to an understanding of literary monuments . . . [or] as a means ultimately to trace the social, moral, intellectual and religious progress of the human race" (cited in Harris, 1981, p. 43). In this, he provided a scientific check on the Trenchean moral enterprise, as well as the Johnsonian faith in literature as forming a guide to the language. Science, Müller held, was on the side of the natural and living sounds of human speech, but this was still to prove a nature shaped by the Victorian imagination.

Another of Müller's indirect links with Trench proved to be on the question of language and race. Although he was later to dissociate himself publicly from the racial implications readily drawn from his work, Müller developed in England what was then an emerging Aryan reading of the Indo-European linguistic tradition, bringing to bear the full force of a German philology, inspired by both forward-looking scientific aspirations and a Romantic interest in the past (Poliakov, 1971). It was a philology which the British greatly admired for its aura of learnedness, although its objectivity has recently come into question for the manner in which it set out to isolate ancient Greece from what was for many the uncomfortable aspect of Semitic and African influence that clearly interfered with its Aryan roots.[1] Linda Dowling pointedly summarizes Müller's beliefs that "language somehow remains unchanged in its power to guarantee human identity and value"; it continues as "a patent of nobility for the Aryans, the imperishable record—and author—of all thought"

(1982, p. 161). It was a widely held sentiment during the heady days of imperialism, and Dowling, in a later work, cites one Victorian who felt that as a result of this Aryan descent, "the Saxon should now rule with uncontrolled sway over that antique land" (referring to India), if only to "impart to his Hindustanic brethren a civilization whose germs had been planted by their common ancestors" (1986, p. 57).

Although it is probably unnecessary to recall how commonplace such attitudes were, I do think that, as part of the "scientific" spirit that guided the *OED*, they need to be kept in mind. To this end, Charles Darwin, whose reputation survived in a way that Müller's did not, provides an excellent instance. When Darwin entered the Victorian fray over language in his *Descent of Man,* published in 1871, he flatly rejected the strain of Victorian thinking that played the descent-into-barbarism against the singular nobility of Aryan ascent: "To believe that man was aboriginally civilized and then suffered utter degradation in so many regions, is to take a pitiably low view of human nature" (1993, p. 511). He also attempted to strip from language the remaining elements of divine intervention in his efforts to set it on a more scientific basis: "The survival or preservation of certain favored words in the struggle for existence is natural selection" (p. 466). However, if Darwin held that "progress has been more general than retrogression," it was still the Western nations of Europe "who stand at the summit of civilization" (p. 507). As for the English people, Darwin was not above granting that natural selection had, on the evidence of colonial success, led to intellectual, energetic, and benevolent advantages over other peoples (p. 508).[2] On another level, the linguistic interests of Trench and Müller were not so far removed from the work of Darwin and the geologist Charles Lyell. They were all, in effect, historicizing nature through their concept of uniformitarianism (as opposed to catastrophic versions of development), with theories of natural phenomena finding their intellectual parallel in the age's philological inquiry into the "evolution" of language. Murray would, after all, later entitle his Romanes Lecture at Oxford "The Evolution of Lexicography" (1970).

The proposed *New English Dictionary* promised to fill out the record of Müller's patent, establishing through the selection of citations the continuities and changes that assured this noble identity, this deeply rooted and evolved value. By 1872, however, Müller was prepared to denounce "the misunderstandings and controversies" that arose from "antiscientific" talk of "an Aryan race, Aryan blood, or Aryan skulls" (cited in Poliakov, 1974, p. 214). Nonetheless, one has only to turn to his later defense of the term in the ninth edition of *The Encyclopædia Britannica* to see how easily this "great family of speech" falls within the language of race, defined in this case by the Indo-Greco-Latin-Germanic-Anglo ascendancy of the English people (Müller, 1900, p. 672). Scientific thinking during the period formed its own battlefield of interests, and Müller was no small force among the educated classes in Victorian England. Whatever isolation from the academic community may have been experienced by the Philological Society's project at Oxford, the dictionary was to detract from, as well as to support in turn, this don's scholarly interests in the comparative philology of national and racial identity.

During this period of negotiations between the Society and the Press, the delegates were increasingly impressed by Murray's levelheadedness and commitment, compared to Furnivall's exasperating diversity of interests. "At present," Murray wrote to the delegates in 1878, "I do a considerable amount of unpaid work in the interest of English Literature, and for its own sake, I have considered, that I ought to reckon giving a portion of time without remuneration . . . as my own contribution to English Literature" (*CWW*, pp. 158–159). During this period of negotiations with Oxford, Furnivall began to refer to Murray as "Mr. Editor."

Early in 1879, much to the relief of Society members, a contract was drawn up between the Philological Society of London and Oxford University Press. It specified that the Society's dictionary would be between 6,000 and 7,000 pages in length, and would be completed in ten years' time with Dr. James Murray as the editor (*TPS*, 1877–78–79, pp. xlix–lix). In turn, the Press agreed to advance the moneys needed to complete the project, including the salaries of Murray and his assistants, to be paid back with interest out of future sales of the work, while allowing the Society a right to 15 percent of the profits. Murray took up the job warily, later describing it as giving up his "liberty to be the slave of the Dictionary" (*CWW*, p. 257).[3]

For the first seven years of what grew into a thirty-eight-year editorship, Murray was forced to divide his time between schoolteaching at Mill Hill, to sustain himself and family, and working on the Society's dictionary, with students and family lending a hand in the work. His *Appeal to the English-speaking and English-reading Public* in 1879 notes that "James Murray's own pupils have supplied him with 5,000 good quotations during the past month." Murray's tenth and youngest child, Jowett, was later to recount a childhood of slip-sorting toward which he showed little resentment: "Hours and hours of our childhood were spent in this useful occupation . . . the standard rate was one penny an hour" (*CWW*, pp. 177, 179). In spite of the support that Murray received from the Press, as well as from family, colleagues, and students, it was obvious that the great dictionary could not be fully built in the spare time of the editor and Society members. In 1884, after the belabored publication of the first fascicle covering only *A-ANT*, the Press moved Murray and the project from Mill Hill School to Oxford, and he began to work full time on the project. For the first few years, members of the university, apart from the delegates of the Press, showed little interest in the project; the appointed committee of consulting scholars did little consulting with Murray (*CWW*, p. 220). However, when the classical scholar and master of Balliol College, Benjamin Jowett, became ex-officio chairman of the delegates in 1882, that changed somewhat. Jowett oversaw the drafting of a one-page "Suggestions for Guidance in Preparing Copy for the Press," which might seem an innocent enough contribution to the project. It was actually a manifesto for a far more exclusive and prescriptive dictionary than had originally been intended, a dictionary that, for example, proscribed slang and scientific terms, unless they were warranted by use in "literature." James Murray could only ask in response, "What is classed as literature?" (*CWW*, p. 221). On the delegate's insistence that citations should be kept to the work of the great authors, Murray retorted, "And with what chance of success should I search for 'famous Quotations' which the reading of 25 years has missed?" (*CWW*, p. 223). Murray stood his ground, insisting on a dictionary given, as he put it, to "exhibiting the facts." Jowett went on to become one of Murray's few academic friends at Oxford. He made Murray a member of Balliol College, and the dissenter Murray worshipped at the chapel when Jowett, a minister of the Church of England, was preaching, while Murray's tenth child was named after Jowett (*CWW*, pp. 243–244). The Oxford philosopher's contribution to the *OED* is perhaps most notably recorded through his translation of Plato, from which 2,000 citations were drawn.

The authority of the dictionary was not to rest in appeals to fixed notions of propriety, of what was fit and best for the language. This was part of Trench's legacy. He, too, had called for a diligent, almost Gradgrindian, adherence to what were taken as the *facts* of the language, which could be established by the great and small published record of the English language. Yet in setting aside Trench's linguistic concerns with the "intimation of the origins at once divine and human" (1856, p. 39), and John Horne Tooke's materialist etymology, Murray could be said to be returning, in effect, to the specific empiricism of John Locke.[4] In *An Essay Concerning Human Understanding* (1689), Locke had argued that the imperfection and abuse of words could be checked by carefully consulting the selected examples of others: "The proper significance and use of terms is best to be learned from those who in their writings and discourses appear to have had the clearest notions, and applied to them their terms with the exactest choice and fitness" (Locke, 1965, p. 289). It is important to note how Locke's liberal support for the free and collective determination of significance placed a special emphasis on the intelligence of the writing classes. While denying individuals, especially those in positions of power, the authority to create a word ("the great Augustus

himself, in the possession of that power which ruled the world, acknowledged that he could not make a new Latin word"), Locke spoke of language growing by "common acceptation" and "tacit consent" in what is
suggestive of a social contract (pp. 232, 233). Locke held that words,
"being no man's private possession," were, in an apt phrase, "the common measure of commerce and communication" (p. 289). Here is the
liberal investiture of the citation's lexicographic sovereignty. Note that
the proper signification and use of terms that appears in the *OED* is not
simply the product of an empirical sense of what is largely common, but
is more specifically located in the "measure of commerce and communication" defined by the publishing enterprise, itself a rich amalgam of interests not least of which was, in the time that passed from Locke to
Murray, a middle class with liberal designs on an evolving democratic
nation-state. After the dictionary had been successfully launched on the
wings of Trench's sacred philology, Murray returned it to a Lockean empiricism which invested its authority and meaning in those who sought to
write the course of English thought and imagination.

Predictably, the empirical record constituted by the Philological Society's materials was not as impartial or fully factual as claimed; it restricted the language of the many and overrepresented the literature of the
few. But perhaps a more troubling element to this new positivist lexicography is its use of scholarship to construct a coherent and continuous
linguistic history for the modern nation out of those many bundles of
citations, and to build it around the voices emanating from around the
political and publishing center of London. Murray and the members of
the Philological Society were committed to creating a Whig history of
English that demonstrated the devolution of a superior language. The
resulting dictionary was far more liberal in its reach, thanks to Murray,
than we have any right to expect from a work of that period, especially as
it was sponsored by Oxford. It was, however, still destined to tell a story
that fit remarkably well with the ideological needs of the modern European nation-state.

Whatever differences in opinion separated Murray and the delegates,
whatever isolation he experienced while living in Oxford, the project's
association with Oxford University Press was an enormous step forward
in the realization of the Philological Society's dream. It was also not without a telling significance for the future of Oxford University Press. A project of this magnitude run by erratic amateurs represented a risky venture
for the delegates of the Press, and as late as 1896, after the publication of
the letter *D*, the balance sheet was still in the red, with £50,000 invested,
compared to £15,000 recovered from sales of the dictionary (Barker,
1978, p. 52). In spite of the obvious risk, there was a logic to Oxford
University Press taking on this project as a commercial, if not as an aca-

demic, venture. Although the Press had been the site for scholarly publishing for over four hundred years, it had often sustained itself financially through a legal monopoly over publication of the Authorized Version of the English Bible, which it shared with Cambridge University and the Royal Printer (Taylor, 1989, p. 314). The Oxford Bible business, supported during the nineteenth century in large part by the efforts of the British and Foreign Bible Society, meant spreading the Word to the world through some 4.5 million copies of the Bible and Testament printed from 1837 to 1847 (Howsam, 1991, p. 118). The Bible was a mainstay for the Press. To take but one measure from Leslie Howsam's study of Bible publication during this period, the ratio of the paper required for printing it, compared to what was needed for all of the other works the Press published, ran close to twenty-to-one (p. 77). This publishing activity also fit in well with the university's training of clergymen for the higher reaches of the Church of England. Yet the closing years of the nineteenth century witnessed a falling off in the Bible market. After the sensational release of the Revised Edition, with one million sold on the day of publication in 1881, the Victorian cult of the Bible began to fade. The major publishers were left for the first time with overstock (Barker, 1978, p. 51). It may well have been that the more far-sighted of the delegates in the late 1870s had realized that, once the market in Bibles began to decline for reasons of both saturation and secularization, the future of the Press might well lie in an Authorized Version of the English Language, a second Book of Books. At the beginning of the nineteenth century, the expanding empire had been envisioned as a market for Bibles: "What a glorious sight!—Great Britain standing in the attitude of presenting the Bible to all the world" is how one pamphleteer described it (cited in Howsam, 1991, p. 3). By the twentieth century, that glory seemed to belong to the English language and its literature alone. On the occasion of the Press's 500th anniversary, and a century after Oxford University Press agreed to publish *A New English Dictionary*, Charles Ryskamp noted the transition in economic dependency between the Press's principal texts: "The success of the Oxford University Press through the ages is inseparably tied to the printing of the Bible and the *Book of Common Prayer*. But in later years the history of the Press was as closely associated with all of the dictionaries, histories, 'companions,' texts and books of verse which bear the name of Oxford" (cited in Barker, 1978, p. vi).

At the same time that the Press undertook to support *A New English Dictionary*, the Philological Society was increasing the public's involvement with the project through its reading and citation program. If the association with Oxford brought a certain exclusiveness to the project, the Society's ongoing reading program maintained its openness to the breadth of the English reading experience. With the publication of the first fascicle of the dictionary, James Murray presented to the Philological Society a detailed list of the 762 contributors who had served between 1879 and 1884, along with a listing of the titles they had read (*TPS*, 1884, pp. 601–642). The index of readers gives a sense of this diverse, dedicated group, united in their efforts to record a certain history of the English language, working from assigned eras and texts as well as freely chosen reading materials. The list includes, among overlapping groups, 278 women, 103 Americans, 89 clergymen, and 63 members of Mill Hill School. These readers were to be found not only in the British Isles and America, but as far afield as Florence, Copenhagen, Ceylon, Japan, Calcutta, New Zealand, and Canada. Thomas Austin, Esq., to take an extreme instance of citational profligacy, gathered some 165,000 citation slips (having culled cites from, among other works, fifty volumes of the Royal Society's *Philosophical Transactions*). Dr. Helwich of Vienna contributed 50,000 slips (favoring works of the Early English Text Society); the Reverend Pierson of Michigan sent 46,000 slips across the Atlantic (from a wide range of works); Murray's eldest son culled 27,000 slips (principally histories), and his wife, Ada, in the midst of raising nine children (destined to become lexicographical assistants), managed to garner 2,000 cites (with special attention paid to the poetry of John Crabbe). By the time the first volume, covering *A–B*, was published in 1888, James Murray was in a position to thank in the preface thirteen hundred readers who had scoured some 5,000 books from across six centuries for citations, compared to the first volume of the Grimm brothers' dictionary of the German language, which credited, as Trench had pointed out to the Philological Society in 1857, "no less than eighty-three volunteer coadjutors" (*TPS*, 1857, p. 69).

One can think of citation culling as an intelligent pastime, like doing crossword puzzles, that possessed the additional incentive of contributing to the historical record of the English language. It went well beyond sending a letter to the *Times* protesting some writer's solecism in an effort to maintain standards in the English language. Here was the chance to lend a hand in establishing the greatness of the English language, as it had been developed and refined over the centuries into a civilizing instrument of great intellectual suppleness and beauty. The remarkable receptiveness to the project, at least among the educated classes, must have comforted Murray amid his sense of isolation at Oxford. The dictionary might advertise on its title page that it was completed "with the assistance of many scholars and men of science," but it bore the more common touch as well, with credit given occasionally to the families of Society members for assisting in the preparation of materials. Elisabeth Murray notes that there were "very many intelligent ladies, lonely widows or spinsters living at home" finding their pleasure in reading for the dictionary as a form of participation in the public life of the nation that was not otherwise available to them (CWW, p. 185). Of the 278 women readers (36 percent of the total) who collected citations for the dictionary, 64 percent were designated as "Miss."

Dr. Murray repaid the readers' efforts through these published acknowledgments and by covering, on request, their postage expenses, or so his 1879 announcement advised.[5] On the other hand, calling on a volunteer corps of readers to build a dictionary had its risks. A number of the historical books distributed by the Philological Society for citation-reading disappeared without a trace of book or reader, other sets of citation slips were left behind when readers moved, while other sets were rendered useless by leaky roofs and poor storage. Some books were read for the occurrence of words beginning with only one letter of the alphabet, and others came back carefully cut up and pasted onto citation slips in a system that at least ensured accuracy even as the two copies required with this method depleted the nation's textual heritage. As it turns out, the lexicographical precedent for this bibliographical abuse was Dictionary Johnson, who after exhausting his own library had the habit of gaining citations by borrowing books from friends and marking them up for his dictionary, leaving the books, as the man's contemporary John Hawkins notes "so defaced as to be scarce worth owning, and yet, some of his friends were glad to receive and entertain them as curiosities" (cited in Reddick, 1990, p. 35). It might suggest a certain tendency on the part of the dictionary to cannibalize the key books in the language, feeding on the authority of those it consumes.

Murray's network of devoted readers formed only the outer reaches of participation in this lexicographic enterprise. In the preface to the first volume, Murray also gratefully acknowledges the assistance of an inner circle of thirty volunteer subeditors who arranged quotations, prepared definitions, and otherwise contributed to the rigorous system of editing that prevailed. Editors, subeditors, and assistants checked each citation for accuracy. In the dictionary itself, each quotation included a full reference to its location, inviting readers to return to the original to check what the lexicographer has deduced for themselves. This was undoubtedly a science of language that sought to establish itself as a public enterprise, rather than the private and commissioned undertaking of an aspiring literary figure such as Johnson presented.

Although Murray was not the writer that Samuel Johnson was, he did use the many prefaces to this serialized dictionary to share what he had learned about the language as each new section went to press. Nor was he above employing the preface to promote his life's work, identifying the distinct advantages of the OED by using charts listing the word and citation figures for "certain other Dictionaries," including Johnson's. The early prefaces became Murray's own philology journal, filled not only with word counts and contributors' names, but with a guide to the etymological highlights of each letter and the principles of lexicography that evolved with the project.

In perhaps the dictionary's most important preface, for the volume A–B, Murray makes it clear that his lexicographical position was, like Samuel Johnson's and Richard Trench's, on the side of description. He echoes their complaint against the use of the dictionary to fix the language, to deter the natural process of word creation:

> A literary language, with its more accessible store of words already in use and sufficient for all ordinary requirements, its more permanent memories and traditions, its constant appeals to authoritative precedent—"Where did you find that word? Can you cite it from any of the masters of English Prose? Is it in the Dictionary? Is it English at all?"—is hostile to word creation. The new word is apt to die almost as soon as it is born, ashamed of its own newness, ashamed of the italics or inverted commas which apologize for its very existence, or question its legitimacy. But such is not the case with natural language.

"The new word is apt to die. . . ." Here Murray approaches Johnsonian heights in lyrical and moral sensibility. And when he asks, "Is it in the Dictionary?" Murray seems to be forswearing such a dictionary-promoting query as in itself hostile to "word creation." The preface amounts to a fine-print disclaimer of the dictionary's policing of the language. Johnson had said as much in his preface, although it did little to deter people from treating his dictionary as a stand-in language academy. Murray, having learned what Johnson realized about the robustness of an ungoverned language, made a similar effort to wash his hands of this inevitable (ab)use of the authoritative dictionary.

But Johnson and Murray, having both spent time teaching school, should have known better than to expect anything less than the use of the dictionary to set a standard for the legitimacy of certain kinds of language usage. At heart, the dictionary is a schoolbook; it contributes to the disciplining of language, as easily as to its study. The Philological Society's dictionary, in its association with Oxford, came to represent a fine and increasingly important bourgeois marriage of scholarly and institutional authority. The dictionary offers a particularly apt basis for making linguistic distinctions among social classes, for ensuring a schooled and disciplined hold on public discourse, and for specifying the order of the known and named world. This was indeed a nation prepared to ask of each word a person might use, at least in the influential medium of print, "Is it in the dictionary?" "Is it English at all?" In dealing with a "highly cultivated living language," Murray recognized without passing judgment in that first major preface that there were levels of acceptability that differed by class of speaker: "There are many claimants to admission into recognized vocabulary (where some of them will certainly one day be received), that are already current coin with some speakers and writers, and not yet 'good English' or even not English at all, to others."

Murray goes on to explain in the preface that while "the aim of this Dictionary" was to show when, how, and in what shape each word "became English," this often presented a problem with more recent, indigenous creations, that is, for words that are actually born of the English language. For such indigenous words, he proposed a rather fascinating and liberal path of social development. As he imagines it, these words often spring to life in the fertile English settings of local dialects and colloquial speech, invented to "serve the needs of the moment." This is language aimed "only at being expressive, and treating memory and precedent as ministers, not as masters." He then imagines the freshly minted term entering "epistolary, journalistic, and finally into general literary use, or from the colloquy of the novel into the literary composition of the novelist, and are registered as 'new words.'" Consider, then, how a new word might take wing, born of, perhaps, a bit of verbal sparring at a crossroads or a colorful exchange at the baker's, and after being heard around the street, it is found in the casual air of a letter. The word might also be hit upon by a harried journalist looking for a vital turn of phrase in the face of a deadline, and finally it is absorbed by the pub-frequenting, paper-reading author who completes a verse with it, fully qualifying the word for inclusion in the dictionary. Drawing on the letter *B*, Murray suggests that such instances as *bam*, *blabber*, *blizzard*, and *blot* may well have followed such a route. With the American term, *blizzard*, for example, he concludes that it is "a modern word, prob. more or less onomatopoeic" that "was apparently in colloquial use in the West much earlier" than Colonel David Crockett's 1843 citation indicates.

While this evolution of new terms seems a very neat process in principle, Murray repeatedly short-circuited it in the *OED* by capturing words for the dictionary before they had completed the cycle and reached maturity. As will become apparent in later chapters of this book, a word may come to be listed while still in its epistolary stage, albeit in a published letter by, say, Lady Montagu, or while it was still in its journalistic phase—and not always from the better papers. The more extreme case of arrested development, and one I will examine in more detail below, was the inclusion of words that had no other apparent life in the language than their bright moment on the Shakespearean stage, often repeated season after season in performances of his plays. The *OED*'s natural history of the language is full of anomalies, and its history of the language in print may indeed be mistaken at times for the very nature of the true language.

Murray's own historical vision of the language is found in his lecture on *The Evolution of English Lexicography* (1970). In this brief history of the dictionary, he draws an analogy between the English dictionary and the constitution. The one, just as the other, "is the creation of no one man, and of no one age; it is a growth that has slowly developed itself down the ages" (1970, pp. 6–7). The history of a language and culture is treated as a natural self-governing process. Interruptions in the growth of English, since Anglo-Saxon times, only serve to emphasize the development, especially if it is the French that are meddling. Murray makes special reference to how the "rich and cultured tongue of Alfred and Aelfric was left for generations without literary employment" after the Norman Conquest (1970, p. 14). By the eighteenth century, however, English had "attained a high degree of literary perfection; a perfect prose style, always a characteristic of maturity . . . capable of expressing clearly and elegantly everything that needed to be expressed in language" (p. 36). Given the classical reference points for the evolution of European civilization at the time, Murray cannot help but add that "the age was compared to the Ciceronian age of Latin and the age of Aristotle and Plato in Greek" (p. 36).[6] But the dictionaries of the eighteenth century were not so perfect as the prose of the age; they still wanted, in Murray's opinion, for a properly scientific spirit. This is the trumpet call for the evolution and entrance of Murray's project: "The Oxford Dictionary, permeated as it is through and through with the scientific method of the century, lexicography as for the present reached its supreme development" (p. 49). He concludes the lecture, which is in effect a genealogy of the *OED*, by drawing attention to the collective cultural forces that speak so elegantly to the superiority of the English nation: "The evolution of English Lexicography has followed with no faltering steps the evolution of English History and the development of English Literature" (p. 51).

Two decades earlier, however, Murray had more frankly linked the productive aspects of imperial and nation-building instincts with the lexicographical project during his presidential address to the Philological Society for 1880: "The language of a civilized nation, the individuals of which are constantly growing in their knowledge of the objects, actions, and customs of other climes and other times, which objects, actions, and customs are constantly becoming the subject matter of new *ideas*, and the theme of new discourse, is constantly adding to the sound-combinations, or *words*, by which it expresses these new ideas, and which are, indeed, the *only* means in existence for expressing them" (*TPS*, 1880, pp. 131–132). Certainly, there were on occasion impressive scholarly turns to this imperial extension of British interests in other climes and other times. Sir William Jones, for example, made perhaps the single most important discovery in eighteenth-century philology when he described the basis of an

Indo-European family of languages in 1786, while serving as a judge of the supreme court in Calcutta's Fort William (Aarsleff, 1983, pp. 115–140). The discovery did little enough to set the two languages on an equal footing—Jones speaks of a "degenerate" and "abased" Indian culture—or to deter the famous Macaulay Minute from 1837 that made English the language of education in the British raj in India (Niranjana, 1992, p. 15). Still, Murray's point that colonial expansion was having a profound effect on the English language is well taken.

There was also the question of English among the English, in what was during the nineteenth century a contest between the realms of the rich and poor within the British Isles. Murray, for his part, held that there are no fixed limits or boundaries to "the Vocabulary of English-speaking men." Prior to the fifteenth century, English "existed only in dialect." But since then, Murray points out, there had evolved a core—"the 'Common Words' of literature and conversation." In the extensive preface to the first volume of the *OED*, Murray supports this notion of a naturally evolved center or core to English vocabulary that exists at the intersection of uncommon parts with an oft-reproduced diagram. COMMON is set in the middle; LITERARY arches above it and COLLOQUIAL below it. Radiating out from this center are five rays—SCIENTIFIC, FOREIGN, DIALECTAL, SLANG, and TECHNICAL—with arrows indicating their extension away from what is "common" to the language. Setting science and dialect on the same linguistic plane, if headed in different directions, is indeed a remarkably dispassionate representation of the cultural universe for a Victorian gentleman. It is impertinent to ask, common to whom or to how many? Equally so, inquiries should not be made into whether one speaker's *common* words are another's *dialect*. "Common," in this case, does not refer to a numerical majority of English speakers, for that was constituted by the lower orders whose speech was richly localized and marked as dialectical for it. "Common" was reserved for the language of print used across the land, and as such common to the educated classes and the language to which they aspired, perhaps more often than they achieved, in their daily discourse.

Murray also came to explain, toward the end of this long preface, the problems presented by the work's primary lexicographical principle—that each word tell its own story. Between the plan and the preface for the dictionary, as Johnson had so markedly established, comes an editor's understanding of the language and lexicography. Murray was particularly frustrated by certain obscure and specialized terms, belonging to "history, customs, fashions, trade or manufactures," which proved reluctant witnesses to their own story, whether one looked hard to their context or relevant reference work: "In many cases, the only thing known about them was contained in the quotations, often merely allusive, which had been collected by the diligence of our readers. They were found in no dictionary, or, if mentioned in some were explained in a way which our quotations evidently showed to be erroneous. The difficulty of obtaining first-hand and authoritative information about these has often been immense and sometimes insurmountable." What is most revealing about this comment is the degree to which it suggests the need, on occasion, for an oral sensibility, for getting to someone who knows this aspect of the language, who can be called upon when citation and reference books break down. This admission also admits limitations to the principle that each word, through its use in the citation, tells its own story. There is always something more to meaning.

In his Romanes Lecture of 1900, Murray offered a revised version of what a lexicographer can reasonably ask of quotations: "Quotations *will* tell the full meaning of a word, *if one has enough of them*; but it takes a great many to be enough, and it takes a reader a long time to read and weigh all the quotations, and to deduce from the meanings which might be put before him in a line or two" (1970, p. 44). There is something in the emphasis and the sense given by "a great many" to suggest that Murray's confidence in the quotation had indeed been tempered by two decades of editing the dictionary. The trick is in moving from specific instances of the word-in-use to a fixed and general definition of only a line or two. There are limits to this conquest of meaning; not all can be inferred from textual instances—when does one have enough citations?—and sometimes very little can be drawn from specific uses. This cautionary note is now something of a given in the trade. Sidney Landau, in his guide to the art and craft of lexicography, states as a counterprinciple to Murray's that, whatever else, "citation files are flawed" (1989, p. 164). There are never enough citations for a word, in part because use is of a different order than definition. The editor of meaning must at some point reluctantly become its author.

In the face of these moments of lexicographical frustration, Murray consoles himself toward the end of the preface by quoting at some length from Johnson's preface, in which the good doctor, after reviewing his grandest aspirations for the language—"to pierce deep into every science"—concludes that "these were the dreams of a poet doomed at last to wake a lexicographer." If Murray had not been a poet before becoming an editor, as had Johnson, he had still fully awakened as an editor-lexicographer, and metamorphosed by his great gift for devoted scholarship and learning into the man responsible for one of the great philological accomplishments of the last two hundred years. He also learned the limits of the feat, finding its apt expression in Johnson's maxim of lexicographic realism—"I set limits to my work, which would in time be ended, though not completed" (p. xii). As it was, Johnson was able and keen to revise his

*Dictionary* through four editions, from 1755 to 1773, with a fifth in preparation at the time of his death (Reddick, 1990). For its part, the OED continues to expand and be amended, with readers from all parts of the globe sending in citations for a third edition of the *Oxford English Dictionary*. There is little sense that Murray's work has been, or ever will be, completed, which would undoubtedly have pleased him.

Despite the considerable voluntary work force that Murray was able to marshal for the project, the composing proceeded slowly. In 1885 Henry Bradley began to assist with the editing from his London home, and he soon took over the completion of the letters *E* and *F*. Eleven years later, he set up as an editor with his own staff at the Clarendon Press in Oxford. A year after Bradley's arrival in Oxford, William Craigie joined the Press as an assistant to Murray, and by 1901 he and a small staff were given responsibility for editing sections of the dictionary, beginning with the letter *Q*. In 1914 they were joined in what was formerly the home of the Ashmoleum Museum by a third editorial group, led by Charles Onions, who had first begun to work with Murray as an assistant in 1895. Murray was busily editing entries for the letter *T*, at the age of seventy-eight, when death finally overtook him in 1915. This great loss to the project was followed by the demise of Henry Bradley in 1923, and *A New English Dictionary* was finally brought to completion within the next five years by Craigie and Onions, with Craigie spending the final three years on the project while working at the University of Chicago.

Elisabeth Murray includes in the biography of her grandfather a series of photographs of James Murray at work on the dictionary that date from the period of World War I, after the man had labored for nearly four decades on the OED and was finally approaching the last quarter of the alphabet and the end of a life devoted to this one work. The quality of the pictures suggests the work of a professional photographer with a tripod, large-format camera, and an eye for carefully positioning his subject, as if to catch unawares the humble editor at work—"Here I am, yes; I'm working right now, but do come in and have a look around, if only for a brief moment." A close look at the photographs reveals not only a summation of Murray's life with the dictionary, but fault lines that run through this lexicographical project like hairline cracks in old crockery.

The now-famous portrait of Murray that appears on the dust jacket of Elisabeth Murray's book is a full-length shot of the elderly editor standing by his high desk. He appears a gentle and scholarly man with kindly eyes and a black frock coat. His reading glasses have slipped halfway down his nose and his snowy beard reaches to his chest. He is wearing his prized University of Edinburgh doctoral cap, presented to him with an honorary degree in 1874. He has a somewhat quizzical look on his face, as he holds in one hand an open book, and in the other, a pen and a citation slip. The slip is likely the work of one of the dictionary's volunteer readers, perhaps from Sussex, Edinburgh, or Boston. The photographer has had Murray turn away from his desk and pose against a backdrop of floor-to-ceiling pigeon holes crammed with bundles of citation slips. The modest citation slip Murray is holding symbolizes the work of well over a thousand readers whose pleasure it was, as part of a literate cottage industry, to copy out short passages from books, magazines, newspapers, and pamphlets, which they had been assigned to read or were selected from their own reading. The book and pen in Murray's hand are a reminder of the tremendous editorial effort that went into verifying the wording and sources for the 1,827,306 citations that were eventually included in the first edition of the dictionary. Sixty subeditors and an equal number of assistants worked over the course of the project to check the accuracy of the citations and organize the entries for the senior editors—Murray, Bradley, Craigie, and Onions—who coordinated this enormous literate effort. Looking at this photograph of editor and citations, no less than in paging through the *OED*, it is easy enough to assume that here is the entirety of the English language and its literature. When the dictionary was finally finished and printed as a complete set in 1933, some eighteen years after Murray's death, it included a ninety-one-page, three-column list of authors and works which, the editors noted, failed to cover all of the citations that were included in the dictionary. Nonetheless, the list is, according to the preface, "a bibliography of English literature such as does not exist elsewhere." This picture of the tireless editor assembling the *OED* out of the whole of English literature, citation by citation, sets out the mythical proportions of the project; it is an image complemented and contradicted, in effect, by a second photograph from the series.

This photograph, revealing another side to the marshaling of authorities, captures the editor standing at his preferred high-desk, looking up at the camera with a slight, wry smile. This time he has a stack of citations and a pen in his hand, as if he were again caught at this Adam-like task of properly naming the things that make up this world. Over his shoulder, three assistants are busy working at a table, while a fourth is writing at a broad, sloped shelf, set between upper and lower bookcases. Both Murray's desk and the shelf that runs around the periphery of this part of the room support a great many open books. Elisabeth Murray describes in her biography how her grandfather worked amid open copies of Johnson's *Dictionary*, Littré's *Dictionnaire de la langue française*, Webster's *American Dictionary of the English Language*, the American *Century Dictionary*, and Nathan Bailey's *Universal Etymological English Dictionary* (CWW, p. 298). In addition to these oft-turned-to reference works, Latin, Greek, German, Danish, and Dutch dictionaries were used to establish etymologies. The open reference books featured in this photograph represent that easy intertextuality that exists among dictionaries, whether the borrowings are accredited, as in the *OED*, or not, as in other dictionaries. Editors have long turned to old lexicons to beget, or at least bolster, new ones.[7]

Murray and the other editors of the *OED*, however, were committed to breaking this cycle by working directly from the use of the English language over the last millennium, rather than relying on the questionable extraction and scholarship of others. The dictionary was to be based on an unmediated contact with the English language, as if meaning had to be carefully extracted from preserved and verified specimens of the language. Murray points out in the "General Explanations" included in the first volume of the *OED* that the dictionary's definitions were intended to be "framed anew upon a study of all the quotations for each word," although he recognized from the beginning that there would be times when this would prove impractical. If firsthand sources could not be found, Murray insisted on acknowledging the dictionary's shortcomings and debts in a manner that distinguished the work's scholarship. If he felt forced to cite another dictionary, he fully acknowledged it, contrary to common practice; if there was little point in creating a definition anew, he credited his predecessor: "In particular, the explanations [definitions] of Dr. Johnson and of his editor Archdeacon Todd have often been adopted unchanged (within inverted commas and marked J. or T.), as have those of N. Bailey, and other early lexicographers to whom it is only right to give credit for original work which has become the common property of all their successors." Throughout this book, I return to this theme of the lexicographer's "original work," as an *editor* of the language, examining not only the sources of citation, but the precise ways in which they serve the framing (anew) of the definitions and the sense we make of the language.

Another quality of the Murray photographs is their way of locating the place in which the dictionary was made. Murray regularly signed the prefaces he wrote for each fascicle and volume as "James A. H. Murray, The Scriptorium, Oxford." The Scriptorium, featured in the photographs, was his pet name for the pigeon-holed, book-crammed workroom that housed his working life. The Scriptorium is his reference to the gothic chambers in which medieval monks spent their lifetimes carefully transcribing and illuminating the Bible and other works, to the greater glory of God, and it compares well enough with the image of Murray and his assistants engaged in copying out by hand what was to be another great book of books for the English language. In this second photograph, Murray stands apart from his assistants in a certain expression of devoutness, with his long dark coat, long white beard, and doctoral cap, suggesting a man engaged in a labor of some other-worldly purpose. On at least one occasion he came to express the spiritual elements he found in the project to his son, Aelfric, explaining to him that he began with "earnest Prayer every morning for help to do my work," to which he added, "to many a long article, but for affectation and the appearance of Pharisaism, I could gladly append *Deo soli sit gloria*" (*CWW*, p. 309). Murray was living out the monastic ethos celebrated by Thomas Carlyle: "Admirable was that of the old Monks, *Laborare est Orare*, Work is Worship" (1912, p. 193). This monastic bent was not uncommon to a Victorian era in search of what Northrop Frye has identified as a "saving remnant" meant to preserve a thread of spiritual authority otherwise threatened by scientific and proletariat forces (1967, p. 135). Murray was not the churchman that Trench had been, nor did he see the dictionary doing God's work in that same explicit way. Publicly, Murray proclaimed himself "a man of science . . . interested in that branch of anthropology that deals with the history of human speech" (*CWW*, p. 292). The mixture of spiritual and scientific investment in the work of editing the dictionary also had a way of appealing to the troubled Victorian mind. The religious doubts that ruffled the educated classes were allayed in part through a new faith in the powers of art and nature, on the one hand, and science and technology, on the other. This theme of an age reevaluating its sources of authority, which forms the subject of this book, defines the intellectual climate in which citations were gathered and a great dictionary was constituted under Murray's direction.

If Murray's use of "scriptorium" suggests that the editing was going on amid the medieval spires of that postcard known as Oxford, the truth was that the work took place in no more than a shed built of corrugated iron (as a fire precaution) in the backyard of the Murrays' North Oxford home. It sat oddly out of place a few steps from the back door of his respectable brick house, set within a large trench that kept it from disturbing the view of Murray's neighbor, a Professor Dicey. One visitor frankly noted that it was "like a tool house, a washhouse, or a stable" (*CWW*, p. 242). Murray had wryly observed that the point of this sunken obscurity was "that no trace of a place of real work shall be seen by fastidious and otiose Oxford" (p. 247). Although Murray was not without friends at Oxford, he suffered the exclusiveness of this ancient academic community. When he came to express his appreciation for the contribution of "men of Academic standing in the States" in his presidential address to the Philological Society in 1880, he added that "we have had no such help from any college or university in Great Britain" (*TPS*, 1880, p. 123).[8] It was only in 1900 that Oxford University appointed Murray to its recently established Board of Studies in English Language and Literature in recognition of the significant contribution the dictionary had made to the subject. He noted with some bitterness that the university waited until he was seventy years old to award him the Oxford doctoral cap that he had half-expected when he first took up residence in Oxford at the age of forty-eight. He spoke of himself as "to a great extent only a sojourner" in that ancient academic community (*CWW*, p. 248).[9] The Philological Society's *New English Dictionary* did not become the *Oxford* English dictionary until the 1933 edition, nor did the country's university community become really involved in the project until the editing of the *Supplement* during the second half of the twentieth century.

In a number of ways, Murray took over the immensely ambitious project of a largely amateur society and turned it into something of a backyard hobby-yacht that grew into an enormous Noah's ark. How is it, one might well ask, that a good part of the English language was assembled in a damp iron shed, lined with bundles of citation slips and shelves of reference books? I am playing up the personal qualities of the project, in all of the faintly romantic aspects that haunt archival pictures of the Scriptorium, to strike a balance with the prevailing, equally romanticized image of a God-given *OED* that circles the globe as the British flagship of the English language. There is an element of truth to both images of the *OED*. It is a far more human document than we sometimes imagine, far more aligned with the failings and ambiguities at the edge of meaning, than we recognize in turning to it. Yet this dictionary also carries with it, as flagships do, the full weight of a nation consumed with the struggles of democracy at home, imperialism abroad, and a culture seeking to mediate the eclipsing of religion by the gospel of science.

A final photograph of Murray at work is included in Elisabeth Murray's book. The photographer has arranged a group portrait in the Scriptorium, with Sir James at its center, another smile on his face. He is flanked by two of his daughters who worked on the project, with three other assistants standing behind them. The caption with the photograph explains that this was, in fact, Murray's last day in the Scriptorium, having been taken some two weeks before his death on July 26, 1915. In spite of his failing health, we might gather from that smile that he knew, with his sense of faith and the burden of experience, that he had conquered the language, and that the dictionary, which he had assembled out of the enormity of the English language, was to have no peer for its scholarship, its depth of inquiry into philology and meaning. Over the course of his thirty-six years in the Scriptorium, he edited 7,207 of the first edition's 15,487 pages. He had spent weeks, as he points out in the preface to the first volume, defining such seemingly slight words as *at* or *be*, and written "ten, twenty, or thirty letters" to track down the meaning of an obscure term. He had hounded the promised work out of less than diligent readers in the Philological Society, watched the eighteenth-century works assigned to the American volunteers go unread through misunderstandings, and dealt with the delegates of the Press who were apparently not above "taking advantage of legal technicalities to escape moral obligations," as a writer in *The Oxford Review* put it at the time (*CWW*, p. 248).

The *OED* was one of the great triumphs of the self-taught Victorian scholar. Murray had risen from his start as an assistant teacher at Hawick in Scotland, after ending his formal schooling at age fourteen. He spent time as a bank clerk in London and as an assistant master at Mill Hill School, all the while continuing to teach himself a number of languages and lecturing at meetings of the Philological Society on dialect forms and the northern influences on Shakespeare's language. Murray's smile in the final photograph has a way of turning back the frustrating years that he had spent wrestling tirelessly, not only with the language, but the people that were helping to put the dictionary together. Yet the photograph misleadingly suggests that here sits and stands the full human scale of the project, focused on the one great man at the head of the venture.

The truth is that this small ensemble of editor, family, and assistants is more notable for those who are missing than those who are present. A massive number of people might have been assembled in the Oxford commons, beginning with the three other editors and their assistants, the nine Murray children who sorted and cited, and their tireless mother, Ada Murray; then on to the numerous students at Mill Hill School and the membership of the Philological Society who toiled at citing and editing; and finally the thousands of readers whom this photographer might have snapped looking up from the citation slips they are copying, their books propped open in their laps. Even if a large part of the project was not to be in Murray's hand, his imprint has remained on many aspects of the dictionary's design. It can be felt in the relentless pursuit of full documentation and first published usage, in the regard for literary usage, and it can be seen in the masterful design of the dictionary's page. If there has been, as I will go on to show, something of a shift in the linguistic authorities cited by the editors of *A Supplement to the Oxford English Dictionary* and the second edition, the *OED* still carries forward the spirit of that Society of gentlemen and ladies, all of whom found their champion in James A. H. Murray.

Apart from these romantic images of editor and reader, it should also be clear that a dictionary of this massive a scale needs to be underwritten or authorized by some greater national purpose, a purpose that was perhaps best articulated in philological terms by Richard Trench, but was fully realized through the efforts of Murray and the Philological Society. The theme is one of creating the nation in one's imagined best self by finding the unifying chords struck by language and literature. Murray's good friend, Walter Skeat, Cambridge philologist and early supporter of the *OED* project, actively promoted the study of the language as opening students' eyes "to the Unity of English, that in English literature there is an unbroken succession of authors from the reign of Alfred to that of Victoria, and that the language which we speak *now* is absolutely *one*, in its essence, with the language that was spoken in the days when the English first invaded the island and defeated and overwhelmed its British inhabitants" (1873, p. xii).

Murray's tenure roughly coincided with the period which historian E. J. Hobsbawm (1987) has identified as the Age of Empire, 1875–1914. The partitioning of the world, as Hobsbawm describes the process among the European powers, bears some comparison with this project to establish the sovereign dominion of the English language, both delineating its bounds and greatly expanding its claim as an administrative and cultural force in the world. During this period, the English language arrived among many people as the purported word of God, the order of military authority, the rule of law, and the currency of trade and exploitation—it was the very carrier of civilization. It was carried abroad by the Bible and the dictionary which served as the two great record books of the English language. In happy conjunction with English literature, they were the mainstays of a properly colonial education with its promise of a ticket to other worlds. So it now stands that the *OED* still has its sovereignty intact, when other empires and emperors have long since departed and the authority of the Bible no longer stands without question.

Shortly after James Murray and Oxford University Press joined forces for the publication of *A New English Dictionary*, the celebrated French historian, Ernest Renan, declared to all of Europe in his famous 1882 lecture, "*Qu'est-ce q'une nation?*" that "a Nation is a spiritual principle," one that "presupposes a past" (1990, pp. 18–19). The *OED* was to be part of the spiritual/scientific presupposition of a British nation that realized itself through its extended claims on the world. The Newtonian law of motion working on the dictionary dictates that it was to be propelled forward, through the twentieth century, by this act of projecting historically a protonational literate imagination. This dictionary's authorization of the English language is found in the particular bonds struck between citation and definition, history and sense. In this way, at least, the authority of the dictionary is not the myth that Ronald Wells (1973) claims it is, simply because the book is intended to possess a descriptive function. If the dictionary does not single-handedly establish the standard of usage for the language, as Wells rightly argues, it definitely contributes, in conjunction with other forces, to the disciplining of language and writer. What distinguishes the *OED* from other dictionaries is its superior rationalization of this authority over the language. Its historical principles, affected through what Raymond Williams calls its "air of massive impersonality," fix the definition of the English language to the citation which, in the first instance, constitutes the national literature and more broadly encompasses the writing trade, the book system (1976, p. 18).

Looking back on the significance of Oxford University Press's publication of the *OED*, Nicholas Barker makes perhaps the ultimate claim for it by proposing that "no other single factor has assured the position of English as the twentieth-century lingua franca" (1978, p. 52). However overstated that may appear, the success of this dictionary does represent a further ideological extension of English, as word and force, throughout the world, moving in this case from the scriptural to the lexicographical and soon followed by the pedagogical, in the form of the ubiquitous school dictionary. James Murray, one might well think, had none of this in mind as he labored in the Scriptorium with all of his scholarly modesty. Yet one can argue that it had been there in Trench's vision for the work of the Philological Society and in Murray's reflections on the resulting project. How those interests have developed since Trench first set out the deficiencies of the English dictionary, how they are divided between the Society and the university, between reader and professor, literary author and journeyman writer, can be found in the pattern of citations that have been selected over the last century and a quarter in constituting the realm and history of the English language. In the next chapter I begin with the citational situation of Shakespeare in the dictionary, to illustrate the role of literary reputation and authority; and in the following chapter I will examine the extraction of meanings by looking at the specific contribution of citations from *The Taming of the Shrew*.

## CHAPTER 4

# Shakespeare's Dictionary

WELL BEFORE the Philological Society's *New English Dictionary* was completed, scholars began turning to the published fascicles in their study of the English language. Otto Jespersen's history of the English language, published in 1906, took considerable advantage of the partially completed work, but not without pointing out apparent weaknesses in the dictionary, including one that arose from the considerable attention paid to William Shakespeare:

> In turning over the pages of the *New English Dictionary*, where every pains has been taken to ascertain the earliest occurrence of each word and of each signification, one is struck by the frequency with which Shakespeare's name is found affixed to the earliest quotation for words or meanings. In many cases this is no doubt due to the fact that Shakespeare's vocabulary has been registered with greater care in Concordances and in Al. Schmidt's invaluable *Shakespeare-Lexicon* than that of any other author, so that his words cannot escape notice, while the same words may occur unnoticed in the pages of many an earlier author. (1982, pp. 210–211)

The irony that Shakespeare's notable presence in the *OED* was determined by the contribution of another lexicon, rather than through the avid reading of his work, is overshadowed by the way this may have skewed the scientific spirit, as Murray called it, that guided the dictionary's coverage of the language. The Philological Society's "Proposal" advises those readers who were in search of citations for the period 1526–1674 to find "a quotation for every word, phrase, idiom &c., in his book that does not occur in the Concordances to the Bible and Shakspere, or that to the Bible only, if the Shakspere Concordance be unprocurable" (*TPS*, 1857, p. 5).[1] Among the Shakespearean concordances available at the time, Schmidt's *Shakespeare-Lexicon* was supplemented by Francis Twiss's from 1805 and Mary Cowden Clarke's from 1845. In addition to Cruden's concordance for the Authorized Version of the Bible mentioned in the proposal, Milton was covered at the time by three indexes, Tennyson by two, and Pope by one (Schäfer, 1980, p. 40). The thoroughness of literary citation that marks the *OED* was certainly aided by this ready flow of material from one reference work to another. The concordance is, after all, little more than a handy one-author dictionary. The index and the concordance are part of the transformation of the book from an event in the language to a tool of reference, citation, and scholarship; they form part of a literate technology that only enhances the intertextuality of the book trade.

A century earlier, Samuel Johnson had taken advantage of the recently published indexes to the Bible and Milton's *Paradise Lost* in preparing a fourth edition of the *Dictionary* that better reflected his current Christian preoccupations (Reddick, 1990, pp. 105–107). Although a Shakespearean index had yet to be composed, it did not prevent Johnson from citing the Elizabethan playwright above all others in his *Dictionary*. An accurate count of citations in Johnson has yet to be completed, and work is underway to create an electronic version of his *Dictionary*. Still, in 1932 Lewis Freed counted the citational sources for the first volume of the two-volume *Dictionary* in his modest Cornell University dissertation, "The Sources of Johnson's Dictionary." Although I present a fuller version of both tables in chapter 6, let me introduce, for the sake of comparison, the citation figures for the five leading authors in the first volume of Johnson's *Dictionary* and the *OED* (see table 4.1 in the Appendix).

Where Johnson set out to build his work as much as possible on the language's best writers and the *OED* intended to include the entirety of English literature, both turned to Shakespeare above all in illustrating English vocabulary in a coincidence of literary taste and linguistic science. Although it does seem that Shakespeare played a far greater role (by percentage of citations) in Johnson's *Dictionary*, he certainly outdistances his nearest rival to an even greater extent in the *OED*. To give a sense of what Shakespeare means to the *OED*, the count of 32,868 Shakespeare citations amounts to nearly 2 percent of the 1,827,306 total for the first edition of the dictionary. His usage also plays a supporting role in roughly 14 percent of the dictionary's 240,000 main entries.[2] The largesse of his contribution to the definition of the language needs to be compared to the published body of his work that spans roughly two decades and employs a vocabulary of 29,066 distinct words (although who knows how many senses), amounting to a relatively modest, if nonetheless rich, linguistic hoard, at least within the context of a millennium's worth of the English language.

It would appear that the editorial staff of the *OED*, taking its lead from Johnson and assisted by a number of concordances to Shakespeare's work, took every opportunity to root the English language in this man's craft. Shakespeare's hold on the *OED* represents the fulfillment, in part, of the Philological Society's 1858 resolution "to make a Dictionary worthy of the English Language." It is as if in answer to their "call upon Englishmen to come forward and write their own dictionary," Shakespeare had risen to the occasion, with the kindly assistance of concordance and dictionary editors, and worked tirelessly to fill out the language. The Society had been, after all, as intent on shaping an English language worthy of a great dictionary as vice versa. And for a leading part in this production, who better than Shakespeare?

This obvious point actually poses a number of challenges to a lexicography intended to be, as Murray announced in 1900, "permeated through and through with the scientific method of the century" (1970, p. 49). Does a poet's use of a word provide a reliable guide to its common sense? Many writers have willingly set poetry off from what might otherwise be understood as the natural life of the language. To take an extreme and modern instance of an aesthetic stance toward verse, the American poet Karl Shapiro proudly sets poetry apart from basic linguistic sense in his essay, "Prosody as Meaning":

> Poetry is not language, but a language *sui generis* which can be understood, paraphrased, or translated only as poetry. Because poetry uses language it is assumed, I think mistakenly, that poetry functions as language. The same word used in a line of prose and a line of poetry is really two different words, not even similar, except in appearance. I would designate the poetry word as "not-word." What we call the sense of poetry is not therefore linguistic sense but something intrinsically and extrinsically different. (1949, p. 338)

Although Shipiro admits to stacking his case by turning to e. e. cummings for his examples, it must still be recognized that, if only in intention, poetry is perhaps not the material out of which to build a natural history of the language. Of course, Shipiro offers only one side of the poetic equation. Presenting something of a counterview is T. S. Eliot, who in his essay, "What Dante Means to Me," insists that Shakespeare alone among English poets served the larger development of the language, while other poets, he allows, enact a form of linguistic abuse:

> The whole study and practice of Dante seems to me to teach that the poet should be the servant of his language, rather than master of it. . . . Of some great poets, and of some great English poets especially, one can say they were privileged by their genius to *abuse* the English language, to develop an idiom so peculiar and even eccentric, that it could be of no use to later poets. Dante seems to me to have a place in Italian literature—which in this respect, only Shakespeare has in ours; that they give body to the soul of the language. . . . To pass on to posterity one's own language, more highly developed, more refined, and more precise than it was before one wrote it, that is the highest achievement of the poet as poet. (Eliot, 1965, p. 133)

This fundamental question of the poet's credibility as a witness to the language appears to have gone unasked in the transactions of the Philological Society during the long period of the dictionary's editing. Yet there are many indications that literature's contribution to knowledge figured among the most profound philosophical questions asked at this time. As Peter Dale describes it, "the essential intellectual history of the nineteenth century may fairly be described as a search for an adequate replacement for the lost Christian totality, an effort to resurrect a saving belief, as Carlyle put it, on the ashes of the French Revolution" (1989, p. 5). For Carlyle, as we shall see, literature offered a point of resurrection, with Shakespeare at its head, and yet this romantic faith in art tells but half the story of this dictionary. Although Dale does not treat the *OED* in his discussion of positivism and the search for a new mode of totality during the Victorian era, he captures the very spirit of the dictionary as he argues for how, due to the proximity to romanticism, "the aesthetic conscious-ness irresistibly asserts itself in the very midst of the positivist project" (p. 31). This resurrected faith in literature found its expression in such leading figures of aesthetic positivism as John Stuart Mill, who does not doubt that "poetry, when it is really such, is truth . . . [and] the truth of poetry is to paint the human soul truly" (Mill, 1963, p. 6). So it was with the *OED*, as it moves between a faith in the poet's word to the strictures of a new positivism. The dictionary, in its scientific and historical princi-ples, engaged in an early form of socio-linguistics, involving a systematic, historical sampling of linguistic data. The unacknowledged compromise of this scientific empiricism, found in the overrepresentation of the poet, betrays Dale's lingering "aesthetic consciousness." It may not be too much to claim that the *OED* represents one attempt to overcome the collapse of the Christian and metaphysical totality through its own over-arching efforts at capturing the whole of the principal organ of reason. This dictionary does seem to meet Dale's insistence on a Victorian inter-section of "aesthetic mode" and "scientific enterprise," rather than per-petuating a rift between the two that was to develop later. It seems natural enough for those who faced the task of reconstructing a fortress of reason and fact to find in Shakespeare's poetic application of genius an indispen-sable aspect of any new conception of humankind. There is no clearer indication of the intertwining spirits of positivism and romanticism than in the Shakespearean concordance itself, which served the *OED* editors so well; it is a research instrument designed to afford a more systematic study of the truth of art.

A factor secondary to the part played by Shakespeare and by literature more generally in the *OED* is found in Ian Small's thesis that during the late Victorian period the "pedagogic and national claims being made for 'English'" became part of a struggle to bring English literature within the authoritative hold of the university (1991, p. 139). In conveying the mighty enthusiasm with which literature was being taken up as a register of national character, Small cites Oxford professor of poetry John Campbell Shairp in a 1882 review of the first volume of the school text, *English Poets*: "The roll of English poetry, reaching through 500 years, contains the essence of the national life—it registers the pulsations of the mighty heart of England during the all those centuries" (Small, 1991, p. 139). It might well seem that the great Oxford dictionary made its institutional contribution by moving from an essentially amateur society to a university press. The thrust of Small's concern for this authoritative taking hold of art's civilizing values is that we often forget how this art met with considerable opposition, not only from those at the universities who felt that English literature did not warrant formal study, but from the aestheticism represented by Walter Pater, James Whistler, and Oscar Wilde. Here were critical voices ready to deny literature's moral value and disparage its service role as they actively campaigned against the formation of a national literary canon. At the very least, Small insists, art's serviceability and social utility in such institutional settings (including, I am suggesting, the dictionary) should not be assumed as the dedicated "roll of English poetry."[3]

All of which is to say that, given that Shakespeare is now perceived as central to the English people's image of the language, it is worthwhile exploring certain weaknesses to the assumptions underwriting the particular investment of authority in the playwright made by the *OED*. What is garnered by the signature of the poet, especially in Shakespeare's case, when text and authorship raise such interesting questions about authenticity and authority? What sort of critical groundwork had been laid out on Shakespeare's behalf that so effectively prepared the way for this monumental use of the poet by the editors of the Society's dictionary? By the Victorian era, well after Johnson's effective use of Shakespeare in his *Dictionary*, there appears to have been little need to question the playwright's testimony on behalf of the English language or, for that matter, the basis on which a dictionary is further authorized by such close coverage of this poet-playwright.

Members of the Society, had they the slightest doubts about the poetics of lexicography, might have taken a cue from Shakespeare himself. Part of his work's charm is its knowing way of speaking against itself as language, theater, and life. Think of Juliet's "What's in a name?"; Macbeth's "There would have been time for such a word . . . signifying nothing"; Hamlet's "To define true madness. What is't but to be nothing but mad"; Falstaff's "What is that word, honour? Air. A trim reckoning"; Caliban's "You taught me language; and my profit on't / Is, I know how to curse." Less well known, perhaps, is Byron's "Taffeta phrases, silken terms precise . . . have blown me full of maggot ostentation, I do forswear them" from *Love's Labor's Lost* and, from *The Merchant of Venice*, Lorenzo's "How every fool can play upon the word." Does this seem the sort of thinking about language that dictionaries are comfortably built upon?

> AUDREY: I do not know what "poetical" is: is it honest in deed and word? is it a true thing?
> TOUCHSTONE: No, truly; for the true poetry is the most feigning . . .
>
> (*As You Like It*, III.iii.14–17)

True and feigning poetry forms one aspect of the divided allegiance to this dictionary. The Philological Society's "Proposal" had been remarkably liberal in setting the scope for a new English dictionary—"We admit as authorities all English books" (*TPS*, 1857, p. 3)—and equally adamant about repudiating "the theory which converts the lexicographer into an arbiter of style" (p. 2). Yet in the actual making of the dictionary, true feigning poetry was admitted first among equals (and even then not everyone's poetry considered equally). Yet the *OED*'s commitment to the language's best poets is but one of its many authoritative facets as a comprehensive dictionary of the language. The dictionary cites in no small measure the work of editors, journalists, and technical writers, although literature holds the front row among the fraternity of writers that are called upon to underwrite the first edition of this dictionary. Certainly by comparison, both Johnson's and Richardson's dictionaries reflect a greater dependence on the citation of great literature, especially as they present more fully engaging extracts than the *OED*. For his part, editor James Murray was especially concerned that the literary citing of "pithy sentences or elegant extracts" might mean sacrificing space required for more comprehensive historical coverage of the language. Yet if the literary citation had to be abbreviated in the *OED*, the dictionary's reference to Shakespeare was still extensive. In this, the dictionary supports an image of the English language as the creative, self-made act of Englishmen, led by the likes of William Shakespeare. The dictionary is Victorian science attuned to the nation-building project, to setting in place a history of the English language that ran back through Shakespeare, covering a thousand years of literary achievement. Such was the goal of "the largest single engine of research working anywhere in the world," as one of Murray's correspondents termed the dictionary's project (cited in Burchfield, 1989, p. 196).

The extensive citing of Shakespeare raises questions about the claims of this dictionary to having laid English out on historical and scientific principles. It may seem too obvious to recall that the plays were written to live in that special linguistic realm of the stage, and their transformation into textual artifacts remains ridden with no small problems and uncertainties. The question of the scripts' textual status is further compounded by issues of authorship, as authorization is very much at question in underwriting a dictionary. Literary critic Marjorie Garber, for example, works with a concept of "Shakespeare's ghost writers," pointing to how his plays offer "a critique of the concept of authorship and in particular the possibility of origin" (1987, p. 26). Her deconstructive turn sets into perspective our (ever-futile) search for origins, especially among readers, for "truth's authentic author" (*Troilus and Cressida*, III.ii.181). The truth verified by signature seems relevant to the historical principles of a dictionary that depends on the testimony of named authors or works for the given use of a word. Garber regards the question of the plays' authorship in psychoanalytic terms that appear to bear equally well on the making of the *OED*: "The search for an author, like any other quest for parentage, reveals more about the searcher than about the sought, for what is demanded is a revisitation of the primal scene" (p. 27). This desire to secure the primal scene for the mother tongue is met by citational features of the *OED*, with Shakespeare as first among the elected fathers.

Questions surrounding the authenticity of paternity, particularly in the over-representation of this patriarch, called for a certain compromise of historical and scientific principles in editing the *OED*. Without decisive evidence on many aspects of Shakespeare's authorship, naming the author of *these* citations represents an act of national trust within the well-documented genealogy of the English language. The playwright's missing signature is, in a sense, called upon to attest to a good part of a newly written history of the English language. Adding to the irony of the *OED* staking its largest literary claim on such a questionable bibliographical foundation is the evidence for Shakespeare's own lack of regard for matters of originality and ownership of the plays. Although he may have had a head for business, he gave little thought to seeing his works properly into print, which was for playwrights at the time a largely profitless and unprotected enterprise.[4]

It might be argued that a mythical genius was part of what was needed by a culture that had pinned most of its cultural reference points to a golden age in a classical world far from the British Isles. As it was, promoters of Shakespeare's art, beginning with Ben Jonson's praise-laden preface to the first collected edition of the plays, compared his work to that of the Greek tragedians.[5] In this way, Shakespeare offered the nation an arched bridge between the Elysian fields of classical civilization and the newfound mercantile empire of the English middle class. Enter the Victorian era, and this connection could be accomplished through the Elizabethan middle-distance on grounds that offended few sensibilities, then and now. Poets play a part in the life of the language, but to what degree in any given period is difficult to ascertain with any confidence. The *OED*'s particular treatment of Shakespeare is rather a model of how lexicographers and readers would have the roots of the language magnificently laid out, as if it were theirs for the shaping. Yet rather than dismiss or discount the Shakespearean citations, we need to understand how this particular authority in the language was critically refashioned over the centuries, since the time Shakespeare first formed part of the poetic breakthrough represented by the Elizabethan theater.

Richard Foster Jones, in *The Triumph of the English Language* (1953), describes in some detail how, in a process that began with the Age of Chaucer in the fourteenth century, the Elizabethans finally secured the place of English as the literary equal to Latin, French, and Italian.[6] In the course of his argument, he cites Thomas Nashe's claim in 1592 that "the Poets of our time . . . haued cleansed our language from barbarisme, and made the vulgar sort here in London . . . to aspire to a richer puritie of speach that communicated with the Comminality of any Nation vnder heauen" (p. 178). Nashe's nationalist sense of the superior Elizabethan contribution to the language is reflected in the citations included in the *OED* from that period. Among the historical periods prior to the time of the actual editing of the dictionary, when contemporary sources abounded, the years around 1600 account for more of the dictionary's earliest citations for new words, as well as citations in general, than from any other period.[7] To appreciate this overcoming of Latin's literate hegemony, one has only to consider that in the year of Shakespeare's birth, 1564, Queen Elizabeth was happy to address her English ministers in Latin as they attended the Cambridge Disputations that year, declaring, "I would have all of you bear this one thing in mind that no road is straighter, none shorter, none more adapted to win the good things of fortune or the good-will of your Prince, then the pursuit of Good Letters" (cited in B. Smith, 1929, p. 498). For some time to come, the pursuit of those richly rewarded "Good Letters," the foundation of humanism, both sacred and secular, and all schooling beyond primary school, was principally the purview of Latin. Many of the writers of the Elizabethan period, as they wrote in English, were engaged in setting the country and its literate activity, in effect, free of a scholastic and papal Latin. This shift had been initiated by the literary labors of Chaucer, Gower, and Langland, some two centuries before, all of whom also play a significant part in the *OED*. But as Jones argues, the Elizabethans saw the English language triumph in this battle of the languages. Not so much did Shakespeare unsettle the grip of ancient Athens and Rome as play to it with his schoolboy Latin tags and classical references. Three centuries later he was being held up by Carlyle, Emerson, and the *OED* as a figure from a golden age who might rightly lead the English people in their own tongue.

In order to appreciate the significance of Shakespeare's Victorian coronation as a king among English poets, one must realize the degree to which his later greatness was a process of "reinventing" the playwright, to use a term from the title of Gary Taylor's book on Shakespeare (1989). The *OED*'s investment in Shakespeare needs to be understood as part of a cultural production of interest and appreciation that resulted in, among other things, the concordances to the poet's plays. Shakespeare, in the two-and-a-half centuries since his death, had gradually been invested with the necessary authority for securing the language in the fashion desired by the Philological Society.

In the late seventeenth century, as Taylor points out in his witty history of "Shakespearotics," the critical word on Shakespeare's language was *obfuscation*, most notably expressed by the poet John Dryden (Taylor, 1989, pp. 33–51). Dryden took a keen interest in the fate of the language and was part of a lobby that petitioned the Royal Society to establish an English-language academy after the manner of the French. When it came to Shakespeare, he was more than a little disturbed by the Elizabethan playwright's sheer bombast and the unreasonableness of his poetry, not to mention his rough use of lowly wheelwright and ragman imagery. The lexicographical point does stand in Shakespeare's favor, as he came to represent a broad range of language on the stage, although it could often be through a form of obvious caricaturing, as with the rude mechanicals in *A Midsummer Night's Dream*. It also needs to be noted that Dryden's complaint may well have something to do with dead competitors, as this poet-playwright was not above turning on the Shakespeare-keen Restoration audience of his own time "which loves poetry," Dryden complains, "but understands it not" (cited by Taylor, 1989, p. 42). In Dryden's critical assessment, Shakespeare "often obscures his meaning by his words, and sometimes makes it unintelligible," suggesting that he is particularly ill-suited to illustrate definitions in a dictionary (cited in Taylor, 1989, p. 43). In defense of both Dryden's judgment and Shakespeare's art, Taylor allows that Dryden faced corrupted editions of Shakespeare's work. Yet if it is true, as Taylor insists, that "we understand Shakespeare, when we do, only by virtue of the labors of centuries of annotators" (p. 43), then a greater degree of irony creeps into the *OED*'s use of a clipped citation from Shakespeare. He who is so in need of annotation becomes, in turn, the great annotator of the language.

Questions about Shakespeare's language during the Restoration period led to theater companies *revising* the vocabulary of his plays to make it comprehensible to the theater audience. Taylor offers examples from Sir William Davenant's reworking of *Hamlet* for his theater company, which included substituting *proclaim* for *bray out*, and *obscurely* for *in hugger mugger* (p. 47). Again, the oddity is that Shakespearean diction does not appear to pose nearly the same challenge for modern readers or playgoers. The Restoration audience had not benefited by an education in annotated editions of the plays; they were, as well, a far broader cross section of society than attends in modern times. This brings us to one of the key aspects of Shakespeare's ultimate suitability as a source of citational authority. His current, if somewhat more restricted, accessibility operates at the direction of the state, through the support of both the school system and public theaters. His considerable presence in the *OED* may depend far more on such interventions than is suggested by the natural evolutionary model of meaning presented by the dictionary.

But before the pervasive influence of the schools, Shakespeare's champion proved to be the periodical press. One of the early breakthroughs in Shakespeare's claim on the history of the language came with the flowering of eighteenth-century journalism. By virtue of excerpt and citation, the *Tatler*, published from 1709 to 1711, turned the playwright into a poet, first establishing how aptly Shakespearean citations could serve a writer in search of a confirming phrase or word. In Taylor's estimation, Shakespeare was used to "cudgel the past and to shame the present" (1989, p. 63). No other figure is called upon as often in the *Tatler's* spirit of Whiggish compromise on the side of civil behavior and liberty. Shakespeare's reputation had undergone a sea change since the Restoration. Where *Julius Caesar* and *Macbeth* were used once to rebuke the excesses of contemporary theater and drive home the virtues of propriety, Shakespeare was then held up, Taylor feels, "as an affirmation of the literary primacy of 'plain and simple' bourgeois humanity" (p. 65). Between these two eras, the extensive editing of the plays, in search of the real and true text, furthered Shakespeare's standing. Indeed, it provided another opportunity for his work to enhance the reputation of others, including a large number of established literary figures such as Pope and Johnson.

With each edition of the plays, the issue increasingly became one of editing either for the stage or page. Pope was most adamant about "the ignorance of the Players, both as his actors, and as his editors" (cited in Taylor, p. 83). His remedy was to edit the plays for their readerliness, consulting as many editions as he could lay his hands on to piece together the ideal text. But Pope's edition is part of what gave that movable literary feast its home as a *text*, to which he appended, for the first time, a glossary. Taylor concludes that with the new era initiated by Pope's edition, "the fullness of Shakespeare's meaning is always just out of reach, postponed until we can read another old book, which would make clear to us some new aspect of what Shakespeare said or—just as significantly—deliberately avoided saying" (p. 87). What was made clear at least was that there was no *singular* Shakespeare—"always just out of reach."

As important as Pope's edition was, Johnson was the one who first demonstrated Shakespeare's lexicographical usefulness, with the playwright accounting for roughly 20 percent of the citations in the *Dictionary*. But in the preface to his edition of Shakespeare's plays, Johnson also provided a critical turning point in understanding the playwright's contribution to the language, providing in essence one of the principal warrants for the *OED*'s use of his work.[8] With Shakespeare, Johnson holds, "drama is the mirror of life." In particular, Johnson finds in the language of the plays a naturalness that indeed qualifies it as a reliable source for a dictionary of the English tongue: "The dialogue of this author . . . is pursued with so much ease and simplicity that it seems scarcely to claim the merit of fiction, but to have been gleaned by diligent selection out of common conversation, and common occurrences" (1968, p. 264). He went on to assure his readers that Shakespeare's "scenes are occupied by men, who act and speak as the reader thinks that he should have spoken and acted on the same occasion" (p. 265). Johnson held that Shakespeare was one of the "original masters of our language," who knew best where to gather the true language of the nation: "If there be, what I believe there is, in every nation, a style which never becomes obsolete, a certain mode of phraseology so consonant and congenial to the analogy and principles of its respective language as to remain settled and unaltered; this style is probably to be sought in the common intercourse of life, among those who speak only to be understood, without ambition of elegance" (pp. 269–270).

The dictionary, too, shares an interest in this classical mimetic sense. We might imagine the effect of a lexicographical mirror taking its image from the Shakespearean glass, reflecting both a circularity of meaning among texts as well as something more of the "common intercourse of life." As it turns out, Johnson is not long in turning against his initial claims, and a few pages farther down the road we find a more modest aside let drop, "whether he represented the real conversation of his time is not easy to determine" (1968, p. 271). In fact, the tone of the preface can often be strikingly defensive of Shakespeare, reminding us that the great poet was not always unassailable. At times, Johnson also shows temperance in his praise of Shakespeare's language, as he notes the "disproportionate pomp of diction" in his narration, and the "commonly cold and weak" nature of his set speeches. The most serious charge for Johnson, in his former pose as a lexicographer in the spirit of John Locke, must be that in Shakespeare "the equality of words to things is very often neglected" (p. 272). There are cracks enough in this mirror, or at least in Johnson's sighting of it, in the works of Shakespeare.

When it comes to the Victorian period, the critical figure central to establishing Shakespeare's cultural authority is Thomas Carlyle. Through a public lecture series given in London during 1840 and published as *On Heroes, Hero-Worship and the Heroic in History* (1841), the first of the great Victorian sages placed Shakespeare squarely within the evolutionary path of civilization's great heroes. Carlyle's initial lecture, "The Hero as Divinity," turned to Scandinavian mythology for its primary instance of the mythical man made into a god. In returning to this distant past, Carlyle was deliberately speaking to contemporary fears that the religious hold on the world was falling away: "The world, which is now divine only to the gifted, was then divine to whosoever would turn his upon it" (Carlyle, n.d., p. 17). After a second lecture, "The Hero as Prophet," which featured Mahomet as his singular example, Carlyle turned fully earthward in his third lecture, casting his regard on the human heroics of the poets, taking Shakespeare and Dante as the "Saints of poetry" who have been rightly canonized for their creative virtues (p. 113). The "Hero as Poet" is by no means the end of Carlyle's history, yet his discussion of the poet proves extremely helpful in understanding what Shakespeare brought to the pages of the *OED*.[9] Carlyle was speaking at a time when there was a distinct need for supplementing traditional values and figures, a time to bring the heroes within reach, a time to reach across the classes through a unifying device such as literature: "We are all poets when we *read* a poem well," Carlyle offers in his discussion of the Hero as Poet, adding that "Nay, all speech even the commonest speech, has something of song in it," with song at the heart of poetry for Carlyle (pp. 108, 110). This Wordsworthian point had been made only a few years earlier by John Stuart Mill in "Thoughts on Poetry and Its Varieties": "For whosoever writes out truly any human feeling writes poetry" (1963, p. 14). Here was poetry firmly affixed to the truth of both language and hear tby the romantic Carlyle and positivist Mill, an affirmation which seemed to signal, in turn, a spiritual enfranchisement of the vernacular. But this populist sentiment did not run deep; there was an assumed difference in Carlyle and Mill between the potential in each of us for poetry and the realized truth of poets. That is, they were prepared to put their faith in the nation's clerisy, as Coleridge identified the new class of intellectual and writer who would guide literature's formation of a new *lingua communis*.[10]

In elevating the poet's position as a political voice, Carlyle does not hesitate to amplify the humble personhood of William Shakespeare, as many have in celebrating his representation of the sturdy English stock: "This is our poor Warwickshire Peasant, who rose to be Manager of a Playhouse, so that he could live without begging" (n.d., p. 148). The stress on the common man with a quill, as well as a nose for opportunity, is part of Carlyle's perceptive and political regard for the power of print: "Literature is our Parliament too. Printing, which comes necessarily out of Writing, I say often, is equivalent to Democracy; invent Writing, Democracy is inevitable. . . . Whoever can speak, speaking now to the whole nation, becomes a power, a branch of government, with inalienable weight in law-making, in all acts of authority. . . . The nation is governed by all that was tongue in the nation: Democracy is virtually *there*" (p. 213). Carlyle believed that Democracy would become "palpably extant" through this truth-will-out power of Printing. It is a power he vests in the poet, first of all, followed by the man of letters, and only then, perhaps, in the fourth estate or the press.

Although the inevitability of Democracy was not explicitly part of the rhetoric that mobilized the *New English Dictionary* project, the dictionary is decidedly Writing's invention, an unmistakable product of Printing, and an enabler of those who would speak to the whole nation. And with the dictionary I would say, following Carlyle, Democracy is *virtually* there. The dictionary is potentially a populist tool that might assist and assure "whoever can speak," as Carlyle put it, extending the power of its readers to speak to the whole nation. But as I have already stressed, this and other Victorian projects ran on an alternating current that seemed equally capable of boosting a rising democracy at home and an expanding empire abroad. Carlyle's language of power and power of language cut both ways. For this enfranchisement of "whoever can speak" refers principally to those who are properly educated, who participate in the literate culture defined by the journals of opinion and review, and who define a new level of democratic participation at home based on property, even as they underwrote highly undemocratic forms of political economy that operated increasingly on a global scale: "Divinity and prophet are past. We are now to see our Hero in the less ambitious, but also less questionable, character of Poet; a character which does not pass. The poet is a heroic figure belonging to all ages. . . . Let Nature send a Hero-soul; in no age is it other than possible that he may be shaped into a Poet" (Carlyle, n.d., p. 104).

Carlyle sets the poet-as-hero a step or two above the position of unacknowledged legislator that had been proposed by Shelley in his famous defense of poetry. "I fancy there is in him" Carlyle claimed, "the Politician, the Thinker, Legislator, Philosopher—in one or the other degree, he could have been, he is all these" (p. 104). Carlyle was determined to find a place for literature, David Riede has argued, "beyond the irresolution of romanticism to a position of genuine authority" (1989, p. 88).[11] Carlyle equates the prophet and the poet in a form of sacred trust: "In some old languages, again, the titles are synonymous; *Vates* means Prophet and Poet. . . . They have penetrated both of them into the sacred mystery of the universe; what Goethe calls 'the open secret'" (p. 106). *The open secret* is a wonderful metaphor for language. In both sacred and profane senses, there is language's refusal to give up its full meaning, if all the more so with the poet who speaks for the world: "Italy produced the one-world voice; we English had the honor of producing the other"

(p. 133). Carlyle set Shakespeare at the heart of a Nature that, then as now, people feared would no longer be heard: "Shakespeare's Art is not Artifice. . . . It grows-up from the deeps of Nature, through the noble sincere soul who is the voice of Nature" (p. 141). This is indeed the Victorian canonization of Shakespeare, an induction into the temple that extends to poet, poetry, language, and nation.

Given the age, one could expect that imperial themes were not far off. Not only does Carlyle set Shakespeare against Mahomet, as the greater hero, but he sends the poet out to conquer Islam: "This Shakespeare may still pretend to be a Priest of Mankind, of Arabia as of other places, for unlimited periods to come!" (Riede, p. 147). Carlyle is carried forward by this theme of global domination in the name of Shakespeare: "For our honor among foreign nations, as an ornament to our English Household, what item is there that we would not surrender rather than him" (p. 147). He does not stop until he feels compelled to put before the nation a rather absurd challenge—"Will you give-up your Indian Empire or your Shakespeare, you English?" (p. 148). It seems that England can have both for the time being, even if Carlyle allows that "the Indian Empire will go, at any rate, some day" (pp. 148–149). But there is still this terrible sense of India, and the empire generally, as a possession and point of cultural pride, just as a set of Shakespeare plays is ornament to the English household. Farsighted Carlyle is fully prepared to regard Shakespeare, on this question of empire, "as a real marketable, tangibly useful possession" (p. 148). Given that "there will be a Saxondom covering great spaces of the Globe," it seems that Shakespeare might "keep all these together into virtually one Nation" (ibid.), a Commonwealth unto King Shakespeare: "We can fancy him as radiant aloft over all the Nations of Englishmen, a thousand years hence" (p. 149). Has Carlyle gone mad here with poetic sacrament—"we are of one blood and kind with him" (p. 150)—or has he found the very ethos of an era which gave rise to an *OED* that, along with the collected works of Shakespeare, set a standard for English libraries around the empire? It is not hard to imagine thunderous applause greeting this panegyric conclusion of Carlyle's third lecture, as his words about poet and empire resounded through the hall on that warm May evening. It was inspiring talk of a people founded on the cult of poetic genius, inheriting an empire that took some part of its warrant from its literary accomplishment. What better model of recognizable merit than selfless Shakespeare? The bourgeois were busily laying the ideological foundations of their own ascendancy, by virtue of competence, capability, education, and history.[12]

Carlyle's equation of the divine and poetic had already found its sharpest expression during the Renaissance with the Italian poet Torquato Tasso's declaration: "There are two creators, God and the Poet" (cited in

Williams, 1961, p. 22). This was part of a long Christian tradition, with Christ cast as the Word incarnate, that developed into the humanism of the Renaissance. So it was that the cultural authority of the poet was especially important to the aspirations of this dictionary. The *OED* was the work of a gentlemen's society with strong clerical representation among the membership. In the British tradition of resisting a language academy, the Philological Society did not seek royal decree or legislative enactment. Instead, it sought reputable and weighty precedents, as in the country's constitutional and legal tradition, and built its case for an "unwritten" constitution of the language upon those cited precedents.

However, for the Victorian era, no less than today, the Shakespeare corpus still formed a bundle of bibliographical quandaries over versions of the text, stages of revision, degrees of collaboration, and cycles of dubious editing. Ralph Waldo Emerson, in an 1850 essay on Shakespeare, warned readers not to apply current standards of invention to the playwright's text. He cites Edmond Malone's scholarly calculations that with the three parts of *Henry VI*, "of 6,043 lines, 1,771 were written by some author preceding Shakespeare; 2,373 by him on the foundation laid by his predecessors; and 1,899 were entirely his own" (Emerson, 1912, p. 92). Emerson concludes that "at that day, our petulant demand for originality was not so much pressed. . . . A great poet, who appears in illiterate times, absorbs into his sphere all the light which is anywhere radiating" (p. 93). It almost suggests that the text should be regarded as a collective historical document of the time rather than the solitary creation of a gifted poet. Still, Emerson, like Carlyle, is prepared to hand to Shakespeare the language's highest laurels when it comes to the "uses of great men": "He, of all men, best understands the English language, and can say what he will" (p. 13). Going a step further, Emerson holds that this understanding of language gives Shakespeare the ability to see into our lives: "He wrote the text of modern life . . . he read the hearts of men and women, their probity, and their second thoughts, and wiles" (p. 100).

The editors of the *OED* certainly gave the bibliographical issue in Shakespeare's case no less attention than prevailed generally. They decided to stay with the "original" spellings of the extant texts, working principally with the Cambridge Shakespeare of 1863–1866, which is particularly rich and authoritative in its offering of footnoted variant readings. Yet as it now stands, Oxford University Press is at variance with itself on the question of Shakespearean textual scholarship (Sam, 1992). Eric Sam traces out the many contradictions that occur in attributions of Shakespeare's authorship and dates of publication between the Oxford Shakespeare, edited by Wells and Taylor, and the second edition of the Oxford dictionary (1992, p. 13). The dating disparities, according to

Sam's calculations, "add up to some ninety years and apply to over 100,000 lines or almost a 1,000,000 words," but then he concludes that they "are not only mutually incompatible but demonstrably wrong" (ibid.). It does not help matters that within the OED itself, the dating of Shakespeare's plays was not regularized until after the letter B (Schäfer, 1980, p. 4).

In his impressive work on the OED's treatment of Shakespeare, Jürgen Schäfer attests to the degree of scholarship that was shown with regard to the Shakespearean question in the actual editing of the dictionary:

> Far from contenting themselves with simply analyzing the established text of the Cambridge and Globe editions, the editors bravely tackled the complicated textual situation. They recorded variant readings in the quartos and folios, discussed major cruxes and sampled quite a number of the emendations of the great editors of the past. In this respect we can only concur with John Dover Wilson's dictum that the O.E.D. is an "incomparable editorial instrument." (1980, p. 18)

Using Shakespeare and his contemporary Thomas Nashe as test cases, Schäfer employs a number of clever and painstaking calculations to ascertain how successful the dictionary's editors had been in their quest for "the illusory grail of absolute first occurrence" for each word (1980, p. 5). He found that in approximately one-third of the OED entries he examined, the earliest citing listed can be antedated by an overlooked source, if only by a few decades (p. 45). To his credit, Murray suspected as much before he had completed the first fascicle, although these suspicions did not travel far beyond the Philological Society. He estimated in his presidential address of 1884 that three-quarters of the entries could be antedated by a matter of decades. All is not lost historically by this realization, but there is just a little less assurance as to the certainty of that earliest date. According to the new Oxford edition of Shakespeare's plays, Nashe also had occasion to collaborate with Shakespeare.

Schäfer describes the dictionary's literary bias along a number of dimensions, the first of which is priority of inclusion: "Words of marginal importance used by these preferred authors are rarely omitted, and their vocabulary is usually assigned main lemma status" (p. 13). As it stands, the OED records virtually every word Shakespeare is known to have written, attributing 1,904 new coinages to the poet in the process. By way of suggesting how the poet's inventiveness might have been overstated, Schäfer establishes that Nashe alone deserves credit for the earlier use of fifty of the first occurrences attributed to Shakespeare (p. 43). As Schäfer notes, the concordance surely made the difference. The Philological Society had actually foreseen the dangers of this dependence on the concordance in their "Proposal." Recalling their instructions to look for words that were not in the biblical and Shakespearean concordances for the 1526–1674 period, they understood that this created what they felt was an "unavoidable defect in our scheme": "It is true that this plan will fail to give the earliest use of those few words which, though used in the Bible or Shakespere, yet were first used by some of the earlier writers of the interval between 1526 and Shakespere" *(TPS, 1857, pp. 5–6)*. Things were indeed weighted in Shakespeare's favor.

This commitment to Shakespeare's lexicon in the *OED* is also reflected in the citational anomaly known as the *hapax legomena,* which is an entry in the dictionary that is based on a single citation, that is, on finding one published instance of the word. Shakespeare's singular use of a word such as *scamel,* with only a second questionable trace of the word found in the citation files, proved warrant enough for an entry in the dictionary (albeit with the headword set in slightly less bold typeface than regular entries):

> **Scamel,** *Obs. rare* -1. Meaning uncertain: the statement in quot. 1866 is of doubtful value. Some have proposed to read *staniel.*
> 1610 SHAKS. *Temp.* II. ii. 176 And sometimes I'le get thee young Scamels from the Rocke. [1866 H. STEVENSON *Birds of Norfolk* II. 260 At Blakeney Mr. Dowell states that bar-tailed godwits are known to the local gunners by the singular appellation of 'Picks' and 'Scamells'. . . He believes by 'Scamells' are meant the females and those found singly in autumn.]

With Stevenson's *Birds of Norfolk* parenthetically discounted, we have only this offer from Shakespeare's Caliban to gather "young scamels," along with filberts, marmoset, and pig-nuts, in his efforts to entice a jester and butler, mistaken for gods, to see "every fertile inch o' th' island." As *OED* entries begin to resemble footnotes to the plays, one can see how it has, in effect, dedicated the language to the poet, setting it at his feet, as Caliban did with his scamels to Stephano and Trinculo.

As further testimony to Shakespeare's particular hold on this dictionary, Schäfer found that the editors created entries for more than half of the twenty *malapropisms* that Shakespeare used in the plays (1980, pp. 15–16). It remains an open question whether a reader of Shakespeare, having found an unannotated edition of the plays, needs a definition for these nonsense words or "humorous blunder," as the *OED* refers to it, as in the obvious use of *pulsidge* in *Henry V*, part II ("You are in an excellent good temperalitie; your Pulsidge beates as extraordinarily, as heart would desire"—with blunderous *temperalitie* earning an entry in the *OED* as well). The question is not so much, when is a "word" not a word. It is, rather, who has had cause to use that supposed word? Another instance of a malapropism gaining a permanent place is found in the entry (again with the headword in a lesser typeface), shown in its entirety, for *impeticos*:

> Impeticos, *v.* A burlesque word put into the mouth of a fool: app. as a perversion of *impocket*, and perh. intended to suggest *petticoat*.
> 1601 SHAKS. *Twel. N.* II. iii. 27, I sent thee sixe pence for thy Lemon [*mod. edd.* leman], hadst it? *Clo.* I did impeticos thy gratillity.

It is hard not to find a tincture of pretense in this treatment of *impeticos* as a word, even a burlesque word, that is "put into the mouth of a fool." Who is the joke on in this case? The *OED*'s coverage of Shakespeare has to be set against the exclusion of well-known vocabulary items of undisputed currency and sense belonging to the community that found its living on the millside of Oxford, among other places. Spare the poet and spoil the tongue. So it is that this dictionary pays homage to the inventive powers of the poet, placing these peculiar speech acts at the center of the language and culture while diverting attention not only from language of the street but from the less sublime texts that facilitated the operations of the East India Company, the Foreign Office, and the Home Office.

The Philological Society's original aim—to contain *"every word occurring in the literature of the language"* (*TPS*, 1857, p. 2, original emphasis)—appears to refer to a broader textual tradition than defined by the strictly literary work of art. Yet it becomes clear, in returning to these earlier statements, about the degree to which the Philological Society was committed to treating the creative writer as the author of the language of influence, of the record of the word, whether alive or dead: "As we are unable to perceive any difference between a dead and living language, so far as lexicographical treatment is concerned, it follows that we cannot refuse to admit words into the Dictionary which may not be sanctioned by the usage of more than one writer. . . . However worthless they may be in themselves, they testify to a tendency of language, and on this account only, if on no other, have a distinct and appreciable value" (*TPS*, 1857, p. 3).

The *OED* was engaged not only in furthering the literary canonization of Shakespeare, a process that had been relatively secured by the time the dictionary was being edited, but it was also assembling documentary evidence of the "distinct and appreciable value" of literature, as the poet gave shape to the English language. It is a fair England, the dictionary may seem to presuppose, that is ruled by a modest, unassuming Shakespeare, artful at every turn of phrase, often magnanimous, and prepared to mete out poetic justice that brings down the unjust. Shakespeare describes the lay of the land, and if he wrote of Padua and Elsinore, it was, we are to understand, still inescapably an English landscape. His election in the *OED* to the position of highest authority in the language, however a fair and widely celebrated candidate he might be both for his art and elusiveness, is allowed to stand as a chapter in the natural history of the language. What of Touchstone's "For the true poetry is the most feigning?" What is the truth of this language, that in the dictionary is triply staged, by playwright, concordance editor, and lexicographer? How much of this world is spoken through the editorial life of literature? The tendency of the dictionary is to define not only the center and bounds of a national literature, but to give it an accelerated force in governing the language.

But then Shakespeare, in turn, had not written his plays and poetry without lexicographical support. DeWitt Starnes has suggested that "perhaps the majority of the classical allusion in Shakespeare's poems and plays came to him secondhand," referring to the playwright's probable use of Thomas Cooper's *Thesavrvs Linvae Romanae and Britannicae* of 1565, a book to be found in the Stratford Grammar School of Shakespeare's day and a work that contains a number of errors that are neatly replicated in a variety of Shakespeare's plays (Starnes, 1963, p. 114; Robertson and Robertson, 1989, p. 29). It was a schoolbook crib for a poet who was perhaps wanting in Latin and Greek, and it reiterates one of the symbiotic relationships within the book trade, between literary work and reference book, poet and scholar, given to a shared and intersecting authority that meets within the realm of the published life of the language, especially as it came to be represented in the *OED*. The dictionary represents one extension of a faith in both an aesthetic and scientific knowing of the world that was especially marked during the spiritually unsettled Victorian era (Dale, 1989). The real test of the relationship between the poet and the editor, however, can best be assessed by giving a close reading to how citation sits with sense in a dictionary entry, which is what I now turn to with a number of entries supported by Shakespeare's *The Taming of the Shrew*.

## CHAPTER 5

# Citing *The Shrew*

THIS CHAPTER turns from the larger literary issues raised by the prevalence of Shakespearean citations in the *OED* to the relationship between the line from a play and a definition in the dictionary. It reviews the role played by nine excerpts from *The Taming of the Shrew* which are used to support the dictionary's entries for *annoy*, *basin*, *bold*, *crave*, *diaper*, *modesty*, *rid*, *smack*, and *softly*. I have chosen these instances to illustrate different ways in which quotations can support the senses given in an entry. While in a few instances the citation provides the perfect complement to the sense given, more often complications arise between the poet's choice of a particular word for a given text and the earnest efforts of the dictionary editor to specify a far more generalized meaning. The dictionary's search for the literal sense of the word can easily run into interference from its poetic use. One need only recall Taylor's point on Pope's editing of the plays that "the fullness of Shakespeare's meaning is always just out of reach" (cited in the previous chapter) to get an inkling of the tenuous relationship that obtains between the two genres—verse and definition. Within any given entry in the dictionary, Shakespeare's fullness has a way of unsettling the logic of a citation-fed definition of the language.

"The aim of this Dictionary," Murray succinctly remarks in the preface to the *OED*'s first volume, "is to furnish an adequate account of the meaning, origin, and history of English words in general use, or known to have been in use at any time during the last seven hundred years." The adequacy of that account rests upon the selection of citations. The proper citation, it is reiterated in various statements of the *OED*'s editorial principles, "*must be extensive enough to carry a complete sense by itself*" (*TPS*, 1857, p. 10, original emphasis). Once a set of these hypothetically complete senses is in hand, rewriting it in the form of a definition becomes the key lexicographical trick. This process of abstracting meaning so that it can be translated across genres amounts to an uprooting of sense from published use in order to revive it in a dictionary entry. An attenuation of meaning seems inevitable and necessary in arriving at what is regarded as the *literal* sense of a word, at what is said to be *denoted* by it in the first instance. Herein lies the citation's contribution to meaning and authority in the dictionary.

The process by which literature, reduced to an abbreviated citation, forms the basis for writing out a dictionary sense is bound to be a difficult one to trace. Johnson, as a critic *cum* lexicographer, sometimes wrote definitions that amounted to little more than interpretations of the passage cited, which was a decided risk in using longer excerpts. The editors of the *OED* were able to steer clear of this mixing of lexicography and literary criticism as they worked from a much larger number of abbreviated excerpts and without the same concentration of literary instances. However, descriptions of the method followed by the editors of the *OED*, in moving from citation to definition, are usually terse, from Murray's "General Explanations" to the following section on the "Editorial Process" of the *Supplement*, included in the front matter of the second edition:

> *Drafting.* This process involved the preparation of a first draft of a dictionary entry for all of the items in a "bundle." Each assistant editor was expected to prepare complete entries, i.e. to ascertain the pronunciation and etymology of each new term where appropriate, to compose a definition, and to select and verify the quotations used. . . . During this process the material available from the quotation file were augmented by further quotations found in the department's library of dictionaries, concordances, and other reference works. Often it was necessary for additional work to be done in other libraries, such as the Bodleian Library in Oxford, the British Library in London, the Library of Congress in Washington, and elsewhere, in order to trace earlier and further quotations and to provide more detailed information for the definition.

The bundles of citations, made up of thirty to fifty items, are sorted by distinctions in meaning that suggest different senses are at work in a given word. In deciding on how the citations for a word fall into different senses and how those senses are to be ordered, thought is given to both chronology and, interestingly enough, the degree of specificity or concreteness in the use of the term. This second feature has been identified by Neil Hultin (1985) in terms of a "law of specification" that generally governed nineteenth-century thinking about the evolution of meaning. This law took a number of forms, including Herbert Spencer's assumption that "in primitive thought the concrete name cannot be separated in thought from the concrete object it belongs to," and Condillac's formulation that meaning moved from the sensuous to the abstract (Hultin, 1985, p. 43). Hultin points out that on more than one occasion, Murray was willing to set this logic of development over the chronological order he found in the citations. Murray held that the "natural" or "actual" order cannot be drawn directly from the citations because they form only a sampling of a word's development: "The historical record is not complete enough," Murray wrote in his "General Explanations" for the *OED*, "to do this, but it is usually sufficient to enable us to infer the actual order." Hultin points out that there is little anthropological evidence of language evolving from the concrete to the abstract (p. 49). But one has to appreciate the comfort of having a few guiding principles in deciding the history of sense for a word when sorting through a bundle of citation slips that, in this case, contain a quotation from *The Taming of the Shrew*.

As it turns out, the actual text of *The Shrew* poses fewer problems today than it did during the era in which the *OED* was edited. At the turn of the century, scholars did not doubt that Shakespeare had worked on this play with a collaborator who was responsible for up to two-fifths of the script, at least by one scholar's estimate (Morris, 1981). Understandably, in the pull between scholarly complexities and literary conventions, the editors of the *OED* set aside the indeterminacy of authorship, although they paid attention to other aspects of Shakespearean bibliographic study at the time. The importance of Shakespeare's unequivocal authority as a source of citations took precedent. And while the dictionary certainly includes anonymous citations, the testimony of an uncontested author was a definite advantage in grounding the citation, giving it a notable voice, a certainty of speech, that served the larger ambitions of the project of constructing a proud and coherent past for the English language.

Since the first edition of the *OED* was completed in 1928, scholars have reassigned *The Taming of the Shrew* in its entirety to Shakespeare, based on the analysis of the "image clusters" and other features of the writing, a conclusion that vindicates the *OED*'s assignment of the text (Morris, 1981, pp. 65–69). This image cluster research also "proves" that the language is Shakespeare's in a way that the basic story is not. Brian Morris, as editor of the Arden edition of the play, concludes that among the many sources for a story of a tamed shrew current at that time, much was borrowed except perhaps this particular version of "killing her in her own humor": "The rest of the main plot is a *melange* of incidents, motifs and commonplaces which would have been common knowledge to the playwright and his audience" (p. 76). This freehanded borrowing of the plot provided, we might imagine, a skeleton on which Shakespeare fleshed out the play of his language. The resulting *Taming of the Shrew* was to serve the sense-making of this dictionary in at least nine ways, as can be shown by citing the appropriate entries from the *OED* and examining what stands between sense and citation.

## BY WAY OF CONTRAST

### Modesty

†1. Moderation; freedom from excess or exaggeration; self-control; clemency, mildness of rule.

**1531** ELYOT *Gov.* I. xxv, Modestie; whiche worde nat beinge known in the englisshe tongue, ne of al them which under stode latin, except they had radde good autours, they improprely named this vertue discretion. **1585** T. WASHINGTON tr. *Nicholay's Voy.* I. xviii. 21 He gouerned with all modestie to the great contentment of the inhabitauntes. **1596** SHAKS. *Tam. Shrew* Induct. i. 94, I am doubtfull of your modesties, Least . . . You break into some merry passion. . . .

Although the particular sense is declared obsolete (†), we can still use *modesty* to begin with an almost ideal case of a definition fully supported by the Shakespearean citation. The opposition struck in the citation from *The Shrew*, between "modesties" and "break into some merry passion," is well captured by the sense given for *modesty*, as a matter of mildness and self-control. In writing this definition, the editor could work from the syntax of contrast in Shakespeare which situates the *modesty* in relation to other dispositions. Where the Thomas Elyot citation offers, with less precision, what modesty is sometimes mistaken for—discretion—the Shakespearean quotation offers a direct opposite among equivalents, between modesty and passion. *The Shrew* citation also has the bonus of affording a slight (modest) but delightful sparkle, reminding us of the vitality of Shakespearean diction. Here it serves not only to enliven the language, but as a more general encouragement to readers of the dictionary to write with a similar vividness, as becomes the English language defined here. Given the helpfulness of the self-contained contrast, it struck me as odd that among my original sample of thirty-six *Shrew* citations, only one other excerpt offered this contrasting feature, in the entry for *decrease*: "His Lands and goods, Which I have bettered rather than descreast" (I.ii.119). The relative absence of this helpful lexical contrast in the citations can be explained, in part, by the brevity of the quotations used in the *OED*. Yet if citations were shortened by the editors to conserve space in the dictionary, it is still hard to imagine that they intentionally eliminated this extremely helpful feature for determining meaning. In the entry for *modesty*, the Shakespearean citation works particularly well with difference, which has always played an important role in the structuring of meaning.[1]

## THROUGH AMPLIFICATION

**Smack,** *sb*.2
**1.** A sharp noise or sound made by separating the lips quickly, esp. in kissing, and in tasting or anticipating food or liquor.
**1570** LEVINS *Manip.* 5 Ye smacke of a kisse, *suauium*. **1596** SHAKS. *Tam. Shrew* III. ii. 180 Hee . . . kist her lips with such a clamorous smacke, that at

the parting all the Church did eccho. **1679** DRYDEN *Limberham* I. i, She has a notable Smack with her! I believe Zeal first taught the Art of Kissing close. . . .

A second form of strong citational support comes from what might be called amplification by context. Shakespeare's use of *smack* resounds with meaning, just as the report of the kiss fills the church with its echo. The citation from *The Shrew* unquestionably enhances the first sense given for *smack*. Shakespeare pins down the aural element for the editors, as *smack* is then defined as a "sound made by separating the lips quickly." Peter Levins's quotation, from only a few years before, is decidedly less specific. Also working against Levins's citation is its origins in a dictionary of English and Latin words, *Manipulus vocabulorum*, which, according to *OED* principles, is a less reliable source of language-in-use than literature or other published works. As Murray explains, citing previous lexicons undermines a dictionary's claim, not only to original scholarship, but to the actual rather than inferred use of the word. In this case, Levins holds the special place of earliest known citation, and his citation might have been thought to cover sixteenth-century usage, following the citation-per-century rule set out for the dictionary. Yet the inclusion of Shakespeare's line is also justified for a sharpness of imagery, missing from Levins and Dryden, and its testimony to actual use, after a theatrical fashion. The precise embodiment of Shakespeare's use is also worth noting, as it falls within the dictionary's "law of specification" as suitable for establishing the earliest sense of a word that was to grow in abstraction and metaphorical sense, until it arrived in 1798 at sense 4, which is based on a single citation drawn from a letter written by Jane Austen—"The ball on Thursday was a very small one indeed, hardly so large as an Oxford Smack"—which the *OED* defines with "(See quot.) *Obs.*" Need more be said?[2] The citation from *The Shrew* vividly anchors the original sense of *smack* in "the sound made by separating the lips quickly," both amplifying the meaning suggested by Levins's only somewhat earlier citation and giving it a location, a public use, outside of the referential spiral of another dictionary.

### AS A GRAMMATICAL DEMONSTRATION

**Softly,** *adv.*
10. Used interjectionally: = SOFT *adv.* 8.
  **1596** SHAKS. *Tam. Shrew* I. ii. 238 Softly my Masters. **1611**—*Wint. T.* IV. iii. 76 Softly, deere sir: good sir, softly. **1671** MILTON *Samson* 115 Softly a while, Let us not break in upon him. . . .

A further instance from *The Taming of the Shrew* of a "happy" citation, to use the Philological Society's adjective, occurs with the tenth sense given for *softly*. The sense hinges on a grammatical point that is aptly demonstrated by the three words cited from the first act of *The Shrew*. It proves to be Shakespeare's syntactical invention at work. No earlier instance of this usage has been found. The sense is not original with Shakespeare, as the cross reference—"= Soft *adv*. 8."—indicates the meaning is equivalent to the eighth sense given for the adverb form of *soft*. There, we find the well-crafted definition of *soft*: "8. Used as an exclamation with imperative force, either to enjoin silence or deprecate haste." The exclamatory and imperative force, suggested by the sense, has been decidedly softened in Shakespeare by the ironic use of "my masters" in the cited speech of servant Tranio, who, boldly dressed up as his master, is addressing the gentlemen suitors, Gremio and Hortensio. The grammar of the interjection is sustained, even if the sense still tends to shade toward a greater gentleness than the one indicated in the dictionary. The second Shakespearean citation does suggest the additional grammatical possibility of using *softly* both to open and close a speech, amounting to a parenthesis of requested quietude. This additional Shakespearean citation by no means exhausts the reserves, as Bartlett's Shakespearean concordance offers at least six other instances of the interjection, *softly*, in the plays of Shakespeare, with none earlier than *The Shrew* (1962, p. 1416).

It is also worth noting that Shakespeare's use of *softly* is drawn from what might be described as the particular grammar of spoken language. The *OED* speaks of the word as "used interjectionally," where *interjection* is defined, under its own entry, as "a natural ejaculation expressive of some feeling or emotion used as a Part of Speech." In defining interjection, it goes on to stress, if in small type, its particular lack of grammatical fit, as the word is "so-called because, when it is used, it is interjected between sentences, clauses, or words, mostly without grammatical connexion." This part-of-speech-without-grammatical-connection blurs a distinction that can occur between spoken and written language with which this dictionary has difficulty dealing, given its exclusive focus on English as a written language. Is Shakespeare's use of language so clearly on the side of text or is this oral element a part of Shakespeare's privilege?[3] As a writer of dialogue for the stage, Shakespeare both complicates the authoritative documentation of a literate language and affords an approved avenue for recording this other form of language. The full speech from *The Shrew* reads: "Softly, my masters, if you be gentlemen, / Do this right; hear me with patience." So it need be with this dictionary's utilization of the Shakespearean citation. There is a transformational grammar of genre at work here by which the playwright becomes the published means of citing a usage drawn from the realm of the spoken word.

## AS ILLUSTRATIVE EXPRESSION

**Bold,** *a.*
3. Phrases. *To make (so) bold, to be (so) bold*: to venture, presume so far
as, take the liberty (*to do* a thing). †*To make* or *be bold with* (*obs.*): to take
liberties, make free with.
. . . **1596** SHAKS. *Tam. Shrew* I. ii. 251 Sir, let me be so bold as aske you.
**1598**—*Merry W.* II. ii. 262, I will first make bold with your money.
**1599**—*Much Ado* III. ii. 8. **1601**—*Jul. C.* II. i. 86, I thinke we are too bold
vpon your Rest. **1613**—*Hen. VIII,* III. ii. 318 You made bold To carry
into Flanders, the Great Seale. . . .

In one sense, this Shakespeare-rich entry for *bold* bears similarities to
the grammatical focus of *softly*. However, there are also semantic implications to the various phrasings defined in this instance. The citation from
*The Shrew*, earliest of the Shakespearean set, effectively demonstrates one
way of using *bold*, in the form of "to be (so) bold." True, the sense given
for the phrase omits any mention of a deferential politeness that governs
this particular expression, especially as it is cited here in a mock exaggeration of what is at stake in asking bold questions, as Hortensio does of
Tranio: "Sir, let me so bold as to ask you, did you ever see Baptista's
daughter?" Yet another lexicographical question raised by this entry is
the extent of the Shakespearean contribution, which for this one sense of
*bold* includes citations from *The Merry Wives of Windsor, Much Ado
About Nothing, Julius Caesar,* and *Henry VIII*. The citing of *Much Ado*,
without the printing of the actual quotation—"I will only be bold with
Benedick for his company"—only adds to the sense of superfluity, although the missing line does illustrate *to be bold with*, which is only
partly covered by the line from *The Merry Wives*. This additional instance may have been cut because it is regarded as an obscure usage, while
the coverage of Shakespeare already seemed excessive. When the editors
consulted their Shakespearean concordance with this entry in mind, they
faced no fewer than forty-two instances of *bold* phrased in these four
ways. Shakespeare, through the assistance of the concordance, was able
to establish the entire range of phrasings, with further support found in
citations as early as Chaucer and as late as Gladstone. Taken as a whole,
this Shakespearean cluster at the center of the entry raises questions about
the dictionary's historical approach. Are we to assume that Shakespeare
alone used all four phrasings in that fertile Elizabethan period for which
he is quoted extensively? The dictionary begins to function, with this instance, as its own abbreviated concordance to the playwright's usage and
diction, again calling into question the relationship between citation and
definition. Is Shakespeare serving the dictionary, or vice versa? It could be

argued that this seesawing relationship, with the emphasis tilting between literature and definition, is a particular strength of a citational dictionary with a taste for fine writing. Although the citations are brief, this quintet of excerpts recalls the show-placing of literature in the dictionaries of Johnson and Richardson. The additional attention given to Shakespeare might well flatter the sensibility of educated readers, reaffirming a part of their personal history of the language within a larger cycle of reference and deference.

### WITH AMBIGUOUS REFERENCE

**Annoy,** *v.*
> **3.** *trans.* To affect (a person) in a way that disturbs his equanimity, hurts his susceptibilities, or causes slight irritation. (Refers to the feeling produced, rather than to the action producing it; hence commonest in the passive *To be annoyed*: to be ruffled in mind, troubled, vexed).
>    . . . *c*1450 LONELICH *Grail* I. 324 3if I wiste my lord not forto anoye.
> **1596** SHAKS. *Tam. Shrew* I. i. 189 She will not be annoy'd with suters.
> **1616** R. C. *Times' Whistle* vii 3156 Soe overioyde That through excesse therof he is annoide. . . .

At times it can seem as if the poet's cleverness of expression disrupts the citation's service to the definition. The third sense of *annoy* is supported by a quick-witted line from *The Shrew* that, in its ambiguity of reference, falls decidedly short of the lexicographical ideal of providing a complete sense in itself. It affords too many senses, which could well be seen as interfering with the sense of the definition. Although the line has the quality of bringing the spirit of the play to mind, what needs to be recognized are the ways in which it is not a good candidate for citation. It lacks the context clues discussed above, such as contrasting syntax or amplification. The association of "suitors" and "annoy" in the citation is not, in itself, immediately helpful. Added to that is the negative cast of the citation (compounded by *annoy*'s own negative turn). And on top of that, there is a smart ambiguity inherent in this particular use of "annoy'd." The double meaning of the word in the phrase works like the famous piece of advice, "Don't waste your time in school." In this case, the naive reader might ask of the citation, is it that she enjoys suitors and won't be put out, or annoyed, in the least, to have them fawning around her? Is it that she simply will not brook them? Or is it that at least there are no suitors around to trouble her? Well, as we know Kate and the meaning of *annoy*, we know how annoyed she can be with suitors and sisters, and this annoyance goes well beyond the feeling produced within her. It refers as much, if not more so, to the suitors having to suffer her annoyance, for the expression of Kate's anger is her very song of freedom:

> My tongue will tell the anger of my heart,
> Or else my heart concealing it will break,
> And rather than it shall, I will be free
> Even to the uttermost, as I please, in words.
>
> (IV.iii.74–80)

The double sense of the citation works extremely well within the larger unit of *The Shrew*. This pithy, ambiguous *annoy'd* is at the heart of Kate's strength as a character; she will not suffer a soppy marriage game that only appears to venerate the bride whom it affectionately confines. Shakespeare's Kate, freshly fashioned out of a popular shrewish tradition, is given to witty and sharp counterthrust. But this high-spiritedness foreshadows the actions of a suitor who will move her beyond annoyance, as Petruchio completes his courting by deprivation and humiliation. It may be fairly said that the meaning of *annoy* in this citation remains deep within the play. The citation offers the *OED* only a reliable proof of the word's use, with a knowledge of the play required to appreciate its contribution to the meaning of the word. One might well ask to what extent can any excerpted line carry "a complete sense" or how, for that matter, a bundle of excerpts can add up to a history of meaning. The citation, and this one especially, can undermine the definitiveness of sense represented in the dictionary, as if a word's sense had trouble surviving once it is plucked from the waters that sustain it. The illustrative quotation signifies an opening move in stalking the meaningfulness of language, with that meaning always lying beyond the isolated word, the abbreviated citation, the singular text. The point is at once obvious, I realize, but it contains within it the constitution of language around a fragile and expansive web of meaning. The *OED* pins down the play of meaning to a fixed set of senses, as if to suggest that the matching of sense to word forms the focus of an articulate life.

## IN PUNNING SUPPORT

**Rid,** *v.*
3. To make (a person or place) free *of* (or *from*) something; to disencumber *of*.
**1569** GOLDING tr. *Heminge's Postill* 10 To the intent to rid his disciples of thys errour. **1596** SHAKS. *Tam. Shrew* I. i. 150 Would I had giuen him the best horse in Padua . . . that would . . . ridde the house of her. **1611**

MIDDLETON & DEKKER *Roaring Girl* V. ii, If I do not . . . Rid him of this disease that now growes on him. . . .

*The Shrew* affords yet another instance of citational ambiguity in its contribution to the third sense of *rid*. A pun, after all, is bound to complicate lexicographical matters. Although the citation preserves the essential syntax—*rid of*—it does demand certain imaginative leaps in arriving at what might be thought of as the proper sense, principally between "rid" and the rare participial adjective for "ride" (with a single supporting citation for this sense of *rid* from 1631). Tying together horse and house with rid and ride seems a fine poetic trick, in which we might imagine this best horse charging through the kitchen, chasing Kate out of her father's house. Or is it that the horse somehow hops onto Kate's shoulders and rides her out the front door? As it stands in the larger context of Gremio's speech, it is, of course, not the horse, but her suitor, that rids the house of Kate: "And would I had given him the best horse in Padua," Gremio declares, "to begin his wooing that would thoroughly woo her, wed her and bed her and ridde the house of her!" Gremio offers this comment in response to Hortensio's proverb; "He that runs fastest, gets the ring." Of the dozen citations included for this sense of *rid*, Shakespeare's alone plays with the word in this way. The effervescent playwright embraces the ready confusion of meanings, shunning the clarity of plain style that one might hope for in such devices as a dictionary. My point has been, however, that the *OED* exhibits multiple allegiances. The editors' scholarly commitment to a strict correlation of word, etymology, definition, and citation is sometimes disturbed by their interests in representing those writers whose pleasure and profession it is to ruffle this logic. At the very least, the dictionary's will-to-clarity, its desire to be definitive, will be disturbed at times by its homage to the language's best literature.

## IN DEFINING SIMPLE OBJECTS

**Basin,** *sb.*

1. A circular vessel of greater width than depth, with sloping or curving sides, used for holding water and other liquids, especially for washing purposes. *Barber's basin*: see BARBER *sb.* 3.

. . . **1513–75 Diurn. Occurr.** (1833) 103 The basing and the lawar. **1596** SHAKS. *Tam. Shrew* II. i. 350 Basons and ewers, to laue her dainty hands. **1616** R. C. *Times' Whis.* iv. 1613 Faire water in a basen. . . .

The name of a simple object would seem to present lexicographers with the paradigmatic case of a word dependably defined by its use. Yet in the case of *basin* it proves another less than straightforward matter of definition. While we might well assume from *The Shrew* citation that basins are what women use for washing their hands, there is little to be learned here about its shape. In fact, neither Shakespeare's nor the other nine citations, from *St. Marher* (1220) to Lane's *Arabian Nights* (1845), make any reference to shape or proportion in their use of *basin*. The sense given in the entry clearly exceeds the cites; it is obviously relying on an extra-literary knowledge of the editor who appreciates how objects are told apart by physical qualities, even if they do not tend to figure that way when people refer to them in writing. Citations do not so much establish the meaning, in this case, as attest to a continuity of use. Since 1220 *basin* has referred, we are asked to trust, to an object with the shape given in the definition. That still leaves the question of what confirms the geometry of a basin's proportions compared to, say, an *ewer* ("a pitcher with a wide spout, used to bring water for washing the hands," a definition which the *OED* borrows with attribution from *Webster's International Dictionary*, and which it supports with a similar set of basin-and-ewer quotes from across the ages). What would perhaps constitute better documentation for this definition of *basin* is a series of dated woodcut illustrations, and certainly English dictionaries have long used illustrations, dating back to Thomas Cooper's sixteenth-century *Thesavrvs*. But here we see the *OED* caught between its commitment to print's authorization of meaning, and the need to make necessary distinctions in its definitions. Which is only to say that the *OED*'s definition of the English language may not be strictly dictated by its texts and authors.

One also finds in this entry an example of how the law of specification can override chronological order, creating a history of meanings that moves forward from the specific to the abstract while running backward in time: *basin* begins, in its first recorded sense from 1220 and with Shakespeare's support, as a domestic object of fixed proportions, while the succeeding senses move more broadly into, for example, "a hollow depression, natural or artificial," and "a circular or oval valley." The dates for the first recorded usages of each new sense move unevenly through time: (1) 1220, (2) 1525 (3) 1413, (4) 1302, (5) 1727, (6) 1662, with (7) defining the metaphorical transformation of *basin* into a helmet, circa 1300. Perhaps this basin-helmet was literally the case, warranting it second rather than seventh place among the senses. Better yet, we might question whether this history of the language is so easily told or predicted by theories of linguistic evolution. Such are the challenges that the *OED*'s current editors face as they are now undertaking a revision of the dictionary's historical record. The inevitable limits of the dictionary's ability to organize a history of meaning around a collection of citations can arise, it turns out, in the definition of the simplest household objects.

## IN EXTENDING A WORD

Diaper, *sb.*
2. A towel, napkin, or cloth of this material; a baby's napkin or 'clout'.
**1596** SHAKS. *Tam. Shrew* I. i. 57 Let one attend him vvith a siluer Bason
Full of Rose-water, and bestrew'd with Flowers, Another beare the Ewer:
the third a Diaper. **1837** HT. MARTINEAU *Soc. Amer.* II. 245 Table and
bed-linen, diapers, blankets. **1889** J. M. DUNCAN *Lect. Dis. Women* ix.
(ed. 4) 54.

To take the definition of domestic objects one step further, with the
entry for *diaper*, Shakespeare appears to have coined the use of the term
as a form of "towel." Again amid basins and ewers, Shakespeare's use of
*diaper* in *The Shrew* breaks with the traditional meaning of the word, as
it designates a special weave of fabric. His apparent innovation is to shift
the word's sense, from fabric to the object made of the fabric, that is, a
towel. It follows from this citation that a *diaper* is the sort of towel that
a certain class of handwashers might employ, and that it is borne by at-
tendants in taking one's toilet. Shakespeare is deploying the common rhetorical device of *metonymy*, as the "White House" stands for the execu-
tive level of the American government. In the first sense given for *diaper*,
as a textile, the citations date from 1502 and speak of "a towell of
dyaper." It seems that Shakespeare's use of *diaper*, as a stand-in for "a
towel of diaper," is transformed by the dictionary from a poetic turn of
phrase to investing a word with a new sense. Yet it would again seem odd
to claim that this sense of *diaper* then came into common usage based on
the evidence presented (with the complete set of citations quoted above).
The citation following Shakespeare's, from Harriet Martineau, comes
some two-and-half centuries later. Martineau's use of *diaper* does suggest
an object that is indeed most likely a towel: "Table and bedlinen, diapers,
blankets." But are we to believe that the word somehow lay dormant for
that period of time, before Martineau discovered it in Shakespeare, or did
*diaper*, in this sense, have a life that only very rarely surfaced in print?
The third and final citation is not much more helpful. Drawn from J. M.
Duncan's 1899 *Clinical Lectures on the Diseases of Women*, the OED
does not provide, out of discretion perhaps, the actual instance of the
word in use, although diaper does appear to be used in the sense of a
napkin, as the missing Duncan citation reads, "You cannot well judge of
these discharges when dried on a diaper . . ." (1889, p. 54).

Lexicographically, we are left to wonder in what sense it can be said
that Shakespeare introduced this new use of *diaper*. Here, the contribution of literary invention to linguistic history seems less than certain.
Sometimes a great poet's minor devices live only for the moment, in the

context of their immediate use, and sometimes they are added to the record of the language as part of a genealogy in the authoring of the language. Equally illusive, especially for North American readers, is the absence of a citation attesting to where and when *diaper* was used in reference to "a baby's napkin."[4] Of course, these slight sins hardly diminish the dictionary's accomplishment, and to his credit, Murray had been all too aware of the shortcomings of the *OED*'s citational coverage. A minor domestic gap, such as this one, with all of its gendered and regional implications in understanding how words and authors find their way into print, simply adds to our awareness of a sometimes less-than-robust relationship found between citation and definition in the making of this dictionary.

## OF TOO FINE A SENSE

Crave, *v.*
2. To ask earnestly, to beg for (a thing), *esp.* as a gift or favour. Const. *of, from (†at)* a person.
. . .
c. To beg to know; ask to be told or informed.
**1596** SHAKS. *Tam. Shrew* II. i. 180 If she denie to wed, Ile craue the day When I shall aske the banes. **1735** POPE *Donne Sat.* iv. 67 'Permit' (he cries) 'no stranger to your fame To crave your sentiment.' **1748** SMOLLET *Rod. Rand.* (1845) 35 He craved my name.

This final instance of *crave* credits Shakespeare with a new subsense of the word. The entry raises questions about the breakdown into distinct senses that troubled me with a few of the earlier examples. Does this process entail making distinctions that at some point become too fine to bear the weight of independent meanings? How is it, we might ask, that the use of *crave* in the citation from *The Shrew* is not adequately covered by the initial definition (2), creating the need for a further subsense (2c)? If Petruchio longs for the day when he can announce the marriage, then it appears that he desires more than a knowledge of the day; he is asking, in effect, for the banns to be performed, published, and the marriage publicly declared.[5] Petruchio is begging, as it were, for a thing to be done, albeit done by the pronouncement of the words. This sense (2c) of "beg to know" is further supported by citations from Pope and Smollet. These do pertain more directly to the given meaning of a request for knowledge, but they, too, might seem to fall as much under the sense given in 2.

The failure of distinction here works the other way as well. Under the second sense of *crave* (2), there is Richard Carew's "Salomon . . . craued wisdom from heaven," which antedates Shakespeare's *The Shrew* citation by two years and seems to possess the informative sense set out in **2c**. But then, too, under sense **2**, Richard Steele's "I the rather make bold to crave your Advice" also seems to fit **2c**. Such overlaps among senses are bound to appear out of the richness of reference that occurs within closely associated units of language. The dividing lines are not easily found, but such is the work of the dictionary. In this case, and it is not an isolated one, it may well be that the editor's decision to introduce a subsense was prompted by a tendency to regard Shakespeare as an inventor of meaning. Certainly, the setting out of ever finer distinctions of sense is an effective way of bringing order to those stacks of thirty to fifty citations that the editors often faced in writing an entry. This methodical disciplining of meaning into entries, senses, and subsenses represents the richness of the English language, even as it is destined to fall short in capturing the shades of meaning among word senses. The multiplication of senses by nuance, on the one hand, suggests that no rough count of entries in the dictionary will ever capture the "size" of the language's vocabulary. Each word is expansive with meaning. On the other hand, this exercise of discrete and numbered senses favors a conception of the word as holding a fixed number of meanings, rather than bringing to the fore its ability, especially in the hands of a Shakespeare, to reach out in a fluid manner across senses, drawing meaning to it, as a mock-groom can *crave* a day, both as a matter of time and knowing.

Given the various ways in which the nine citations from *The Shrew* work in the *OED*, we might surmise that Shakespeare's poetic bag of literary subtleties raises a number of lexicographical issues, from sense-making to fair representation. What can often seem to be the spontaneity of a poetic device is cast in the dictionary as an effective coinage in the master's hands. Yet we cannot know with Shakespeare's re-sensing of *diaper*, anymore than with the 1,900 terms he is credited with originating, the degree to which the word already possessed a certain currency in the sense used by the poet. This is to ask after the ways in which the writer is both witness to, and originator of, the language. The short answer to this complex question has typically been to accept the myth of literary invention and influence that can be traced across the centuries of citations in the dictionary. Isn't Martineau's much later use of the word *diaper* proof of Shakespeare's invention, or is she the source of a second invention of the term? It could well be that Martineau's use of *diaper* represents the more effective introduction of the term into the vocabulary. Or we might allow them both creator status, raising interesting questions about gender equity in the history of authorship.[6]

It may seem perfectly natural that the most celebrated poet in the language receives the most extensive coverage in its best dictionary. This coverage has been accomplished through the support of other reference works and by suspending, at times, principles otherwise meant to ensure the scientific force of the work. In Shakespeare's name, the dictionary breaks the one-a-century rule for citations; it uses multiple instances from a single author; it fosters dubious subsenses and uses ambiguous citations; it offers citations that fail to substantiate definitions. These transgressions certainly occur with citations from other writers as well. But it is important to appreciate, in the first instance, what has been made of William Shakespeare as a guarantor of the language. Going to such lengths, as I do, over a little lexicographic *diapering* and *craving* is necessary to expose one set of seams in the dictionary's fixing of citation to meaning. The editorial staff of the *OED* was certainly not making up the definitions of the language, nor were they simply framing them with quotations like decorative ribbons. Yet they must have been all too aware of how in each instance they could produce only approximations of the lexicographical ideal. And around that human earnestness has sprung up our unshakable regard for the dictionary, as the definition is proved by the words of the published. Murray's own lexicographic inclinations had clearly been to pursue the language on a much broader basis than the work of the celebrated writer. This modest editor stood for the uneven marriage of national cultural aspirations and a new science of descriptive linguistics interested in the whole of the language. Yet as Shakespeare is the figurehead set at the prow of the *OED*, it is literature that leads in the authorization of this dictionary's image of an English power and burden carried far and wide. It was *the language of Shakespeare*, after all, that was carried abroad as part of Britain's civilizing mission:

> Abhorred slave,
> Which any print of goodness wilt not take,
> Being capable of all ill! I pitied thee,
> Took pains to make thee speak, taught thee each hour
> One thing or other: When thou didst not, savage
> Know thine own meaning, but would gabble like
> A thing most brutish, I endow'd thy purposes
> With words that made them known . . .
>
> (*Tempest*, I.ii.352–358)

As will be well known among readers of this dictionary, the defiant Caliban is not cowed by Prospero's indignancy, striking back with that famous line that I had recourse to use in the previous chapter: "You taught me language; and my profit on't / Is, I know how to curse." As it turns out with this national dictionary, it was not until the time of the *Supplement* that the language of either colonial native or cursing became fully welcomed in this dictionary. The *OED*'s celebration of Shakespeare, and the literary artist in more general terms, entails a certain romantic heroism that is meant to transcend the legal and institutional systems in which we often find ourselves and our language. As the English teacher working between school bells enthusiastically celebrates Shelley's wild embrace of freedom through his poetry, so the *OED* goes to great length to place the history of the language in the hands of those authors who appear to write their own destiny and meaning. Of course, this grounding of the English language in Shakespeare was not merely the Victorian enthusiasm of Murray and the editorial team working on the dictionary in Oxford. The *OED* represents an accumulation of critical concern with literature and nation; it carries this spirit forward into the current determination of the language by the dictionary, more so today, interestingly enough, than for the Victorians who created it, as they were able to assemble the early fascicles and volumes only for their bookcases.

When the final volume of the first edition of the *OED* was published in 1928, the delegates of Oxford University Press issued a statement about the language of the dictionary that clearly placed it in the hands of poet and Bible in its claim for the universality of the dictionary's English: "It is perhaps less generally appreciated that what makes the Dictionary unique is its historical method; it is a dictionary not of our English, but of all English: the English of Chaucer, of the Bible, and of Shakespeare is unfolded in it with the same wealth of illustration as is devoted to the most modern author" (cited in Burchfield, 1989, p. 166). If among all classes of society, the hold of poetry on the language has waned since Victorian times, Shakespeare alone can be thought to retain a special place through, in part, state and corporate sponsorship. The earlier efforts of Thomas Carlyle to forge a common culture around such a hero of poetic creation continues unabated. The *OED*, as much as any instrument from the nineteenth century, contributes to the overrepresentation and investment in this singularly constituted poet, declared to be "of all English." We might imagine that a desire for a form of meaning and authority that exceeds our own words is met by the larger-than-life stature of this poet-as-hero, all the more so as he has come to be cited by *The Oxford English Dictionary* as "this star of England" in the writing of the nation.

> Thus far, with rough and all-unable pen,
>   Our bending author hath pursued the story,
> In little room confining mighty men,
>   Mangling by starts the full course of their glory.
> Small time, but in that small most greatly lived
>   This star of England: Fortune made his sword;
> By which the world's best garden he achieved.
>
> (*Henry V*, Epilogue)

## CHAPTER 6

# A Victorian Canon:
# The Authors

IN MOVING with this and subsequent chapters into a mildly statistical treatment of *The Oxford English Dictionary*, I take my lead from James Murray. However much he was a man of words and meanings, he took decided pride in measures of magnitude with this dictionary. This excerpt from his "Report on the Dictionary" to the 1881 Annual Meeting of the Philological Society is not atypical:

> The weight of the 817,625 slips, thin paper as they are, is close upon 15 cwt., and the cost of their postage to Readers and back again, £54 , 10s.; that, laid end to end, they extend a distance of 87 miles, and that, supposing them each to take up only half a minute of the Editor's time in reading them and dealing with them, their inspection would occupy 850 days of 8 hours each, or about three working years. (*TPS*, 1881, p. 261)

He directs these comments to "members of a statistical turn of mind," which had indeed become a popular interest of the times. Numerous measures of people's social situation were being conducted, many for the first time, by commission and society. The belief was that by amassing the figures on the state of people's lives one could begin to manage them properly. Numbers were seen as a measure of control over what seemed the burgeoning immensities of modern life. Given the spirit of the times, it is no more surprising to find Murray mentally laying slips end to end than to come across Henry Mayhew's table, "Showing the Quantity of Refuse Bought, Collected, or Found in the Streets of London," in *London Labour and London Poor* from 1865, which attests to a Victorian recycling program for everything from bone (3,000,000 pounds annually) to tea leaves (78,000 pounds).

For his part, Murray took every opportunity to report the number of words, slips, readers, quotations, combinations, and cross-references assembled for this project. He counted his progress in entries, column-inches, fascicles, and volumes, as if the dictionary were his tower of Babylon building its way to heaven. He also put the numbers to work in the promotion of the dictionary. Beginning with volume 3 of the *OED*, each preface included a table comparing figures for his dictionary with those of Johnson's *Dictionary* (1755), Cassell's *Encyclopædic Dictionary* (1879–

1888), Whitney's *Century Dictionary* (1889–1891), and Funk and Wagnalls's, *Standard Dictionary of the English Language* (1893–1895). The
tables offered the statistics for what might be mistaken, in sporting terms,
for the International Dictionary League. And with each volume, Murray
and his team at the *New English Dictionary on Historical Principles*
headed the league in all categories by a considerable margin (fig. 6.1).

Nor would Murray's habit of keeping count die out at Oxford. It lives
on with each new generation of editors. In the preface to the second edition of the dictionary, John Simpson and Edmund Weiner go into some
numerical detail in describing the time spent on preparing the electronic
version of the dictionary. It is true that they speak in terms of *person-
years* (a term backed in the *Supplement* by a 1970 citation from *Scientific
American*), but they are still talking Murray's language:

> Data capture took 120 person-years; computer development took 14 per-
> son-years, automatic processing of the text took ten months; interactive inte-
> gration took 7 person-years; the two rounds of proof-reading, undertaken
> by 50 people, each took 60 person-years; and the final composition of the
> integrated text involved the setting of approximately 20,000,000 characters
> per week.

By virtue of these spent person-years, we now have the opportunity to
take the measure of the *OED* in ways Murray would not have dreamed
possible. My work with these computer-generated statistics amounts to
an initial and fairly crude pass through the data, focusing on the twenty
most-cited authors and titles from among the citations used in the *OED*
between 1884 and 1989. These figures offer one version of how a century's worth of editors at Oxford has constructed the history, the scope
and range, of the English language. The leading authors of the first edition of the *OED* form a parade that begins with those who took a literary
stand, at some risk, by writing in the English language, most notably from
the Golden Age of Chaucer. The story is also about the less-celebrated
contribution to the shaping of the language made by translators, editors,
scholars, and other text workers. These writers worked a more prosaic
side of the language, which proves equally indispensable in forming a
solid foundation for English. Yet a third area of interest in examining the
citational record of the dictionary is a body of overlooked linguistic and
literate activity, largely for reasons of gender, class and profession, which
I am holding for discussion until chapter 11. Taken together, the chapters
that follow amount to a short course in the history of British and American publishing, covering familiar ground, from Chaucer to Faulkner,
along with more obscure pockets of activity. The profiles of author, book,
and periodical that follow offer a particular understanding of language
and nation that is dominated by classical and religious influences, the

Figure 6.1  "For the Sake of Comparison . . ." from the Preface to Vol. III (D-E), *OED 1*

For the sake of comparison with Dr. Johnson's Dictionary, and with some more recent lexicographical works, the following figures have been carefully compiled for the letter D.

|  | Johnson | Cassell's Encyclopædic | Century Dict. | Funk's 'Standard' | Here. |
|---|---|---|---|---|---|
| Words recorded in D | 2,684 | 10,089 | 10,705 | 11,181 | 19,051 |
| Words illustrated by quotations | 2,136 | 5,251 | 4,977 | 1,313 | 16,128 |
| Number of illustrative quotations | 6,529 | 9,178 | 12,471 | 1,815 | 85,466 |

The number of quotations under D in Richardson's Dictionary, where the first serious effort was made to show the history of words by quotations, is 7,988.

*Source:* James A. H. Murray and Henry Bradley (Eds.), *A New English Dictionary*, Vol. III, Oxford: Clarendon Press, 1897, p. xi.

working of art and politics, the rise of a new class, and the making of a standard out of a vernacular literacy.

The concern of this chapter, however, is with the authors who dominate the first edition of the dictionary, as a Victorian record of invention and authority in the language. If Messrs. Coleridge, Furnivall, Murray, Bradley, Craigie, and Onions *edited* the *New English Dictionary*, then the work is *written* by a collection of poets, prose stylists, (other) lexicographers, and translators drawn from across five centuries of publishing (see table 6.1 in the Appendix). As with the shorter version of this table (table 4.1 in the Appendix), the poet prevails, taking up eight of the top twenty positions, or as many as ten, by crediting the poetry of Johnson and Scott. Add Dickens, as the sole novelist, and the panoply of literary greats confirms the well-known bias toward art-speech in this scientific record of the English language. Whatever the *OED* has borrowed from these great writers for the authorization of meaning and use, it has more than returned to them by setting out, word by word, their contribution to the English language. The literary figures who hold the top three positions in Johnson's *Dictionary*—Shakespeare, Dryden, and Milton—stand here as well among the top figures, although their hold on the proportion of the total citations drops by a factor of ten, from 30 to 3 percent (see table 6.2 in the Appendix). But then Johnson pursued his own interests in the language rather than "historical principles." The top authors in the *OED* are the product of a large assembly of readers, subeditors, and editors, backed by a Philological Society concerned with creating a legitimate history of origins and continuities. They represent the culmination of a Victorian philological inquiry among dedicated amateurs and emerging academic specialists. But there was still a playing of favorites.

The list of the most prominent authors in the *OED* represents a historical portrayal of the language, as assembled by more than a thousand readers over the course of seventy years. The results of this reading program that included both assigned and freely chosen texts was bound to include a few surprises, even among the poets. William Cowper, for example, reaches the same citational plane of influence in the *OED* as Pope and Spenser. Although this may well be attributed to the qualities of Cowper's great poem, *The Task*, published in 1784, a work that begins its six books of rural delights with the evolution of the sofa, there are also other factors at work in the citational process. The detailed "List of Readers" that James Murray presented to the Philological Society (*TPS*, 1884) reveals that Cowper's poem was read, obviously with great diligence and citing, by a Miss Lees of Sidlow, south of London, who submitted 1,550 citations (having also read Brewster's *Natural Magic* and *Optics* for the dictionary). As the eighteenth century was delegated by the Society in large part to American readers, we might conclude that Miss Lees read Cowper out of her own delight in *The Task*, perhaps drawn to the deeply troubled life led by this gentleman-poet. While Cowper was read by others for citations, we might still speculate that Miss Lees's interest in *The Task* made a difference. So it is, whether for thoroughly philological reasons or not, Cowper stands with Pope as one of the two principal contributors to the *OED* from the eighteenth century.

> **1784** COWPER *Task* I. 19 *Joint-stools* were then created; on three legs Upborne they stood. Three legs upholding firm A massy slab, in fashion square or round.
> [Note: The italicization of the word under definition.]

However, rather than pick away at the inclusion of one or another of the well-cited figures from the list, I have decided to work selectively with three themes that underlie the work of a number of those who have done more than their share in constituting the English language (having already dealt at some length with Shakespeare in previous chapters). The first of these themes covers the emergent glories of authordom, during the earliest of English literature's golden ages; the second is represented by the gothic and classical historicism of Spenser, Milton, and Scott; and the third dwells on the considerable impact of translation on the English language.

I

England's plenitude of literary golden ages—Chaucerian, Elizabethan, and Augustan—is well represented in the *OED*'s list of leading authors. But the first, and in some ways foremost, of the golden ages in establishing English literature's claim to greatness occurred during the latter half of the fourteenth century. The age of Chaucer did much to break the literary hold of Latin and French and open the way to the development of an English literary Renaissance. This period is represented in the table of leading authors by Chaucer, John Wyclif, John de Trevisa, and William Langland, while the poet John Lydgate falls short of the list by roughly one hundred citations. Among the top titles in the *OED* (see table 7.1 in the Appendix), to get ahead of myself a little, the works from the golden age of the fourteenth century include Langland's *Piers Plowman*, Trevisa's translation of *De proprietatibus rerum* and *Polychronicon*, John Gower's *Confessio Amantis*, and the anonymous translation of *The Gest Historiale of the Destruction of Troy*. These were authors and translators who, under a patronage system, succeeded in anglicizing a corner of the country's manuscript culture, as they each sought to reach a broader audience. It was a productive period, accounting for close to 20 percent of the citations from among the top authors and titles. The trade in texts was divided between the two sources of authority current at the time, the church and the court. Of the authors, Langland, Wyclif, Geoffrey, and Lydgate were ecclesiastics of varying degrees of fidelity to the church. However, rather than go through them all, I want to consider the instances of Chaucer and Wyclif as exemplifying a division of formative forces in the history of the language. Chaucer was the literary figure of remarkable tales and court patronage, while Wyclif was the rebellious priest, who broke with the Roman Church on such textual matters as translating the Bible into the language of the people. Together, the poet and rebel contribute a significant chapter to the nation's history project. Their prince-and-pauper story is about making English stock out of such linguistic resources from abroad as fine Italian verse and a Latinate Bible.

Geoffrey Chaucer's literary inventiveness in English occurs within the context of his translations, adaptations, conscious borrowings, and subtle reworkings that critics have long noted as enriching his work (Bassnett-McGuire, 1980, p. 53). The court's patronage of his poetry may well have played an instrumental role in the very choice of English as the poet's language.[1] What is being repeatedly cited in the name of Chaucer, then, is a particular linguistic and social process, as well as perhaps the more obvious aspect of the man's literary genius within this freshly written language. At an early point in his poetic career, he fell under the influence of Dante, taking a good deal from this champion of vernacular verse, as well as from French models, to fashion his influential poetry in the English language. It was during this Italian period that he composed *Troilus and Criseyde*, a neoclassical love story set in Troy which Chaucer lifted principally from Boccaccio's *Filostrato* of 1340 (and passed on to Shakespeare and Dryden). *The Canterbury Tales*, drawn from a myriad of classical, French, and Italian fables and tales, came after he had moved on to a classicist version of the heroic couplet. Although Chaucer did translate a few complete works from other languages, his poetry represents another, more imaginative form of transcription, from both the classical period and contemporary work imported from the continent in his search for what Dante (1981) called *de vulgari eloquentia* in drawing up his Latin defense of the great poetry written in Italian. In the spirit of this English Golden Age of poetry, Chaucer was intent on bringing to fruition the beauty of what Dante referred to as "our first true speech" (albeit in a tongue much closer to the revered Latin).

Chaucer was, however, well aware of the risks of writing literature in a language that had yet to be standardized in the manner of Latin.

Toward the conclusion of *Troilus* (1958), the narrator prays that the story just told will not be destroyed by the very diversity of English:

> And for ther is so greet diversitee
> In Englissh, and in writing of oure tonge,
> So praye I God that noon miswrite thee
>
> (V.ii.1793–95)

The last line, with its prayer for fidelity in writing, is cited by the *OED* to illustrate the definition of *miswrite*. This apprehension over the state of a diverse English was to stay with those who wrote and read in this language, as they were to later turn to the nation's lexicographers, asking them to take this linguistic anarchy in hand. Such conservatism had been Johnson's original intent with his *Dictionary*, although by the time he had finished the project, he was prepared to recognize the virtue of the language's copious energy and capacity for change.

The actual nature of Chaucer's contribution to English literature was debated well into the sixteenth century, particularly around the proper Englishness of his vocabulary. Many called upon the authority of Chaucer to warrant their own inventions in the language, as Brian Melbacke writes in his *Philotimus* of 1583: "If I haue vsed any rare and obsolete words, they are eyther such as the Coryphees of our English writers, *Chaucer* and *Lidgate*, haue vsed before me, and now are decayed for want of practise; or else such as by apt translation out of *Greekes* and *Latins*" (cited in Jones, 1953, p. 118, original emphasis). Equally so, the great Elizabethan translator of Homer, George Chapman, was prepared to claim that "Chaucer (by whom we will needes authorize our true english) had more newe wordes for his time then any man needes to deuise now" (cited in Jones, 1953, p. 209). Yet this very need to call on such authorization suggests that contrary views were current at the time, and Jones does report that an "antiquarian hostility to neologizing" stood opposed to Chaucer's still-fresh coinages. Jones gives the example of another Elizabethan, Richard Verstegan, who called for a proper recognition of English's German roots and thus was all too ready to censure Chaucer for being "a great mingler of English with French" (p. 260). Others during the period, such as Roger Ascham, John Skelton, and Sir Thomas Elyot, were prepared to deny that any substantial inroads had been made during the Age of Chaucer against the basic rudeness of the English language (pp. 3–31). The frequent borrowings of Chaucer and other poets of the age were cast as a literary necessity given the paucity of English at the time, but it was a cross-cultural inventiveness later condemned as trading in *inkhorn* terms with its pretense of learning. The *OED*, for its part, is unequivocal in locating the English language in such accomplished poets as Chaucer. What is not apparent in examining the entries in the dictionary is the degree to which the poets' inventiveness comes out of the daring appropriation of their art and politics. In this Chaucer gives the English language a secure and proud moment of its own self-invention that tells only part of the story through the citations that authorize the language within the dictionary.

Outside of Chaucer's courtly fashions, and yet equally given to challenging the Latinate hold on written discourse, is the religious reformer John Wyclif (with his name often rendered Wycliffe). Wyclif's place in the table of leading authors is the product of a collective effort on the part of Wyclifites, who were drawn from among his Oxford followers, as well as his own efforts. Together, in the 1380s, they translated the entire Bible into English for the first time, with Wyclif's precise contribution somewhat difficult to establish. Such forms of Wyclifism were officially condemned in 1382, which was apparently to give pause more generally to those writing in English (Bennett, 1992, p. 7). The more certain of the citations from Wyclif come from his sermons in which he took up verbal arms against those forms of authority that, to his thinking, lacked grace; he was not afraid to name the wicked, whether they were popes, kings, or priests. Wyclif's sermons represent a powerful mix of spoken and written language. Whether transcribed on the fly by an agile scribe, or worked up from his notes on the request of followers, the sermons carried with them the sense of impassioned delivery. He turned the church's own didacticism against it in the name of a higher morality. "Why he was not burnt alive no one knows" is the rather uncharacteristic interjection made on his behalf in *The Oxford Companion to English Literature* (Harvey, 1967, p. 901). The church, as well as the state, was not yet mobilized, as it would be after the advent of the printing press, to control the written word. So it was that the next significant translation of the New Testament, published in 1526, was by William Tindale, who was executed for heresy in 1536.[2]

The sermons, no less than the Wyclifite Bible, were part of a resistance in the British Isles to the hold of a latter-day Rome, part of a cultural struggle that repeatedly finds itself, pamphlet by broadside, carried out through an engaged print culture. The sermon, in particular, continued as a source of outspokenness, conservative and heretical, Catholic and Calvinist; it is an early form of spoken essay and editorial, certainly the first that many people, literate and illiterate, experienced as they grew up. When the English Bible fell under the patent of the King's Printer during the Reformation, the sermon became the center and substance of a free market in popular religious publishing (Feather, 1988, p. 23). The *OED* features 10,431 citations from works by various authors which bear the title *Sermons*, with Wyclif's foremost among them (compared to 20,160 citations for the various translations of the Bible). Wyclif was determined to give the English people access to sacred texts and to the articulation of injustices in their own life, which was sufficient to ensure a contribution to the *OED* that ranked with Chaucer's far more literary language. Wyclif represents a part of the heroic past of the English language, inspired by traditional and biblical forms, yet determined to make them over in their reach for new levels of meaning.

> *c.* 1380 WYCLIF *Sel. Wks.* III 234 O if God so scharply biddes þese *negatifes* . . , who are more heretikes þen þese þat done hit ageynes hym?

While Chaucer and Wyclif represent radically different aspects of the writing trade, they meet in the dictionary as fashioners of a late fourteenth-century English informed by imported influences and vernacular interests, gentle satire and incensed passion, craft and exigency, art and fire. Building a history of the language through citations, as there is really no other way of documenting the past, means locating words in the history of authorship and books. As long as we do not mistake this for the whole of language, for the entirety of its historical life, then we can realize how the Golden Age of Chaucer, dominated by poets, translators, and a rebel-priest, offers a particular sense of the English past. It tells of a nation forged out of well-turned verse and outspoken nay-saying, a heroic image that may well comfort the educated classes who use the dictionary today no less than it did during Victorian times when the construction of this history began.

II

The guiding light for Richard Helgerson's *Forms of Nationhood: The Elizabethan Writing of England* (1992) is a query posed by Edmund Spenser in 1580: "Why a God's name may not we, as else the Greeks, have the kingdom of our own language?" (p. 1). The question suggests yet another version of the literary project in England, from the Age of Chaucer to the "Proposal for a New English Dictionary." Among leading contributors to the *OED*, this striving for "the kingdom of our own language" through a focus on the past informs the writing of Spenser, Milton, and Scott as three of the leading contributors to the *OED*. Edmund Spenser's interests in the "writing of England" during Elizabethan times, as Helgerson casts it, resembles the national project that the *OED* was meant to consolidate, bringing to bear the work of those who collectively wrote out a *United Kingdom* for the British Isles no less than for use of the world at large. Spenser's poetic contribution to a sovereign English language brought together a number of classical and gothic claims to the throne of the English pen. The classical meters and themes of his early comedies earned him the title of "the Virgil of England." From there he went on to gothic themes of Prince Arthur's chivalrous knight errantry within the lingering Virgilian tones of *The Faerie Queen*. Spenser set in motion, in Helgerson's terms, "the dialectic of Greek and Goth [that] remained central to England's self-understanding and self-representation" (1992, p. 55). For some, however, it was simply "old rustic language," as his contemporary Philip Sidney first named it on reading Spenser's *Shepheardes Calendar* (cited in Helgerson, 1992, p. 42). But where else was Spenser to turn? Sovereignty over a people or a language is a matter of establishing a lineage, which in the case of Spenser's poetry took the form of a deliberate archaism in diction and setting. The eponymous heroine of *The Faerie Queen*, a "mayden" seemingly Elizabethan, is not actually present in this epic and unfinished poem. She serves, in absentia, as a sovereign continually inscribed through the deeds of others in her name; she represents a circulation of authority through a process of citation or invocation. The meaning achieved through this suspension of direct reference, in the place between the off-stage presence of the queen and the work done in her name, seems to hold a parallel with the work of the poet and the lexicographer, both of whom, in these instances, reach back to earlier times for their warrants and precedents.

**1590** SPENSER *F. Q.* I. iv. 15 Yet the stout Faery mongst the *middest* crowd Thought all their glorie vaine in knightly vew.

Less than a century later, Milton had struck yet another path in the effort to return English verse to its roots. In *Paradise Lost*, he seemed intent on rejecting Spenser's "barbarous" rhyme, his "long and tedious havoc fabled knights / in battle feigned" (*P. L.*, 9.30–31), just as he turned his back on the pattern of Shakespeare's richly imaginative poetry (Guillory, 1983). Composing verse in English and Latin, Milton preferred a return of his native tongue to some form of original and pellucid state, taking much from its Latin connections, and yet developing a "plain style," as at least one critic argues, with "a diction that is native and pithy rather than polysyllabic and Latinate" (Tricomi, 1986, p. 135). Without being drawn too far into the critical debates that still smolder over which traditions prevailed and which were resisted, it is important to note how the poetic authorities, in making such a substantial contribution to the *OED*, were of radically different minds about what was foremost in the English language and what they felt compelled to make of it. Milton remained intent on restoring English to a purer state, hoping perhaps that this language, no less than his poetry, would do the same for the English people. His eighteenth-century editor, Thomas Newton, declared with little hesitation that this pious poet "frequently . . . uses words in their proper and primary signification" (cited in J. Leonard, 1990, p. 233).

This prelapsarian project, of returning language to a time before the Fall—to a time when words possessed their original meanings—may only seem ill-fated. The *OED* was to allow Milton just such a place in reshaping the record of the language, as in the case of *error*:

> 1667 MILTON *P.L.* IV. 239 The crisped Brooks, Rowling .. With mazie *error* under pendant shades.

Milton's Latinate use of *error* (in the sense of "the action of roaming or wandering") is marked, "Now only *poet.*" followed in small-type with the note, "The primary sense now only Latin; in Fr. and Eng. it occurs only as a conscious imitation of Latin." Milton's vocabulary represents a conscious attack on the errors of a wandering (Shakespearean) fancy in the language. He is intent on powers of the imagination that are disciplined by reason and uncluttered by ornament:

> 1667 MILTON *P.L.* IV. 318 How have ye .. banisht from mans life .. Simplicitie and *spotless* innocence.

This sense of banished simplicity in Milton is, as Stanley Fish describes it, very much an issue of connecting words and meanings: "The loss of the perfect language is more than anything else the sign of the fall, since in Eden speech is the outward manifestation of the inner Paradise. . . . The congruency between the word and the thing implies a congruency between the mind and the thing" (1967, p. 118). Fish is pointing to elements in *Paradise Lost* that may be thought to resemble the original project for the *OED*, as inspired by the Reverend Richard Trench, that is, of finding the mind and morality of (English) humankind by rooting the language in its proper history.

If Samuel Johnson had studiously avoided citing Milton's polemical prose works in his *Dictionary*, the *OED* has leaned the other way (Reddick, 1990). Jack Gray, in working on Milton at the Waterloo Centre for the New *OED*, has ascertained that of the 637 Milton citations credited as the earliest found for the word being defined, only one-third are from the poetic works (1989). Milton's predilection for Latinate constructions—giving rise to a run of negated terms on the order of *unadopted*, *unadorned*, and *unaided*—account for no less than one-quarter of the first-credited citations. Gray also found evidence of the greater inventiveness of Milton's fiery prose in the dictionary's single-citation entries. Of Milton's 141 instances of these *hapax legomena*—including *adamantean*, *affatuated*, *antagony*, *aphorismer*, and so on—only eight are drawn from his poetry:

> 1643 MILTON *Divorce* I. x, Minds that can not unite .. two incoherent and *incombining* dispositions.

The point in terms of the *OED*'s oft-ascribed literary bias is worth emphasizing: in tracking inventiveness in the language, the dictionary gives more weight to Milton's Puritan pamphleteering, his topical interventions in issues of publication, divorce, schooling, and heresy, than to the timeless spiritual longing of Adam and Eve. This is not a product of the editors' interests or of self-directed readers keen on Milton's prose, but the direct result of working from a concordance to his writing. As timely as the pamphlets were for the English Revolution and Restoration, Milton's own theory of a backward-looking diction has a way of skewing the *OED*'s historical record of the English language.

Given the supporting role played by the concordances for Milton and Shakespeare, Walter Scott may arguably represent the best-read figure for citations in the dictionary. His position among cited authors, without the benefit of an alphabetical guide to his language, provides another indication of the qualities that distinguished the writers who above all were trusted informants for the history of the language forged by the *OED*. During the early decades of the nineteenth century, it had been claimed by some, the English literary banner was carried jointly by Walter Scott and William Shakespeare (Fumaroli, 1992, p. 5). Yet if we take Carlyle as our Victorian guide, as we did with Shakespeare, we find this critic quite certain by 1837 that Scott was not a great writer, but one who managed to avoid "a popularity of the populace" and attract "almost all of the intelligent of the civilized countries" (n.d., p. 56).[3] Whatever Scott lacked, for Carlyle, in ideas, it was his "perfection of extemporaneous writing" that distinguished him. Here was the writer-as-hero producing works that "were written faster and better paid than any other books in the world" (p. 99). That this demi-god of the circulating library was not writing Literature, but "the phraseology, fashion of arms, of dress and life, belonging to one age" which he "brought suddenly with singular vividness before the eyes of another" (p. 101).[4] So it was that Scott, like Spenser and Milton before him, took as his literary project a similar line of recovery and restoration work. His considerable presence in the *OED* is as the author of the Waverly Novels, full of a rich and often archaic Scottish detail and diction, as well as for vivid narrative poems such as *The Lady of the Lake* and *Marmion*.

> 1808 SCOTT *Marm.* I. i, Their armour .. *Flash'd* back again the western blaze.

Scott's vision of a romantic and daring past created a literary sensation that contributed to a vision of Scotland as part of a brave and heroic time. If his work is regarded as gothic melodrama today, Scott was revered for recapturing a lost heroic temper, stocking his story with archaisms and antiquarian delights that reintroduced words and senses otherwise lost into general use. This selective incorporation of Scott's language into the common vocabulary of the dictionary as part of its historical record of the *English* language might be imagined as extending the act of union both backward and forward in time:

> 1805 SCOTT *Last Minstr.* VI. xi, *It* was an English Ladye bright . . And she would marry a Scottish knight.

The literary reconstruction of the past exemplified by Spenser, Milton, and Scott has become, even in its most archaic elements, part of the modern history of the language recorded in the *OED*. Their work also represents the close association of artistic creation and scholarly record, in a joint venture at forging new links with the glories of a carefully constituted past.

## III

The third and final source of citations I will consider in this chapter on the leading authors in the *OED* are the English translations of Greek, Latin, and French works. From the fourteenth to the eighteenth centuries, translation proves a consistent source of invention and affirmation of meaning in the *OED*. It is commonly known that much of the vocabulary of English was imported after the original formation of Anglo-Saxon, with estimates for the proportion of "loan words" running as high as two-thirds. Less well known is the degree to which direct translation proved to be the vehicle of this newfound English. One can on occasion find literary historians, such as Douglas Bush, giving translation its due: "From the beginning of English history the translation of ancient and modern books had been a main agent in the development of religious and secular culture and of literary style" (1945, p. 56). Yet more often the translator's contribution to the development of the English language goes overlooked. Owen Barfield, in his classic *History in English Words*, based in large part on the *OED*, celebrates the enrichment of the language by, above all, the poet, using Chaucer as his example: "A modern poet, looking back on that time can scarcely help envying a writer like Chaucer with this enormous store of fresh, unspoiled English words ready to his hand and unlimited treasury across the channel from which he could pick a brand-new one whenever he wanted it" (1926, p. 53). That Chaucer and a good many other poets and writers picked their "brand-new" words through direct acts of translating foreign-language texts into English is not commented upon in this celebration of the English imagination, nor is it noted that not only poets but unassuming translators served the language equally well in this regard, or so the record provided by the *OED* reveals. The triumph of the English language took place not only through the creative stylings of borrowed themes by the great poets. When Polonius introduces to Hamlet, "the best actors in the world ... for tragical-comical-historical-pastoral, scene individable, or poem unlimited," they are actors especially adept at Seneca and Plautus, in translation.

The prevalence of citations from translated works raises a number of interesting questions about the historical record of the language as it tends to confound the contributions of invention and scholarship, while raising questions about the growth of an indigenous and native tongue. During the period in which the *OED* was being edited, Matthew Arnold was insisting that "the first duty [of the translator] is to be faithful," although he wisely adds that "the question at issue ... is, in what faithfulness consists" (1895, p. 143). In looking back at the record offered by the *OED*, it might be said that keeping the Arnoldian faith has meant the selective cultivation of a particular heritage. The translations that dominate the *OED* are classical, clerical, and French. The English took their literate lead not only from previous conquerors, but from those after whom they sought to fashion themselves. The classical impress on English culture and vocabulary is found, for example, in the fact that, among the twenty leading books cited by the *OED* (presented in the next chapter), one-quarter of the citations are from Greek and Latin works translated into English. In taking stock of this influx, Arnold does not hesitate to claim, in language that recalls Richard Verstegan's contrary position, introduced above, that "we owe to the Latin element in our language most of that very rapidity and clear decisiveness by which it is contradistinguished from the German, and in sympathy with the languages of Greece and Rome" (1895, p. 147).

The contribution of translation to the *OED* takes the form of three rather different forces at work on the language. The first of these, with translations from Latin, is that the translator challenges the hold of this scholastic language on literate culture, especially as it restricts, in effect, access to written language, as a powerful form of participation in the society. The translation of the Bible from Latin, as well as Greek and Hebrew, meant taking a stand on the ability of both the people and their language to engage sacred forms of meaning in a direct and unmediated manner. Of all the acts of translation, the English Bible looms largest in the history of language, nation, and empire. The Bible dominates the list of leading books in the dictionary. It figures in Wyclif's placement near the top of the author's list, and it accounts for the size of Miles Coverdale's contribution, the man credited, not without dispute, for being the first to translate the entirety of the Bible into English, working from Latin and, with his Lutheran leanings, German versions of the text. As such, it has to do with a spiritual impulse married to a democratic tendency based on a trust in the individual to turn this newfound articulateness to good purpose. This popularizing aspect to translation, which dates back to King Alfred, later gained another impetus from the market forces of the printing press.

A second, more conservative force to translation is a desire to move in the other direction, that is, to align the vernacular tongue with the more exclusive literate language, distancing the written vernacular in its vocabulary and themes from those who live by the spoken word alone. The deliberate emulation and imitation of a classical language can be seen to interrupt the sort of indigenous evolution of native English, which James Murray describes in the dictionary's "General Explanations," as moving from the home and street, to the writing of letters, and finally on to the printed page. The classical affiliation, too, has something to do with the publishing market, as the printer favors proven, high-profile titles, working from a more prestigious language and playing on the formation of a "middle" class of literate language consumers who have enough of the classics to know their inestimable worth.

A third force at work through translation from the classics is the desire to bring the unfailing wisdom that comes from studying the wise and good lives of that first Golden Age to the people at large. Translation was part reclamation, part education. Although the disciplined study of the classics was not to be well established in the elite schools of England until the nineteenth century, thanks in good part to Thomas Arnold, it had long been recognized that, as Martin Bernal puts it, "contemplation of all aspects of Greek and Roman Life was supposed to have beneficial educational and moral effect on the boys who were to be the rulers of the Britain and Empire" (1987, p. 317). To work with the classics, even in translation, provided a focus for moral development for students, to take up a later educational theme that was developed by Thomas' son, Matthew Arnold, as I have discussed elsewhere (Willinsky 1991), for the teaching of poetry in state-sponsored schools.

From among our list of those responsible for citations in translation, we might begin with the instance of the celebrated poets and classicist-translators, John Dryden and Alexander Pope. Dryden's translation of Virgil (including the *Pastorals*, *Georgics*, and *Aeneis*) and Pope's working of Homer (*The Odyssey* and *The Iliad*) prove to be among these two poets' strongest contributions to the *OED*, if only because of the substantial size of the texts involved. These considerable translations were not, as it turns out, among the authors' early apprenticeship pieces but work of their poetic maturity. The purposes of these translations were various. Judith Sloman, for instance, writes of Dryden's need to "reveal and conceal himself at the same time, and creative translation provided one answer," referring to a political period in which the author was feeling a little uncomfortable, in his conversion to Catholicism, with anything but "oblique self-expression," as she puts it (1985, p. 7). Sloman also refers to the reliable source of the bookseller's coin, "in good silver," that Virgil proved for Dryden in his later years (p. 26). Dryden himself claimed translation as the material of freeborn subjects, as it "is so very useful to an enquiring people, and for the improvement and spreading of knowledge which is none the worse preservatives against slavery" (cited by Sloman, 1985, p. 27).

Pope dwells in his preface to *The Iliad* on Homer's inventiveness as the soul of the epic's perfection, emphasizing the foundational quality of the poet's language, invoking the poet-as-Adam myth that informs the *OED* on a larger scale: "We acknowledge him the father of poetical diction, the first who taught that language of the gods to men. . . . Aristotle had reason to say, he was the only poet who had found out living words" (1870, p. xii). Pope invites us to imagine Homer forging a proto-national language out of local dialects: "He was not satisfied with his language as he found it settled in any one part of Greece but searched through its different dialects with this particular view, to beautify and perfect his numbers" (pp. xii–xiii). Having established Homer's own immense linguistic accomplishment, Pope then promulgates a theory of translation which eschews "the use of modern terms of war and government" in favor of a more distressed surface of antiquity: "Perhaps the mixture of some Graecisms and old words, after the manner of Milton, if done without too much affectation, might not have an ill effect in a version of this particular work, which most of any other seems to require a venerable antique cast" (p. xix). Remaining faithful to Homer means giving readers a sense of the slightly foreign and archaic in a journey back in time that will not overtax them (as would reading the original) while moving the nation forward with its classical affiliations proudly showing. This progressive conservative agenda was to be part of the distinguished work accomplished by Dryden's *The Works of Virgil* and Pope's *Iliad* both in the first instance, and then again with their considerable citation in the *OED*.

The Dryden and Pope translations of these classical texts are only two of many versions featured in the dictionary. *The Aeneid* ranks tenth among titles cited, by virtue of a series of translations (see table 7.1 in the Appendix). Along with Pope's versions of Homer, at least eight translations of *The Iliad* and *The Odyssey* are cited in the *OED*, from Thomas Hobbes's in the seventeenth century to a nineteenth-century version by William Morris, with an additional entry in the anonymous *The Destruction of Troy*. Greek and Latin terms flowed into English by this constant exercise of poets, scholars, and dedicated translators. More generally, however, the trade in translations was about confirming the English language and people as capable of participating in ancient nobility. The strength of classicist translation in the *OED* reflects a conscious effort among elements of this formative English culture to shape itself around the ancient culture of Greece and Rome, in that Holy Roman Empire, "of which," T. S. Eliot later claimed, "we are all still citizens." By the nineteenth century, the cultivation of the Greco-Roman spirit in Great Britain had developed into an exaggerated dichotomy between Hellenic and Hebraic cultures.[5] No one made more of this separation than Matthew Arnold in *Culture and Anarchy*, where he used it as a way of explaining the nature of the English people, namely a mixture of properties (translated) from both "races," and where they should be headed, namely more fully into the Hellenic. The nation's past is shaped by the conscious cultural interests of the present in word and deed. In translating Homer, Pope and Morris wanted not only to keep the ancient Greek stories alive within the English language, but to re-create in English their own vision of Greece as a glorious and lost past, as the very land of civilization's virgin birth.

Yet it was not only the poets who carried the torch from Athens and Rome. Of those who introduced and kept alive this classicism within the English language, no one did more than Philemon Holland, headmaster of Coventry Free-School and physician, but better known as "the Translator Generall in his Age" (Bush, 1945, p. 57). This eclectic Elizabethan managed to contribute more to the English language, as recorded by the *OED*, than Pope, Spenser, or Johnson, all by virtue of a half-dozen well-executed translations from Greek and Latin. His policy was to avoid "any affected phrase," as he put it, favoring instead "a meane and popular style" which meant, through a rather odd twist, lifting into print a number of common English words in response to the eloquent Latin (cited by Bassnett-McGuire, 1980, p. 57). Yet Holland was open about his nationalist and populist intentions. In his prefaces, he directly confronts the disparagers of this easy distribution of learning through the use of the "vulgar tongue," treating their attacks as unwarranted and dangerous: "Why should any man therefore take offence hereat, and envie this good to his naturall countrey, which was first meant for the whole world?" (cited by Bennett, 1970, III, p. 69). Holland unabashedly dedicates his popular translation of Pliny the Elder's *Natural History of the World* to the pleasure and learning of "the rude paisant of the country, fitted for the painefull artizan in town and citie; pertinent to the bodily health of man woman and child" (ibid.). The Latin original, dating back to the year A.D. 77, is an odd and assorted compendium of some twenty thousand facts drawn from the work of one hundred Latin writers. It is written in a language all the more enriched, one imagines, by the way in which those "facts" were rather freely recorded by Pliny with many of them regarded as obsolete and somewhat absurd, *The Oxford Classical Dictionary* notes, even in Roman times:

1601 Holland *Pliny* II. 365 Bast dogs haire down to a *bend* or piece of cloth, and fasten the same close to the said forehead.

With translations from French into English, which stand close to being equal to the classical languages in influence, we find printers, pedagogues, and lexicographers entering the list of substantial contributors to the *OED*. Although far better known for bringing the miracle of movable type to England, William Caxton actually began to dabble in printing to do something with his translations which he undertook "to eschew sloth and idleness," as he put it, learning to set his own work in type during 1475 while in Bruges, with *The recuyell of the historyes of Troye*. When he set up his shop in Westminster a year later, he was soon printing his Latin and French translations, creating, in effect, an English-language market for printed books. His rendition of J. de Voragaine's *Golden Legende* proved to be the largest book he published, running to nine hundred pages, leaving him, "halfe desparate to have accomplished it" (cited in Crotch, p. 70).

Another on the list attuned to the French presence is Jehan Palsgrave, a graduate of Oxford, where translation was valued little enough, and instructor to Princess Mary, sister of Henry VIII. His thousand-page *Lesclarcissement de la langue françoyse* was intended as a guide and dictionary for English teachers, such as himself, to help their charges perfect their French. The bulk of it is dedicated to demonstrating the nuances of every inflection within the parts of speech, and at least in the opinion of H. S. Bennett, the French language has yet to be more thoroughly or better served than by Palsgrave (1969, I, p. 94). However the French themselves have come to regard Palsgrave's book, it has certainly served well as a repository of obsolete English words and expressions for the editors of the dictionary.

One might imagine that lexicography is itself a kind of translation process with that same trick of rendering a potentially remote text into a second language of meaning. The translations of Wyclif, Caxton, Dryden, Holland, Trevisa, Pope, Palsgrave, and Coverdale (and there will be more to follow in the list of the top titles in the *OED*) all show a determination in this history of the English language to extend the privilege of learning and delight. The place of translation on this list lends credence to George Steiner's argument in *After Babel* (1975) that this interlanguage movement extends the native language through what he refers to as an alchemy of translation that has a metaphysical element to it:

> In order to accomplish this alchemy, a translation must, in regard to its own language, retain a vital strangeness and "otherness." Very little in Holderlin's *Antigone* is "like" ordinary German; Marianne Moore's readings of La Fontaine are thornhedges apart from colloquial American English. The

translator enriches his tongue by allowing the source language to penetrate and modify it. But he does far more: he extends his native idiom towards the hidden absolute of meaning. (1975, pp. 64–65)

Whether English is moving closer to "the hidden absolute of meaning" through this traffic in translation or simply adding to its vocabulary is more difficult to establish. Taking his lead from the Jewish textual tradition of the Kabbala, Steiner treats translation as an act of interpretation. He reminds us of Walter Benjamin's insistence that we are always reading between the lines for what we imagine as the immediacy of meaning. This desire for the time before the tower of Babel, when the world was suffused with one true language, is part of our interest in linguistic supports such as translations and dictionaries: "In the meantime, the very need for translation was like the mark of Cain, a witness to man's exile from *harmonia mundi*" (Steiner, 1975, p. 62).

For John Wyclif and Miles Coverdale, biblical translation meant trusting the capacity of people to find their own way with the Word. For Pope, it was the guarantor of classicist civility against signs of encroaching decay. Translation is about access and preservation. It has to do with what is silenced and who is heard in the championing of certain texts by representation through translation and citation. Britain, with its history of Roman colonization and Norman invasion, was ready to bring Latin and French back into a sixteenth- and early seventeenth-century England on its own terms, through the English language. And they were often profitable terms at that, as these texts offered printers and booksellers brand-name recognition, often doubly so for author and translator, in a culture concerned with a form of self-colonization. By comparison, translators and lexicographers working on Persian, Sanskrit, and Chinese texts, although by no means absent from the *OED*, were not part of the larger equation of meaning intended to affirm English cultural connections with classical civilization.[6] In this regard, we might consider as typical the statement of Edward Fitzgerald about translating from the Persian, which he made in 1851, eight years before anonymously publishing his version of *The Rubàiyàt of Omar Khayyàm*: "It is an amusement to me to take what liberties I like with these Persians, who, (as I think), are not Poets enough to frighten one from such excursions, and who really do want a little Art to shape them" (cited in Bassnett-McGuire, 1980, p. 3).

After reviewing the principal contributors to the *OED* from English's first Golden Age, its historicist tradition, and its accomplished translators, it seems worth commenting on the rather startling absence of the Romantics, with the debatable exception of Scott. The list of leading authors is not simply a literary who's who. One has to look well down the list of the top authors to find that first among the leading Romantic poets is Lord Byron, who ranks thirty-sixth among the contributors to the first edition (with 4,027 citations), followed by Shelley and Coleridge. With fewer than 2,000 citations, Wordsworth's explicit rejection of archly poetic diction and dramatic narrative may have made him a less than favored author among readers for the dictionary. To be "a man speaking to men" and as such, "to imitate, and as far as is possible, to adopt the very language of men," may keep one from finding a substantial place in a record of the language devoted to the published record (Wordsworth, 1927, pp. 178, 173).[7] At the very least, he failed to find a champion among the readers for the *OED*. While at least four readers scoured Byron's work for citations, judging from Murray's "List of Readers" for 1884, Wordsworth seems to have had J. H. Nodal of Heaton Moor, who read his *Description of the Lakes*, and Miss C. Richardson of Grasmere, who is described as offering "a few quotations" in his name (*TPS*, 1884, p. 631). It is hard to know if this is a failure of interest in this Romantic poet or a measure of his failure to provide helpful instances of language in use.

1798 WORDSW. *Old Cumb. Beggar* 108 The *easy* man Who sits at his own door,—and . . Feeds in the sunshine.

This shortchanging of the Romantic poets' inventiveness, after the *OED*'s readers and editors awarded so much lexicographical attention to the Victorian quartet of Charles Dickens, Alfred Tennyson, Thomas Carlyle, and Thomas Macaulay, provides some sense of how aspects of literary taste can govern a great dictionary. If English literature was not yet an academic matter in the universities during this period, it was among the most hotly debated topics of magazines and reviews, carried out with a vehemence that could cost a poet dearly: "*Blackwood's* did not kill John Keats," Louis Dudek asserts of the magazine's criticism of the Romantics in the early nineteenth century, "but the cruelty and insensitivity with which the Edinburgh critics attacked the poet has not been easy to excuse" (1960, p. 88). Carlyle had pronounced against the Romantics in his essay on Scott as "the sickliest of recorded ages, when British Literature lay all puking and sprawling in Werterism [Wertherism?], Byronism, and other Sentimentalism tearful or spasmodic (fruit of internal *wind*)" (n.d., p. 69). Francis Jeffrey, editor of the *Edinburgh*, was equally intent on bringing Wordsworth and Coleridge low at every opportunity (Gross, 1991, p. 13). This critical disparagement may well have left its mark on the *OED*, and yet the Romantics, as much as any literary figure considered in this chapter, have continued to live on in the language. Perhaps the devotees of Wordsworth, Shelley, or Keats need to lead a lexical reconsideration, a re-reading for citational purposes, of the Romantic contribution to the history of the English language.

The larger point, however, lies in the degree to which the *Oxford English Dictionary* remains very much the product of the late-Victorian period, as much as it is a display case for the whole of the English language and those who wrote it. The leading figures in this citational display are divided between the celebrated literary author and the translator who brings a secondary tradition of biblical and classical proportions to bear on the language. Together, they tell a tale that is perhaps most effectively summed up, in all of its mythical proportions, by Sir Arthur Quiller Couch, who became in 1912 one of Cambridge's first professors of English literature. He insisted on the remarkable integrity of this newborn national discipline—"our living poetry and prose"—an integrity driven by the self-fashioned geography of a jointly gothic and classical antiquity, all musingly stirred by an adopted ancient mother:

> From Anglo-Saxon prose, from Anglo-Saxon poetry, our living poetry and prose have, save linguistically, no derivation ... whatever the agency—whether through Wyatt, or Spenser, Marlowe or Shakespeare, or Donne, or Milton, or Dryden, or Pope, or Johnson, or even Wordsworth—always our literature has obeyed, however unconsciously, the precept *Antiquam exquisite matrem*, "seek back to the ancient mother"; always it has recreated itself, kept itself pure and strong, by harking back to bathe in those native—yes, native—Mediterranean springs. (Cited in Crowley, 1989, p. 40)

## CHAPTER 7

# A Victorian Canon:
## The Titles

IN SPITE OF the impression that one might gain from the last chapter, the notable and named author is not everything in *The Oxford English Dictionary*. The dictionary's entries are filled out, not only by excerpts from little-known journalists, historians, scholars, editors, translators, but by the anonymous citations of encyclopedias, periodicals, early English texts, and collective translations of the Bible. Examining the titles that have been most often cited in the *OED* has a way of setting the contributions of these obscure and anonymous writers alongside the authors of *The Faerie Queen* and *Paradise Lost*. The substantial citation of reference works and periodicals lends weight to a two-tiered view of the historical record of the English language established by the *OED*. In the first instance, the dictionary has privileged the literary construction of the language, but it has done so, in comparison to other lexicographical works, with a far greater regard for a broader history of English publishing activity. The leading titles of the *OED* make it plain how the publishing trade as a whole has been entrusted by the editors, if without equal representation from all segments, to authorize its history of the English language. The leading books and periodicals cited in this dictionary demonstrate how the cultural trinity of literary, sacred, and classical works are tempered by what ultimately developed in the nineteenth century into a textual superstructure built out of the reference trade, the working press, and the journalism of opinion. Even as the *OED* expands the historical principles of the language's formation, it manages to place the language firmly in the hands of the writing and reading classes, as if to set the final seal on their enfranchisement and power, both at home and as a force in the world.

Among the titles that figure heavily in the dictionary, reference works and periodicals posed a special challenge to the project of building a historical record of the language. As I observed earlier, Murray was not pleased with having to rely on quotations from dictionaries and reference works. He felt it diminished the immediacy or firsthandedness of the citation that was supposed to connect the *OED* to the life of the language. Nonetheless, reference books to this day remain a mainstay among sources of citations, suggesting the especially effective circulation of meaning within genres. On the other hand, the delegates of Oxford University Press were not at all comfortable with the use of citations from the *Times* or *Daily News*. Such ephemeral sources hardly seemed suitable for giving direction to the dictionary. James Murray dismissed this as sheer snobbery, permitting newspaper and other periodical titles to become the authorizing signature for a great number of citations from the Victorian era in the *OED*.

To further complicate matters with these citations, neither reference books nor periodicals were, with only a few exceptions, part of the planned reading program designed to gather materials for the dictionary. The citations from the reference books are the in-house work of the dictionary's editorial staff filling in a lacuna in the search for citations from primary texts, while the periodical titles represent the reading habits and active choices of readers for the dictionary. These two citational sources act as a check on the otherwise notable literary bias of the dictionary, even as they reveal another side to the authorization-of-meaning question raised by the citation process. Here the working press tempers the aggrandizing tendencies of this proud and selective tradition. As a means of distinguishing between these influences on the dictionary, this chapter works with separate lists divided between the leading book and periodical titles, considering each, in turn, for what they reveal about the construction of the *OED*.

I

The top twenty book titles in the dictionary are roughly distributed among spiritual, classical, and practical themes, with literary motifs inspiring the work of the first two (see table 7.1 in the Appendix). The spiritual theme, crowned by the Bible, is supported as well by the four long poems on the list—*Piers Plowman, Paradise Lost, The Faerie Queen,* and the less well known *Confessio Amantis* by John Gower, with its mix of love themes and the priestly confession of the seven deadly sins, rendered after the fashion of Chaucer. That the Bible and Shakespeare can be said to lead among citational sources for this dictionary fits the classic image of English literacy, because one tends to imagine the quintessential English family, however reduced in means, still in proud possession of this two-work library. How could one better capture the riches of the English language than with the Bible and a collected Shakespeare, unless, at least during this century, with the two-volume *Shorter Oxford Dictionary*? As the Authorized Version dominates the list of translations, it also accentuates the contribution of the Elizabethan period to the particular triumph of the English language. The editors of the *OED* were able to draw on the Bible to capture some five centuries worth of translation-into-English, from the Wyclif Bible in 1345 through the early Protestant versions of Tindale and Coverdale in the early sixteenth century and the consolidation of the King James version, before arriving at the Revised Edition, which coincided with the editing of the *OED*. One of the ironies of this history of biblical renderings is that Tindale's translation of the New Testament, published in 1526 and 1534 (and cited some 2,000 times in the *OED*), for which, as I noted, he paid with his life, became the source for perhaps as much as 80 percent of the King James Version of the New Testament and, based on his incomplete work, a part of the Old (Wansbrough, 1992, p. 7). In a process of incorporation that has its parallels with the dictionary, this fatally subversive body of work, aimed at the "boy who driveth the plough," as Tindale is said to have remarked, thus fathered many an expression of both literary beauty and moral guidance, as well as the authoritative version of the Word.

There is, as well, on the list the relatively obscure spiritual guide, *Ancrene Riwle*. Dating from 1225, it amounts to a prescription for worship that takes the form of a wise cleric speaking to three nuns about the ways, in the words of one commentator, "to stimulate and control the acts of penance and love in daily life" (Ackerman and Dahood, 1984). Among its contributions is the earliest citation covering the vivid *spouse-breach*, an adulterous term that survived into the seventeenth century:

> *a* 1225 *Ancr. R.* 56 [David] forȝet him suluen, so þet he dude . . . one Bersabee *spus bruche*.

The classical influences on this list of books are felt through Virgil's *Aeneid*, principally in Gavin Douglas's translation, but also in *The Destruction of Troy*, the earliest-cited version of which is attributed to Joseph of Exeter from circa 1400.[1] Homeric and Virgilian themes figure as a common bridge between an emerging English state and the political formations of classical antiquity. During the seventeenth century, the language debate centered on whether it was nobler to be descended from Trojans or Germans. Richard Verstegan led the pro-Saxon forces, mocking the British antiquarians and their regard for classics "as yf they properly appertayned vnto Englishmen, which in no wise they do or can do, for their offsprings and decents are wholy different" (cited in Jones, 1953, pp. 224–225). "The English tongue is extracted," Verstegan claimed in his 1605 *Restitvtion of Decayed Intelligence* "as the nation, from the Germans" (p. 234). Much of the citational evidence gathered by the Victorians seemed to prove otherwise. While the Philological Society had long been drawn to a philology nurtured at the German universities, it was by then a science that was actively engaged in fashioning Germanic culture around the glory that was Greece and Rome.

The eleven reference books on the list are led by *Cursor Mundi*, a fourteenth-century encyclopedic course or "cursor" on the nature of the world. It takes the form of a 5,000-line poetic rendering of biblical history covering "the seven ages of the world," from Creation to the Day of Doom. In the prologue to the poem, the narrator apologizes for using the north-country language of Northumbria, but he seeks to reach the unlearned English folk whose lives are in need of this wisdom as a source of spiritual salvation. By 1874, Rev. Richard Morris, the work's EETS editor, felt comfortable describing it as a "store-house of religious legends, and abound[ing] in quaint conceits gathered from many sources" (Morris, 1893, p. ix). Two other ancient encyclopedic works on the list are Bartholomæus Anglicus's *De proprietatibus rerum* and Ranulf Highden's *Polychronicon*. These Latin works were translated into English by John de Trevisa during the fourteenth century under the patronage of Lord Berkeley. They became part of an expanding English manuscript trade in the vernacular language that was drawn to the book's ability not only to carry the holy word or the profane tale, but to warehouse enormous amounts of fascinating information in what sometimes amounted to a flea market of fact and fancy.

Three of the dictionaries on the list are of historical note. The first among these is the *Promptorium parvulorum sive clericorum, lexicon Anglo-Latinum princeps*, a fifteenth-century "children's storeroom" of nearly 10,000 English-Latin equivalencies attributed to the Dominican friar Geoffrey the Grammarian. This early schoolbook/dictionary distinguished itself from other guides by working from English into Latin, rather than the reverse, suggesting that it was designed to assist students in writing Latin compositions rather than simply reading and translating them. A second of the dictionaries is Randle Cotgrave's *Dictionarie of the French and English Tongues*, which has warranted under Cotgrave's entry in *The Dictionary of National Biography* both the praise that it is "unusually careful and intelligent piece," and the caution that it is "not free from ludicrous mistakes." Murray did allow that foreign-language dictionaries, however flawed, ranked a little better than monolingual ones as citational sources: "They are not first-class witnesses, but often the best we can get, and in such cases as Palsgrave and Cotgrave, we are glad to get them" (*TPS*, 1880, p. 126).

Thomas Blount's *Glossographia: Or a Dictionary Interpreting All such Hard Words . . . As Are Now Used* is the sole general dictionary on the list. As if dictionaries were not enough of a problem as a source of citations for a historical dictionary determined to establish a reliable record of the language, the *Glossographia*'s 10,000 entries turn out to be largely plagiarized. Blount, who spent two decades assembling the work, readily admits "to have extracted the quintessence of Scapula, Minsheu,

Cotgrave, Florio, Thomas," while failing to credit Bullokar, Holyoke, and Camden from whom he also borrowed freely (Robertson and Robertson, 1989, p. 15). Blount has some claim to being the first to use a citation in English-language lexicography, as he notes, for example, with his entry for *habergion*, "It is used in Scripture, *Rev. 19.9.*" He, in turn, is cited in the *OED*, on occasion, as the sole source for some unusual and questionable turns in the language:

> 1656 BLOUNT *Glossogr.*, *Parent*, obedient, dutiful, serviceable.

If cite the dictionary he must, James Murray was always forthright about it, especially compared to Blount, allowing the reader to know and judge this element in the history of the word and the language. When he did have occasion to cite one of Johnson's senses directly within a definition, as he did some 850 times by my calculations, it was with abbreviated attribution.[2] The lexicographic tradition in Great Britain, as attested to by Blount and others, has long been to lift freely and indiscriminately from one's predecessors. To this day, editors' trading in the definitions of others remains a highly charged topic, as *Supplement* editor Robert Burchfield (1984) makes apparent in his modern survey of "who plagiarizes whom," discussed in chapter 3.

Yet another aspect of the lexicographer's contribution to the record of the language, although it fell somewhat short of the top twenty list, is the citation marked *Mod.* This term, standing for *Modern*, constitutes the title for 2,588 apparent quotations. As such it represents a subtle intervention on the part of the *OED*'s editors who created instances of modern usage when the citation files otherwise failed them. They resorted to this device for roughly one percent of the first edition's entries, as editor becomes author in such instances. On examination, the *Mod.* citations prove to be a relatively harmless set of instances, with a few exceptions:

> Mod. *Anthropometrically*, the two races show important differences.

It does not help that in this case it is the only citation to legitimate the word, clearly contravening standard *OED* principles. There is a *Mod.* citation from the letter *T*, the last section on which Murray was to work shortly before his death, which suggests he may have let slip a final jab at the professors who had given so little to the *OED*:

> Mod. They endow '*tame professors*' to advocate their views.

All told, the prominence of the dictionaries and encyclopedias in the list of titles points to a genealogy of genre, to the easy transmission within common forms, facilitated in this case through alphabetical indexing and cross-referencing in the handy packaging of information. This reliance on reference works may seem removed from the more immediate mystery of extracting meaning from the living and historical body of the language with which the *OED* originally intended to grapple, but that may be to hold to a false distinction, to a mythical belief in the primacy of art and authorship as the fount of knowledge and understanding. The reference work, too, constitutes what we know of the world and word. This canonical mix of what might be understood as primary and secondary works provides proof of the otherwise unheralded contributions of editor, compiler, cataloger, and lexicographer, who hold their own with Milton and Spenser as influences on the record of the English language. Here, then, is the idea of the writers' guild that forms for this dictionary a responsible witness to the language. From the Bible to the *Glossographia*, the individual titles that have contributed the most to the *OED*'s history of meaning affirm its commitment to the word fixed on the page, from the earliest compendiums of knowledge to the encyclopedias and dictionaries that remain mainstays of the book trade. This is not the celebrated side of English-language-and-literature to which the *OED* is more often taken to attest proudly. The dictionary's mix of prosaic and poetic titles, albeit weighted toward the literary and sacred, reflects the commitment of the Philological Society to attempt a complete coverage of the English language.

## II

The Victorian era has been characterized as a "journalizing" society, with the burgeoning of the magazine trade "the verbal equivalent of urbanism" (Shattock and Wolff, 1982, p. xiv). The 25,000 periodicals that came to circulate during this era were the result not only of a growing urbanization but of related improvements in printing technology and the spread of literacy. Although questions were raised by the delegates about the suitability of such ephemera for a history of the language, this publishing phenomenon came to dominate the choice of authorizing quotations selected from nineteenth-century publications for the *OED*. The considerable citation of magazines and newspapers in the dictionary can perhaps be attributed to a certain democracy of the word that was taking hold among the educated classes of the British Isles. More precisely, periodicals opened the doors not only to many more readers but to thousands of aspiring writers who sought to fill the pages of periodicals, allowing, ultimately, for a much wider array of contributors to the history of the language. *The Wellesley Index to Victorian Periodicals, 1824–1900*, in its analysis of forty-seven reviews and magazines, manages to identify some 12,000 contributors from the period (Houghton, 1966). The list of the top-twenty periodicals that best served the *OED* reflect choices that cluster around a certain class of publication and reader (see table 7.2 in the Appendix). As the periodical, more than any other text in the dictionary, reflects the personal interests of readers for the work, rather than the editors' systematic reading program, it seems all the more worthwhile to inquire into the nature of this publishing activity.

The review and magazine developed largely out of a symbiotic relationship with the book. The *Athenæum*, to take a leading instance, kept its readers abreast of recent literary activity on a weekly basis, reviewing some 240 novels over the course of a year (with at least half of them by women in 1883), while occasionally giving shorter notice to over one hundred titles in a single issue (Casey, 1985). In this highly reciprocal relationship among printed forms, the reviews fed off the books, producing critical opinions that gave shape, in turn, to an author's subsequent work. At the same time, review essays were collected into books, while yet other books were launched through carefully planned periodical serialization. "Books are largely made up of republished review articles," Mark Pattison observes in his own 1877 review article. "Even when this is not the case, the substance of the ideas expanded in the octavo volume will generally be found to have been first put out in the magazine article of thirty pages" (cited in Houghton, 1982, p. 21). Even the *OED*, as I noted earlier, was initially serialized in the manner of novels and encyclopedias of the era, with well over one hundred fascicles, beginning with *A–ANT*, and concluding some forty years later. The popular novelist and journalist Arnold Bennett was moved to declare the *OED* "the longest sensational serial ever written" (cited in Aarsleff, 1988, p. 34).[3]

An aspect of the periodical's influence on the *OED* that is missing from table 7.2 (see Appendix) can be found in the considerable number of citations from Carlyle, Dickens, Macaulay, and Tennyson that first appeared in periodicals. Carlyle, most of whose writings would first appear in a magazine, bemoaned the fact that "my Editors of Periodicals [including *Fraser's Magazine*, *Edinburgh Review*, the *Foreign Quarterly*, and *Foreign Review*] are my Booksellers, who purchase and publish my *Books* for me; a monstrous method, yet still a method" (cited in Houghton, 1982, p. 19).[4] Dickens, of course, proved to be both a child of journalism and father to the periodical's stunningly successful serialized novel, beginning with *Pickwick Papers*. Tennyson's Arthurian epic, *Idylls of the King*, unfolded in various outlets over a period of some forty years from 1842 to 1885, as he gradually filled in the various pieces of his tale of King Arthur. In Tennyson's well-known sensitivity to critical reviews, one can find a shaping of the language between poet and critic that Robert Browning could not resist mocking: "Tennyson reads the *Quarterly* and does as they bid him, with the most solemn face in the world— out goes this, in goes that, all is changed and ranged" (cited in Woolford,

1982, p. 137, n. 41). As a result, perhaps, the work of the poet laureate was praised by critics at the time as the "offspring of Christianity and civilization" given to evoking "national honour and patriotism" (cited in Hughes and Lund, 1991, p. 131). It is that close relationship among texts, among books and periodicals, authors and critics, that gets caught in the web of the *OED*, even as its use of the citation seems to indicate the solitary invention of the author.

**1842** TENNYSON *Walking to Mail* 18 He . . sick of home went *overseas* for change.

Among the various forms of periodicals, the literary review was at the intellectual center of this activity, contributing to the formation of what Walter Houghton has termed the "articulate classes" (1982). Its particular service to its readers is frankly rendered by John Morely in an issue of the *Fortnightly Review* from 1876, as he discussed a recent volume of Thomas Macaulay's essays that had originally appeared in just such periodicals:

> Macaulay came upon the world of letters just as the middle classes were expanding into enormous prosperity, were vastly increasing in numbers and were becoming more alive than they had ever been before to literary interests. His Essays are as good as a library; they make an incomparable manual and vademecum for a busy uneducated man, who has curiosity and enlightenment enough to wish to know a little about the great lives and great thoughts, the shining words and many-coloured complexities of action, that have marked the journey of man through the ages. (Cited in Houghton, 1982, p. 4)

It may sound more like a class desiring-to-be-articulate, feeling an insecure want of education, as well as a need for some assurance in its progress along the great "journey of man." An appetite for opinion and education, for the ready sense of self-improvement and participation, was met by the periodical. Judging by their circulation, the Victorian magazines of opinion had a rather limited readership, with the circulation of *Blackwood's*, *Fraser's*, and the *Spectator* remaining at well under 10,000 copies an issue.

The Victorian newspaper, represented on table 7.2 (see Appendix) by the *Daily News*, the *London Gazette*, the *Pall Mall Gazette*, the *Westminster Gazette*, and the *Times*, was certainly a prominent part of the print landscape. By 1860, London had the benefit of nine morning and six evening papers, and by the 1880s there were 150 dailies available to readers across the country (Brown, 1985). Among those who gathered citations for the dictionary, Frederick Furnivall seems to have found a particular pleasure in citing the newspaper that goes back to the very beginning of the project. Murray knew that it would be foolish, with the newspaper citations in hand, to deny their worth in documenting recent uses of the language. Although the papers were not part of the assigned reading program, he did ask members of the Society, in his presidential address of 1880, "to register the words that strike them in the leading Daily and Weekly Papers, the magazines and scientific periodicals" (*TPS*, 1880–81, p. 129). The "List of Readers and Books Read by Them, 1879–1884" includes few references to periodicals (*TPS*, 1884, pp. 601–642). Among the works read by Thomas Austin, the exceptionally voracious gatherer of well over 100,000 citations, are Cobbett's *Political Register, Harper's Magazine, Mercantile Marine Magazine, London Gazette, Contemporary Review*, and fifty volumes of the *Philosophical Transactions of the Royal Society*. But the list makes plain that his interest in scouring periodical literature for citations is the exception. Murray himself was a regular reader of the *Daily News*, the only known instance of this editor's own reading habits substantially shaping the citational record, and he reports that "I never read the leaders of the daily papers without finding some word worth extracting" (*TPS*, 1880–81, pp. 147, 129). So it is, perhaps, that the *Daily News* tops the other papers as a citation source.

The first reviews that Murray received for the early sections of the *New English Dictionary* included criticism of the newspaper citation. "Considerable indignation has been expended on quotations from modern newspapers" was how Murray put it to the Society in 1884. "*Modern*, I say, for I do not see that any objection is raised to our liberal quotations from the *London Gazette* of two centuries ago, or from the anonymous pamphlets of the Commonwealth period, which age has since hallowed" (*TPS*, 1884, p. 524). Murray summarily dismisses the criticism as "by far the silliest that the Dictionary has elicited," adding that "I am certain that posterity will agree with me, and that the time will come when this criticism will be pointed out as a most remarkable instance of the inability of men to acknowledge contemporary facts and read the sign of the times" (ibid.). I think that his critic had read the times, as it were, and was dismayed by the fact that the language was being overrun by the daily news. The newspaper, more so than other forms of print, represented the increasing influence of a commercial culture mixed with the democratic tendencies inherent in a free press.[5] There was considerable growth for newspapers and democracy in Great Britain, and the editors of the dictionary at Oxford did not miss the linguistic significance of this development, at least as it has been played out in the polite press. *OED* editor Henry Bradley, in his *The Making of English*, felt compelled to defend the merits of the "much-decried 'newspaper English,'" which included "many subtle contrivances of sentence-structure" (1904, p. 239). As it turned out, the role of the newspaper was only to increase with the supplements and second edition.

By the time the final volume of the *OED* was published in 1928, the earlier concerns expressed by delegates of the Press over the use of the newspaper appear to have been forgotten. On the completion of the *OED*, the Press proudly announced that the dictionary's citations from the *Times* attested to the general acceptance and currency of the vocabulary found within its covers. The Press went so far as to claim that "any respectable and recognized publication—book or newspaper—may very likely be more apt for the lexicographer's purpose than a literary masterpiece" (*CWW*, pp. 223–224). As it was, the *Times*'s degree of acceptance and currency had long been open to challenge, in terms of exactly whose respectable interests and language it captured. One can find novelist Margaret Oliphant complaining in 1863 that the paper took "it for granted that all their readers dine out at splendid tables, and are used to a solemn attendant behind their backs" (cited in Phillipps, 1984, p. 112).

1880 *Times* 21 Sept. 4/4 Slippers, called pumps, which have only one *sole* and no insole, are also sewed in the old-fashioned way.

But if the *Times*, as a journalistic bastion of aristocratic taste and conservative opinion, was a favorite with those who did the promotional work for Oxford University Press, it was not the preferred paper among readers for the dictionary. It stands fifth among newspapers. The *Daily News*, with twice the cites of the *Times* and greater sales on the streets, had reflected the liberal interests of its three wealthy owners since they had acquired it in 1868 (Brown, 1985, p. 64). It was the only London paper to support the English protest against Bulgarian atrocities in 1876, and in the early years of this century, it launched a daily appeal for donated goods to assist the unemployed in the East End of London and sponsored a six-week exhibition on "sweated labour" at the Queen's Hall (Harrison, 1982, p. 274). The ideological mix achieved by the *OED*'s citation of both the *Times* and *Daily News* resulted from readers and editors following their own inclinations in their daily reading. Perhaps a few of them found a need for such a balance in their own literate lives, although it should not be forgotten that the *Times* and *Daily News* by no means exhaust the entire political range of press activities of the day. One of the more successful organs of liberal opinion favored by the *OED* was the *Pall Mall Gazette*. Widely read among the ruling classes, it promoted reform at home and a strengthening of the empire abroad. The paper actively campaigned against the harshness of urban poverty during the 1880s in such exposés as "The Bitter Cry of Outcast London," while promoting a refurbishing of the "front line" of the empire with "The

Truth about the Navy" (cited in Baylen, 1987). There is no simple or single political line running through this list of leading periodicals cited by the *OED*, except perhaps as it falls between Whig and Tory interests.

> 1890 *Pall Mall G*. 25 Nov. 3/1 'Progress of all through all, under the leading of the best and wisest', was his [Mazzini's] definition of *democracy*.

One point of interest for lexicographers in these newspapers was that the "New Journalism" of the age often backed its advocacy with tough investigative reporting that took it to the scene of a language and life that did not otherwise touch the readers of these publications. According to historian Roger Wallins, the novelists of social conscience, including Dickens, Gaskell, and Disraeli, followed the lead of *Blackwood's* and *Fraser's* in writing about the costs of the industrial revolution while the periodicals drew, in turn, on the government commissions that actually documented with eyewitness reports the horrors of the times (1975). In terms of the *OED*'s coverage of the language, the readers for the dictionary attended to magazines and serialized novels, paying little mind to the commissions that published *Report on the Employment of Children in Factories* (1833); *The Moral and Physical Condition of Working Class in Manchester, Westminster* (1833–34); and the *Report on the Sanitary Conditions of the Labouring Classes* (1842). The documents produced by these "theaters of power" were often filled with the poignant transcripts of survivors, and fugitives, who spoke to the Victorian conscience in a voice that was perhaps unavailable in any other form (Ashforth, 1990). Here was common usage and diction in the documented form required of this dictionary. The language captured in the reports, however, was not cited in the *OED*, perhaps out of a preference that the same story be artfully worked over by the writer for the consumption of readers.[6]

To examine a specific instance of the periodical's service to this dictionary of historical principles, we might look at the relatively innocent entry for *trousers*. Here the sharp eye of the journalist dominates the citations for this item of fashion. The sense of "a loose fitting garment of cloth worn by men," is initially supported by the *London Gazette* from 1681— "John Clark a stout Man, . . in . . a pair of Buck skin Leather Breeches . . (sometime wearing trousers over his Breeches) rid away on a Grey Gelding." Although other sources are called upon, the *Gentleman's Magazine* in its inaugural year 1731 reports that "instead of Breeches, he proposes that the ladies should wear Trowsers which will be particularly convenient for those who have not handsome legs." By 1786, the same magazine reports on "twenty-five boys belonging to the Marine Society, in new jackets and trowsers." With an eye for more than fashion, the *Gentleman's Magazine* was the most successful magazine of the eighteenth century, finding its relatively vast readership among provincial gentry and tradesmen of the provinces.[7] The citations from its pages attest to a sphere of influence in fashion and language, as the periodical worked with the novel in gaining a hold on the English imagination. They offered a record not only of English life, but of the life of trousered readers, awarding it published authority and significance. This assembly of citations continues the initial reassurance provided by a gentleman's magazine by making it all part of the history of the English language.

In coming to appreciate the contribution of the English press to the *OED*, it is interesting to note John Gross's point that "it would be hard to exaggerate the part played by Scotsmen" (1991, p. 19). He goes on to describe their role in founding the great quarterly reviews and heading up weeklies, as well as in serving as the initial editors, for example, of the *Spectator*, the *Economist*, and the *Saturday Review*. The secret may well have been the education system and specifically the humanities class that trained the young in vigorous debates over issues of "history, literature, physics, metaphysics, and everything," as one gentleman testified before the Royal Commission on Scottish universities in 1826 (cited by Gross, 1991, p. 19). To this work among the periodicals, one can add the contribution of the Scottish encyclopedists represented in table 7.1 (see Appendix). Taken in conjunction with James Murray's own contribution, the Scots can be said to have exercised a considerable influence on the dictionary. By the nineteenth century, although it may not be readily apparent in the *OED*, the locus of the language had already begun to shift away from the center, as English was to continue to prosper from the trade over the borders of its ongoing formation. Such are the complex elements of national identity and formation that can be traced through the making of the *OED*, citation by citation.

Beyond the newspaper and review journal, a third area of periodical contribution to the *OED* is the more specialized set of scientific, scholarly, and technical titles. While Murray had explicitly proscribed scientific and technical vocabulary as falling outside the common range of the language to which the dictionary was committed, he readily accepted a considerable number of citations from *Nature*, the Royal Society's *Philosophical Transactions*, and the Sydenham Society's *Lexicon of Medicine and Allied Sciences*. Given Murray's policy on scientific and technical language, the considerable place of these publications in the *OED* was earned on two accounts. First, they were read by interested observers of the sciences and philosophy, rather than simply by professionals employed in those fields. Second, these more specialized sources must have provided a good number of first citations for words that had eventually found their way into the common parlance and citation files of the *OED* and then needed to be traced back to an earlier source. Elisabeth Murray reports that in the case of *appendicitis*, her grandfather consulted with

Oxford's Regius Professor of Medicine before deciding to reject the term as too technical for the *OED*. It was destined to be part of popular usage after the coronation of Edward VII was postponed in 1902 due to the inflamed appendage (*CWW*, p. 222).

One title that cuts across the grain of the other periodicals on the list is the *Penny Cyclopædia of the Society for the Diffusion of Useful Knowledge*. Published between 1833 and 1846, it alone among the top-twenty periodicals was targeted for consumption by the industrial classes. The well-meaning Society for the Diffusion of Useful Knowledge (SDUK) had been formed in 1826 by Lord Brougham and a few fellow Parliamentarians who felt that such a publishing enterprise was, in Brougham's words, "eminently conducive to allaying the reckless spirit which, in 1830, was leading multitudes to destroy property and break up machines" (cited in Altick, 1957, p. 271). Useful to whom was to remain a question among the skeptical. As part of its civic duty, the Society introduced a new level of cheap and "enlightening" literature. The *Cyclopædia* amounted to a weekly compendium of the exotic and the domestic, with illustrated features on natural history, practical pieces on health, as well as uplifting works on the fine arts and literature. This serialized encyclopedia—in a marketing ploy found in supermarkets today—began in 1833 with respectable sales of 75,000 per penny number, with the number falling off to 20,000 by its completion in 1844.[8] To what degree the SDUK publications were "eminently conducive to allaying the reckless spirit" of the working class, in Knight's phrase, is difficult to say (p. 272). Richard Altick reports that commercial publishers "accused them of trying to set up a monopoly and 'threatening to destroy the legitimate thrones and dominions of the empire of books'" (1957, p. 272). The *Penny Cyclopædia* was intended as useful knowledge in an apolitical appreciation of Greek literature and bee architecture, albeit societies founded on the labor of slaves and drones. That the *OED* editors purchased a set of the *Penny Cyclopædia* for their office, and then garnered some 3,700 citations of useful knowledge is a reminder of which side triumphed in the political struggle, between a working- and middle-class press, over literacy among the industrial classes during the years leading up to the Chartist movement:

> 1834 *Penny Cycl.* II. 71/2 The *prongbuck* inhabits all the western parts of North America from the 53° of north latitude to the plains of Mexico and California.

The period prior to the commencement of the *New English Dictionary* had been occupied with questions of public expression, enfranchisement, and education. The literate formation and advancement of public interests was an embattled territory, and the weapons of the governing classes were both repressive, with the inequitable "taxes on knowledge," and evangelically philanthropic, through such organizations as Brougham's SDUK. It does not seem out of place to consider the *OED*'s interested inquiry into whose language was to shape the emerging democratic state. Here was a book attuned to the written word, to the growing Corporation of the Goosequill, as Thackeray termed the English press of the day. In a later chapter, I will address the concerted effort of working-class interests during the nineteenth century to forge a counter-formation of journalistic opinion, much of which goes unnamed in the *OED*. Even with these gaps, the accomplishment of this dictionary is in how far it did travel in assembling a layered canon of published authorities—literary, sacred, translated, referential, and periodical. The citational authorities are declared by the dictionary to have defined the trade in words, and thus the very basis of a literate culture, especially as it is viewed through Victorian eyes. That history was "Founded Mainly on the Materials Collected by the Philological Society . . . with the Assistance of Many Scholars and Men of Science," as the title page of the first and subsequent title pages of the *New English Dictionary*'s fascicles declared. It was shaped around a vision of English culture that had been preserved in the university libraries, resuscitated by text-editing societies, and carefully documented in scholarly reference works. Here were the materials out of which a canon was formed through the earnest efforts of amateurs, students of the language, concerned to see the true record of its scope and accomplishment set down. The resulting canon was to govern, in effect, the definition of the English phenomenon, the force of which was increasingly being felt around the globe.

The Victorian canon embodied in the *OED* is not easily summarized. It stretches from the golden age of Chaucer to the *Daily News*. It is dictated by the arts and sciences of the age, by a complex and troubled cultural climate that found particular expression in the work of Richard Trench and Max Müller, Frederick Furnivall and James Murray, Thomas Carlyle and Charles Darwin. At one end, there is a lofty and inspiring artfulness to this canon. The literary arts are overrepresented in the citations drawn from Shakespeare and filled out in the earnest recovery of many classical and sacred works from the history of the West. But art is only one of the governing ideals of the canon; the scientific and historical principles dictated a wide range of texts as forming the record of the English language. There is, as well, a relentlessly material element to this particular process of canon formation, insofar as the very means of production, we might say, became the guiding citational light of the project. James Murray and the other editors employed by the Press were engaged in establishing the authority of their own claim—that is, of the word trade as a whole—on English language and culture. They may be said to have done so on behalf of a larger class of interested readers, a good number of whom had eagerly responded to the initial call to participate in this project. This collaboration among amateurs and volunteers, editors and readers, was bound to create a diffuse, if heartfelt, canon of authorizing works. Of the patterns that can be detected, there is a shift with the citations from the Victorian era, which is not surprisingly the most heavily sampled period in the dictionary, from the influence of the book, as a primary force in the language, to the periodical, in a trend that will only grow with twentieth-century efforts at modernizing the dictionary, as we shall see in the chapters that follow.

## CHAPTER 8

# A Supplement to
# The Oxford English Dictionary,
# 1957–1986

ONE MEASURE of the change and continuity that marks this great lexicographical project is told by the stories of the editors, James Murray and Robert Burchfield. As the *Supplement*'s chief architect, Robert Burchfield does not call to mind Jude the Obscure, as the Thomas Hardy character whom James Murray somewhat resembles in his difficulties of getting on at Oxford in the early years. Burchfield, a New Zealander by birth, is from considerably farther away than Murray, and yet his work on the dictionary was to be far more a part of this beautiful but difficult university town. Burchfield arrived at Oxford in 1949 under the graces of a Rhodes Scholarship. He stayed on to become a lecturer in English language at Christ Church. Before actually joining the Press, he assisted Charles Onions, the last surviving editor of the *OED*, on a number of projects, including *The Oxford English Dictionary of Etymology*. Like Murray, Burchfield gained editorial experience preparing an early English text, in this case the late-twelfth-century collection of homilies known as *Ormulum*. He worked on it under the university supervision of J.R.R. Tolkien, although it was finally left incomplete and unpublished (Burchfield, 1989, p. 189). As a result of an article that brought to light a word from the *Ormulum* "hitherto unknown even to the editors of the *OED*," Burchfield was asked to serve as secretary of the Early English Text Society, which had played such an influential role in the life of Murray and the *OED*. A year later, in 1957, Burchfield was approached by Oxford University Press to assume the editorship of a three-volume supplement to the *OED*: "It had hardly dawned on me that there was a chasm between the comfortable familiar complexities of Old East Norse and the *Ormulum* on the one hand and the hunting out and editing of the modern words like *stereophonic, supermarket,* and *zap* on the other" (p. 191). With the sense of both foreboding and breathtaking challenge that must have been felt by Johnson and Murray on the eve of such a decision, Burchfield decided to enter the lexicographical trade, finding himself at the head of one of the language's major projects.

In a number of ways, Robert Burchfield represented what was to be supplemented. He was from a British Commonwealth country, as well as being an Oxford man and a college don. The *Supplement* was to be a thoroughly Oxonian project that looked beyond the British Isles, even as it stood much closer to the heart of the University community than James Murray might have imagined possible. For all of that, Burchfield maintained a strong allegiance to the patterns established by Murray and the Philological Society, both in the general approach to defining the language and in the specific organization of the dictionary page. Although when it came to starting the project, Burchfield found he had little more than "a bare little room and a desk and a telephone": "All that lay to hand were the remarks of Dean Trench, F. J. Furnivall, and especially J. A. H. Murray, on, first, some deficiencies in English dictionaries and then, in the prefaces of the *OED* fascicles and in the *Transactions of the Philological Society*, descriptions of the various methods adopted for the assembling of evidence for the *OED*, together with some account of the editorial policy" (1989, p. 190). That is, Burchfield also came to lexicography, as Murray and Johnson had, in the manner of the curious amateur, lending native wit and commitment to this international project. His doctorate was awarded, as had been Murray's, in an honorary fashion, once the work was well underway rather than preceding it. Burchfield also followed Murray's lead in the more prosaic aspects of the prefaces, with the word counts and the acknowledgment of readers' citational contributions.

The English Dictionary Department at Oxford University Press was in Burchfield's day more than a little removed from Murray's Scriptorium off Banbury Road. The operation was soon located at 37a St. Giles', across the road from St. John's College, in what Burchfield proudly describes as "a splendid spacious Georgian mansion in central Oxford." In visiting the offices, I found that the building housed a mixture of tradition and innovation that influenced the day-to-day work of assembling dictionaries. While I was examining citation files in a ground-floor office during my first morning there, I was at one point jarred by a clattering of dishes down the hall of this otherwise hushed house. Everyone was soon called to the kitchen, where we were greeted by a tea-granny who poured boiling water into cups of instant coffee as we marched by with our tickets in hand. A good part of the dictionary staff of about thirty people then stood in a room of filing cabinets, sipping coffee and quietly chatting about the dictionary trade and other matters. In the afternoon, the ritual was repeated with tea. Between the call for coffee and tea, I was invited into the basement below the tea room, where I found that the status of new words was being checked through a computer and phone link to massive electronic databases in London and the United States, scanning current American and British periodicals running back to the early 1980s. The number of instances for each new term was printed out, along with citation-sized chunks of text and variant spellings, for use by the editors, in a process that was setting a new standard for keeping up with the language (F. Shapiro, 1986). This contrasting mixture of afternoon tea and high-speed computer searches was reflected in the *Supplement* citation files with which I worked, as hastily penciled citations on odd bits of paper followed computerized excerpts from the *New York Times*.

The reading program that Burchfield had reactivated in 1957, after it had been closed down in 1933, produced well over two million citations. At the time of my visit, the program was overseen by senior editor John Simpson, who held a Master's degree in medieval studies from York University. In our discussion together, Simpson explained that unlike the other publishing houses I'd visited in researching contemporary lexicographical practices, the English Dictionary Department of Oxford University Press did not set aside regular office hours for an internal reading program (Willinsky, 1988a). The Press continued to depend on readers to cover the language, with some recently added backup from the computer. Simpson commented that a reading and marking program by his staff was needed, but that it was impossible to achieve while working to complete the *Supplement*. As it was, the fifteen to twenty paid readers in the field, along with those irrepressible, if irregular, volunteers who sent in their own findings, generated more than enough cites to fill the days of his staff. Although regular readers now receive proper remuneration rather than simply having their postage covered as in Murray's day, traces of the Philological Society's original thriftiness remain. Readers are often sent to their local library with no more than a list of books from which to choose their reading. Few free books are to be had for reviewing, as had been the case, I discovered, with American dictionary publishers. On the other hand, Simpson expressed a certain degree of patience with the understandable inefficiencies of the Press's cottage-industry readers. Though they are not as systematic or accurate in their coverage as the lexicographer might hope, the external reading program remains the mainstay of Oxford's connection to the development of the language. To compensate for some of the inevitable deficiencies, Burchfield resorted to having key works read twice, instructing readers with other important works "to follow what was virtually a concordance procedure" (1973, p. 99).

Simpson estimated the rate of productivity for his department during the final years of the *Supplement* to be approximately 120,000 citations per year, with about 10 to 20 percent made up of unsolicited contributions from what can best be described as interested friends of the language. Reflecting its stature as a respected institution in the language, the

*OED* had also attracted substantial donations of textual materials from the public, which continued to provide it with a rich, if somewhat oddly distributed, assortment of resources in the language. Atcheson Hench, of the University of Virginia, bequeathed to the Press his large collection of the *Baltimore Sun* and other American newspapers from the 1930s and 1940s, which only began to make their contribution to the dictionary and the language with the second volume of the *Supplement*. There had also been Dr. H. Orsman's extensive collection of 12,000 citations of New Zealand English. Burchfield notes in the preface to the second volume that "we have given somewhat more attention in this volume than in the last to the special vocabulary of the West Indies and, nearer home, of Scotland." This swing in attention, for the benefit of the letters *H* through *N*, is taken in stride, without drawing a comment from the editor on what this sudden infusion means for the dictionary as a whole.

There is so much language to sample that serendipity is bound to play its part, particularly with special vocabularies that come far from home. The unevenness of coverage apparently detracts little from the lexicographer's function, as Burchfield describes it in the Preface to the second volume of the *Supplement*, "to form a permanent record of the language of our time." The Press also continued, as it had with the original project, to issue lists of words that required citations (usually of an earlier date) in the Press's house magazine, the *Periodical*. This process of locating quotations, as editorial staff member Yvonne Warburton notes, "on which so much of the quality of the Supplements rests has always suffered from a kind of invisibility in the final product" (1986, p. 94). When Burchfield came to include a seven-level diagram of the dictionary's editorial process (from "sorting" citations to "numbering" entries) in the final *Supplement* preface, he omits the gathering of citations. He does, however, discuss in the preface the range of publications that were consulted: "The sources included all important literary works (in both prose and verse) of the period, a wide range of scientific books and journals, and large numbers of newspapers and periodicals, ranging from *The Times* to publications which emanate from the so-called 'underground.'" One can note the resolution of tone when it came to literature—"all important literary works"—and the patronizing nod toward the "so-called 'underground press.'" As had been the case with Murray, a single (literary) citation could ensure a word's inclusion in the *Supplement*, or as Burchfield has put it, "I have been as much concerned about the unparalleled intransitive use of the verb *unleave* ('to lose or shed leaves') in G. M. Hopkins' line 'Margaret, are you grieving / over the Goldengrove unleaving' as Murray was to record Milton's unparalleled use of the word *unlibidinous*" (1986, p. 24). In something of a reversal of the pressure put on Murray to keep to the literary path, Burchfield reports that there was resistance from "some of my colleagues with the project and by one or two reviewers" to his policy that "the language of great writers, including poets, should be registered, even once-uses, virtually in concordance form" (1989, p. 195). The *OED* has long been on the side of those who have subjected themselves to English literature ("the resistance did not come," Burchfield notes, "from those who subjected themselves to the study of the works of the great writers of the past as part of the discipline of studying English language and literature"), with the dictionary doing its part, beginning in the Victorian era, to bring this subject to the forefront of the national curriculum. The dictionary's special relationship to literature, in which it serves at times as a concordance, continues to reflect a Johnsonian faith in the best authors' right to define the language, in a conscious choosing of the poet as hero. On more than one occasion, Burchfield was to affirm that the English language "can be used with majesty and power, free of all fault, by our greatest writers" (1982, p. vi).

Another point of continuity with the original project was the preservation of print as the final arbiter of usage. While print is by all means the sole record of language use in the past, going beyond living memory, the argument for its exclusive claim as proof-of-use does not hold as well for contemporary language at work in an electromagnetic age. Nonetheless, the print policy was retained by the Press for the *Supplement* with the somewhat contradictory intervention of computer technology to assist the editors in holding to this Victorian principle. Although a "camera script" from the BBC might appear on a list for the Press's reading program, strictly oral citations are still excluded from this mirror of the language because, as Simpson described it to me, there is no proper means of verification. Not surprisingly, this can lead to a certain awkwardness in representing words that have what we might term an oral sensibility to them. With the entry for *smackeroo*, usage is documented through indirect citation—"*Amer. Speech* (1942) XVII. 14/1 gives citations of *smackeroo* 'dollar' used on U.S. radio programmes in 1940 and 1941"—followed by a "proper" citation from the *American Thesaurus of Slang* published in the same year. There has to be that textual attribution, which acts to authorize what was only spoken, or sung in this case, with a note and citation for *hincty*:

> Connection with clipped forms of "handkerchief-head" (= an Uncle Tom Negro) has been suggested but the phonetic development is incapable of demonstration.
> **1924** in W. C. Handy *Treasury of Blues* (1949) 144 We'll I am *hinkty* and I'm low down too.

The scholarly rule at Oxford is that everything must be checked and verified, that doubts and indeterminacies must be reported. In rigorously pursuing this matter of verification, the Press retained the services of seven free-lance researchers, the best known of whom is George Chow-dharay-Best, credited as a major source of citations for the *Supplement* during the period in which he was employed as a free-lance researcher at the British Library before becoming a permanent staff member of the Press. The professional citation checkers are divided between Britain and the United States, with one each at the Bodleian and the Radcliffe Medical Library, two at the Library of Congress, and one in Boston and New York. These researchers, it is stressed, are engaged in "genuine research," that is, in pursuing the earliest sources for the use of a term as well as verifying quotations that have been sent in or retrieved electronically. In going through the citation files, I found that the workers were apt to leave polite little notes on a given slip they had checked—always quick to apologize with an opening "sorry" when the suspected earlier citing was not to be found. These bibliographical sleuths above all know their libraries, it was explained to me, and make it their business and pleasure to intuit where any given word will be found. At least two of the free-lancers had moved up a career ladder from librarian and researcher to lexicographer.[1]

There was also an expansion of the consultation process. Burchfield acknowledges in his preface to the first volume the assistance he received in verifying citations provided by language centers and overseas libraries, naming the University of Sydney and the Turnbull in Wellington, New Zealand. He also introduced a new section into the acknowledgments entitled "Outside Consultants," consisting of well over one hundred names, many prefaced by Dr. or Professor. For his part, James Murray had consulted with the director of the Royal Botanic Gardens at Kew and the Deputy Keeper of the Rolls, among others; he wrote to Tennyson, Meredith, and Hardy on meanings within their own work (*CWW*, p. 201). In the first volume, Murray acknowledged "the ready good-will and helpful co-operation of man scholars and specialists," listing a number of English, German, and American professors. But, given the autonomy of the Philological Society, the appointment of university experts as a panel of "outside consultants" would have been highly unlikely from either their or Murray's perspective.

Another indication of a cultural shift in what constitutes the center of the language came with the hiring of editors whose backgrounds fell outside of the humanities. With the *Supplement*, the Press hired editors with a strong background in the sciences, an area of specialized language that had been regarded, with exceptions, as beyond the scope of the *OED*'s "common" vocabulary. It signaled the increasingly important role of science in our daily lives and its place in the education of the people. What it meant for the dictionary is that a prefix such as *iso-* requires some 320 scientific citations to attest to the variety found in a century's worth of use, followed by thirteen pages of variants, from *isobar* to *isozyme*.

Change came through over forms as well. Marghanita Laski, for example, can be said to have substantially reshaped the modern reading program and, to a degree, the *Supplement* itself. Although she was to leave her own mark on the citations, her tremendous devotion to the OED as a voluntary reader also represents a strong link to the original project. Having written about her work as a devoted gatherer of citations, she provides numerous insights into the relationships among literature, reader, and dictionary. She was a journalist and novelist by trade, who found the time between 1959 and 1971 to "card," as she put it, more than 100,000 words, reaching perhaps double that number over the course of the *Supplement*'s publication. She was the ultimate voluntary reader for the dictionary, obsessive in her interest in the language and intent on setting her own path for the good of the dictionary. When she did approach the Press, on one occasion, about payment for this enormous service, she felt compelled to decline the offer of a contract when she realized that it meant that her reading for the dictionary would be directed by its editors. Still, in recognition of her contribution and independence as a reader, she did eventually receive an honorarium from the Press, as well as payment for serving as a "critical reader" at the proof stage in the publication of the *Supplement*. She was described as an example of a "habitual and critical reader of the dictionary," employed to check the finished copy for comprehensibility and accuracy.

In a series Laski did on "reading for the OED" in *The Times Literary Supplement* in 1968, she describes how in 1958 she got caught in the web while flipping through the Press's reactivated call to the public for help with words needing earlier citations. She realized that the 1946 listing of *alleycat* could be antedated by Don Marquis' *Archy and Mehitabel*, and before long she was sending in two hundred citation slips per week. In a footnote to the first preface of the *Supplement*, Burchfield describes the eclectic reach of her reading:

> Miss Laski's reading included, for example, almost all the works of some twentieth-century authors (e.g. G. B. Shaw, Max Beerbohm, Virginia Woolf, Aldous Huxley) and numerous modern crime novels. She read extensively in the literature of the nineteenth century, both novels (e.g. Dickens, C. M. Yonge) and letters (Mrs. Gaskell, George Eliot, G. M. Hopkins). She also read widely in the general field of the domestic arts (old catalogues, books on gardening, embroidery, etc.) and various modern newspapers and journals (*Guardian*, *Vogue*, etc.).

Laski was concerned enough with the project to try in a number of ways to reshape the work. She reports sending in citations for words which she had only heard in a speech or on radio, such as *fab*, *grotty*, and *goody goody gumdrop*. The editors, true to their historical regard for print, were able to find printed sources for all three expressions. In other instances, she speaks of trying to influence the editorial direction of the dictionary, "if only by sheer weight of cards" (1968, p. 38). Her efforts to have the great train names recorded, such as the *Flying Scotsman*, were a failure. She was also not above planting words in her work, helping to restore *berate*, *v.*, which the *OED* claimed obsolete, by placing it in one of her book reviews, although other instances did turn up. Her use of *carded* in the *TLS* article is cited in the *Supplement*, although without attribution to her name. In terms of her impact on the reading program at Oxford, I was told by Sara Tulloch, who succeeded Simpson as director of the reading program, that her predilection for detective novels, and the wealth of instances she found therein, was enough to ensure that, after she had stopped reading for Oxford, this genre would be added to the list of works that guides the reading program. In chapter 9, which deals with the leading authors in the *Supplement* and again in chapter 11, covering the contribution of women authors, it will become apparent how the thoroughness of Laski's reading is reflected in the constitution of the dictionary. As a writer herself, she did receive some recognition of her own way with words in, for example, the first and only citation for the sixty-fourth sense of *come* ("Of a play, film, etc.: to reach the end of a run"):

1952 M. LASKI *Village*, vii. 121 They say it's a really good film and it *comes* off tomorrow.

When I had the opportunity to examine the citation files for the *Supplement* at Oxford, it was not long before I began to recognize her handwriting, the ballpoint pen (when many still held to fountain pens), and the writing curling up the page as if she'd scribbled out the citation while holding a newspaper or detective novel in her lap as a portable desk. For a combination like *tack room*, she might account for as many as seven of the twenty-two citations gathered in the files, having found it across a twenty-year period in such sources as *Snare in the Rock*, *Nerve*, *For Kicks*, *Bonecrack*, and a more genteel *Country Life*. Of these, the editors selected the 1964 Dick Francis *Nerve* citation for inclusion in the entry; it was really a model of a defining use: "It was a tack room. Every stable had one .. the place where the saddles and bridles are kept." Laski also had a way of giving real breadth to a bundle of citations. With *taboo*, for example, the other citations in the file are from *American Speech*, *General Linguistics*, *Language*, and the *Introduction to Theoretical Linguistics*, while Laski manages to introduce an instance from a work with the title, *Destiny Obscure*. She alone could show that a word had entered the realm of popular culture, although the point, in this case, was lost to the editors and her citation failed to gain a place in the entry on *taboo*. Similarly with *tachograph*, her entry from *Pel under Pressure* breaks with the other technical and journalistic citations, and yet again fails to find a place in the dictionary. This sort of distribution of use by genre was not much of a lexicographical issue at Oxford. However, with a less technical term, such as *tabnab* ("A cake, bun or pastry; a savory snack"), both of her citations, one from Malcolm Lowry and the other from Bonfiglioli's *All the Tea in China*, are included. Her citations from *Gone with the Wind* and *Pangolin* provide proof in the *Supplement* for a new sense of *tackily* ("in a tasteless or vulgar style; shabbily, dowdily"). One might be tempted to say that as she read, she managed to add to the record of the language.

Certainly her citation-laden reading taught her a good deal about a writer's diction. She notes that Virginia Woolf produced few "cards" (with only 239 citations recorded in the second edition of the *OED*); she found Graham Greene offered little by way of original or distinct usage. More interestingly perhaps, she notes that writers appeared to suffer "a loss of ear as the years go by; where an early work may be rich, a late one usually gives almost nothing, as people continue to write in the vocabulary of their youth" (1968, p. 38). Laski also has lessons to teach on social class, literature, and the path of language influence: "One should always look more closely when working-class characters are speaking, because novelists have generally listened to the kinds of things working-class people say; with their own class they more readily rely on stock" (ibid.). She concluded the first of her *TLS* columns with the anecdote about a party held at the completion of the *OED* to which the surviving readers were invited: "Two of these, it is said, were unable to come. One had spent his reading years in a lunatic asylum, the other in gaol" (p. 39). Based on her experiences as a reader for the dictionary, she made four rather demanding recommendations: (1) all literature after 1600 needs to be read again; (2) the trivia of past centuries needs consulting; (3) a perpetual trust be established to support ongoing revisions of the *OED*; and (4) the compilers of the dictionary eschew computers (1972, p. 1226). It has turned out that Oxford's involvement with computers has facilitated, if not helped finance, the ongoing revision of the *OED*, and will, one suspects, be utilized in a second pass through post-1600 texts, as more of these works become available in machine-readable form.

In his preface to the final volume of the *Supplement*, Burchfield summarizes his main departure from the lexicographical policies of Murray as a "decision to try to locate and list the vocabulary of all English-speaking countries, and not merely that of the United Kingdom." In a later summary of the project, he added that he had "established a network of outside readers to ensure that the new vocabulary of all English-speaking countries received adequate attention" (1988, p. 50). The elements of overstatement here are of the same order as the Philological Society's original claim that "the first requirement of every lexicon is that it should contain *every word occurring in the literature of the language it professes to illustrate*" (*TPS*, 1857–58, p. 4, original emphasis). It might seem advisable to approach with modesty the task of monitoring a language on this historical and geographical scale. After the project was completed, as often happens, Burchfield was prepared to admit shortcomings that paralleled his predecessor's: "Like Dr. Murray I have attempted to compile a *Lexicon totius Anglicitatis*, bounded by practical considerations and by some uncrossable boundaries, and like him I have doubtlessly failed" (1989, p. 196). On the new vocabulary of the English-speaking countries, it was my observation that the reading program systematically increased its coverage of world English in 1988 through steps that included appointing two readers to cover such non-British sources of the English language as Nigeria, Jamaica, and India. The World English Program, as it is called, supplements, rather than replaces, the nineteenth-century view of Great Britain's gift of a civilizing influence on language and culture. While I might question the reasonableness of Burchfield's claim to have tried to locate and list the extent of this world language, the *Supplement* certainly does show a greater receptivity to the language that was left behind with the shrinking of the empire, as if governed both by a recognition of a postcolonial world and a greater democratic spirit of the global marketplace.

Burchfield was perhaps more successful in opening the *Supplement* to forms of the language that were thoroughly indigenous to the United Kingdom and yet had been previously expended on grounds of propriety. In the preface to the fourth volume, Burchfield rather overstates Murray's coverage of the English language: "There were no exclusion zones, no censoring, no blindfoldings, except for the absence of two famous four-letter (sexual) words. Dr. Murray, his colleagues and his contributors dredged up the whole of the accessible vocabulary of English (the sexual words apart) and had done their best to record them systematically in the *OED*." Although Burchfield discretely leaves those two words unnamed, one can rightly presume they were included in the *Supplement*. He was later to describe, in *Unlocking the English Language*, how "sexual words and colloquial and coarse words referring to excretory functions were 'controversial' in the *OED*, and as a result not all of them were admitted, but they are no longer so" (1989, p. 84). While most of the excretory words that I know, and a few I was unaware of, are defined and well supported by respectable citation in the *OED*, the "two famous four-

letter (sexual) words" that were introduced in the *Supplement* raise interesting issues of citational authority and editorial propriety.

Shortly after the definition of the two words in the first volume of the
*Supplement*, Burchfield was prepared to deal openly with the issue. In an
article for *The Times Literary Supplement*, he describes how he was originally of the opinion, in 1957 when he began the project, "that the time
had not come for the inclusion of the taboo words *cunt* and *fuck*" (1972,
p. 1233). Shortly thereafter, in 1960, the words were before the courts in
a crucial literary freedom-of-artistic-expression case brought on by the
Penguin Books publication of a paperback version of D. H. Lawrence's
*Lady Chatterly's Lover*. It is worth noting that the paperback edition
provoked the legal charges, three decades after the book's original hard-
back publication, bringing to mind nineteenth-century apprehensions
about the dangers of ready access to print among those in need of regula-
tion, such as the young and the masses. The courts did manage to approve
the printed status of the taboo words in what was deemed to be the appropriate setting of literature. However, this was still not enough for
Burchfield, who was prepared to argue against including the two terms
for the "not necessarily decisive" reasons that the OED already "excluded a wide range of low slang and no doubt out of a sense of 'decent
reticence'" (ibid.).

As Burchfield tells it, the balance was finally tipped in favor of including the two words by the dictionary's newly established consultants.
Burchfield tested the waters with the *Supplement*'s consultants by asking
them to judge an entry for *bugger* (moving alphabetically as these things
go) that added its ruder senses to the legal definition included in the OED
("Now only as a technical term in criminal law"). The entry received
general approval, with its linguistic marker, "coarse slang," coming in for
special commendation from the experts (p. 1233). This approval was sufficient for Burchfield.

His report on this process includes the fact that in 1969, the editors of
the counter-culture magazine *Oz* wrote to the delegates of Oxford University Press, asking why their newly purchased *Shorter Oxford English
Dictionary* did not contain the word *fuck*. A Mr. Davin replied by pointing out that not only was it still uncommon in "serious dictionaries" (not
quite true, Burchfield notes), but that the inclusion of four-letter words
risked having the book banned: "Even now their inclusion might still
have this effect in some countries and failing this, might mean that their
market became restricted in, for example, schools" (cited by Burchfield,
1972, p. 1233). Davin did mention that it would soon be found in the
forthcoming *Supplement*, which one presumes did not have to keep the
extensive school market in mind. He did leave out one surprise for
the editors of *OZ* about the sources of authority for entry:

*a* 1503 DUNBAR *Poems* LXXV 13. Be his feiris he wald haue *fukkit.*

. . .

1928 D. H. LAWRENCE *Lady Chatterley* iv. 44 Fellows with swaying waists fucking little jazz girls.

. . .

1969 *Oz* May 13/1 (Advt.), Pete Quesnal, late of St. Nicholas, where the fuck are you.

The pattern of linguistic license that Burchfield established in this case went from a long history of literary use through judicial approval to the commendation of expert consultants and then into the dictionary. From there, on to perhaps the even larger step of writing about it in the *Times Literary Supplement.* The entries in the *Supplement* for these two controversial terms established their (masculine) literary pedigrees running back through such notables as D. H. Lawrence, James Joyce, Robert Burns, John Rochester, Horace Walpole, and Robert Dunbar. As common to schoolyard English as these two terms are, they needed more than literary testimonials to ensure their place in the permanent record of the language. Although Burchfield suggests that only in these two famous cases did such a convoluted process occur, it suggests how ad hoc procedures are called into play in dealing with untamed zones of language use. For all of its scientific and historical principles, the dictionary is bound to follow and sometimes take the lead with the sensibilities of its readers. Nearly two decades later, when the *Economist* came around to reviewing the second edition of the *OED*, it was still referring to the "f-word" and "c-word," while noting the absence of these two euphemistic hyphenations in the dictionary, as if to distract attention from its own awkwardness over this lingering sense of propriety ("Dressing Old Words New," 1989).[2]

Finally, in treating these flagship terms of the taboo, Burchfield fails to discuss what this particular gain in linguistic realism and sexual liberation means for women. Some senses of the two terms unequivocally denigrate women, with support from the works of Henry Miller and Samuel Beckett, among others, lending them literary authority [*cunt*: "2. Applied to a person, esp. a woman, as a term of vulgar abuse"; *fuck*: "1b. *concr.* A person (usu. a woman) considered in sexual terms"]. In fairness, there is a similarly negative sense given for the corresponding *prick*, similarly defined with citations by men (it also contains an obsolete sense of vulgar endearment from the seventeenth century). But *prick* was included in the original *OED*, as the term was presumably judged not so powerful or threatening in its offensiveness. While the *Supplement*'s treatment of these two opprobrious terms is true enough to the spirit and history of their use, there was little effort on the modern editors' part to pick up on later efforts at redefinitions of the particularly misogynist use of the feminine form, as in Germaine Greer's "Lady Love Your Cunt," which was first published in *Suck* in 1969. Greer took issue with what she had little trouble identifying as "cunt-hatred" in pornography, a phenomenon she felt had its corresponding attitude in medicine (1986, pp. 74–77). Resorting to such a deliberate selection of counter-citations on ideological grounds may well seem to raise its own questions of appropriateness. However, this was precisely the strategy Oxford was to employ, I believe, with another controversial term that also had its day in court.

Whatever problems Burchfield foresaw over the inclusion of the last linguistic taboo words in English, greater problems were to be had with a term that had been all too thoroughly defined in religious and racial terms. In 1971, the definition of *Jew* was the source of an unsuccessful legal challenge launched against Oxford University Press by an English businessman (Burchfield, 1989, p. 17). Burchfield was caught between what he felt was a need to illustrate the common uses of the word, which often enough ran to anti-Semitism, and a desire to distance the Press from participating in, or seeming to contribute to, those sentiments. As sensitive as the issue is, it provides some insight into the powerful ability of citations to carry the secret life of the language, which I intend to introduce here before more fully exploring it in the next chapter, where I deal with the leading authors of the *Supplement*.

As the entry for *Jew* was structured in the original *OED*, the first sense given is supported by relatively neutral citations, including the judicious selection of Shylock's, "What is the reason? I am a Iewe. Hath not a Iewe eyes?" from the original spelling in *Merchant of Venice*. And yet the accompanying small type gives decided prominence to the separateness of the "Hebrew race" from Christian states, as well as allowing the negative features of more colloquial usage to bleed into this first and supposedly literal sense:

> 1. A person of Hebrew race; an Israelite.
> Orig. a Hebrew of the kingdom of Judah. . . . Applied comparatively rarely to the ancient nation before the exile (cf. Hebrew A. 1), but the commonest name for contemporary or modern representatives of the race; almost always connoting their religion and other characteristics which distinguish them from the people among whom they live, and thus often opposed to *Christian*, and (esp. in early use) expressing a more or less opprobrious sense.

Burchfield's revision of the entry in the *Supplement* was to drop those final remarks in the note about "characteristics" and to reserve the first sense for the neutral, nonracial definition of the word: "A person of Hebrew descent; one whose religion is Judaism; an Israelite." He then cre-

ated a second, unavoidably opprobrious sense—"a grasping or extortion-
ate person"—for which he included the status markers "*transferred sense
and offensive*," along with a historical explanation of the Jewish people's
economic status in Europe that might go some distance to explaining how
this sense had been brought on by Christian powers. The *Supplement* also
has additional citations that sustain the negative senses, as well as an
unusually long, ten-line citation on the rabbinical definition of a *Jew* from
John Randall Baker's 1974 book, *Race*. The editor, in this case, appears
to be falling back on an encyclopedic approach to counteract the bad
taste left by simply reporting usage.

Under the *Supplement*'s entry for the verb form of *Jew*—"Also, to
drive a hard bargain. Also, *intr.*, to haggle. Phr. *to jew down*, to beat
down in price"—there is the small-type note, "These uses are now considered to be offensive" followed by twenty additional newfound citations
to be added to the original *OED* entry. The citations range from a 1824
diary entry of C. Harding to *The New Society* of 1972—"I got jewed
down . . over the cheap offer." What still seems a little odd is that the
editor's note continues to set the Jew apart by stating that it is "now considered offensive," which perhaps means now even by gentiles, whereas
before it offended only Jews or, worse, did not offend them. There is also
a form of counter-evidence to the fact that it is "now considered offensive" with citations drawn from respectable magazines and authors of the
day. This raises a series of interesting dilemmas for the precise textual
status of a citation in which it becomes difficult to surmise the context in
which the words were written. It remains impossible to be certain that the
excerpt from *The New Society* is (1) set off as dialogue in a work of
fiction, (2) reporting what someone actually said, in 1972 or historically,
or (3) used directly by the writer. Such questions do seem to matter when
judging the currency and use of controversial terms.

At other places in this entry, the *Supplement* shows greater sensitivity
in selecting citations. In doing so, it carries on a tradition found in the
*OED*'s use of the famous *Merchant of Venice* citation noted earlier. In
this case, the *Supplement* calls on Leo Rosten to register a point about
offensive tendencies in the language:

> **1968** L. ROSTEN *Joys of Yiddish* 142 Just as some Gentiles use '*Jew*' as a
> contemptuous synonym for too-shrewd, sly bargaining ('He tried to Jew the
> price down,' is about as unappetizing an idiom as I know), so some Jews use
> *goy* in a pejorative sense.

The selection of what is in effect a counter-citation, especially a citation
from among the party suffering the definition, does seem a constructive
response to redressing the weight of disparaging use. Whether it is a warranted form of affirmative action on the part of the dictionary's editors

is a question that must be considered in light of the often privileged treatment of literature as an integral component of the nation-building project.

This is hardly the only instance in the *Supplement*'s treatment of racism. This updating of the *OED* provides additional citations, running to nearly two pages for the original entry on *nigger*. The editors do add a note granting an unusual semantic allowance for the one who is using the term: "Except in Black English vernacular, where [*nigger*] remains common, now virtually restricted to contexts of deliberate and contemptuous ethnic abuse." Without taking from the citations, then, a line is drawn between then and now, allowing for that moment of redefinition, that intervention in the "natural" history of meaning by which defaming senses do, through a considerable mobilization of those defamed, become restricted to the "now." But the point also made by the *Supplement*'s note—and I appreciate the challenge of wording these asides—is that this restriction does not apply to "Black English vernacular," which is to say that when blacks use the word they are speaking something else again.

1973 *Black World* Aug. 61/1 Even credit-card *niggers* didn' really trust banks.

Still, it should be made clear that the editors of the *Supplement* worked hard at finding a measure of fair representation in ways that are not easily missed.

1934 G. B. SHAW *On Rocks* II. 70 Pandranath: you are only a silly *nigger* pretending to be an English gentleman. *Ibid*. 71, I am called nigger by this dirty faced barbarian whose forefathers were naked savages worshipping acorns and mistletoe . . whilst my people were spreading the highest enlightenment yet reached by the human race from the temples of Brahma . . . You call me nigger, sneering at my colour because you have none. The jackdaw has lost his tail and would persuade the world that his defect is a quality.
. . . .
1972 D. ONYEAMA *Nigger at Eton* iii. 83, I remember that in conversation, some boys occasionally used 'nigger' in reference to black people. I never dreamt that it was a racial name and generally used with contempt; I just reckoned it was a harmless slang word for a black man.

The *Supplement* unfortunately fails to provide citational support for the modern reclamation of *black*, to displace *Negro*. The most recent citation supporting the dictionary's definition of a *black*, as "a person of 'black' skin," dates back to the pre-Civil War period:

1856 OLMSTED *Slave States* 129 The free *black* does not, in general, feel himself superior to the slave.

It is only as an adjective that a number of twentieth-century *black* combinations are included in the *Supplement*, such as *Black English*, *black power*, and *black theology*. The dictionary does little better with the racial sense of *white*, with three modern citations restricted to illustrating *poor white*, although it also includes instances of *white* combinations, as in *white settlers* and *white supremacists*.

In reviewing the *Supplement*'s coverage of the vocabulary of race and religion, it is not that I imagine anyone swayed in their regard for others by the weight of citations. The entries indicate, on the one hand, how deeply ingrained in the language this history of prejudice runs, and, on the other hand, how the editors respond to the challenge of a redefined situation through small-type notes, the addition of historical context, and the deliberate citation of the counter-instances. Still, in concluding his review of the question of controversial vocabulary, Burchfield's stance is tough and unbowed: " 'Offensiveness' to a particular group or faction is unacceptable as a ground for the exclusion of any word or class of words" (1989, p. 104). There remains his determined sense of "offensiveness," with its demeaning quotation marks. Is it part of *their* problem, this particular group or faction, with being of Jewish or African American descent? References to the objections of groups or factions do not come up in the rather different editorial regard for the famous four-letter duo discussed above. Perhaps the simple use of a label such as *rac. epith.* (*racist epithet*), like *obs. rare*, to demarcate these opprobrious terms would avoid what is otherwise a slight awkwardness of designation on the part of the Press.

In bringing the Philological Society's original project fully into the twentieth century through a four-volume *Supplement*, Oxford University Press combined the labors of diligent readers and high-speed computers, of library researchers and expert consultants; it took to monitoring a language that spanned the posthumously published verse of Gerard Manley Hopkins to the on-line service of the *Washington Post*. Not without controversy did it try to shake itself loose of the earlier ethos of Richard Trench's theologically inspired philology and his Victorian articulation of national and racial interests. The struggle of disassociation is not over; the break is by no means complete. Still, the *Supplement to the Oxford English Dictionary* is about changing definitions of language, authority, nation, and science. It is about traditional and electronic formations of knowledge, old and new sources of citations from a publishing industry engaged in the circulation of meanings and senses. The reading program remains the frontline in the editors' coverage of the language. The citation, however approximate its relation to the sense given in the entry, however vaguely understood in its excerpted form, however overendowed with meaning, still stands as part of the definition of the language. It affirms that here, in this work, by this writer, a word has joined in the circulation of meaning. As we shall see in the next chapter, which examines the leading citational sources in the *Supplement,* the English landscape is no longer the unmitigated focal point of the language, nor do its native poets unquestioningly command its vocabulary. Modern citation, it will be seen, continues to raise complex questions of representation for the privileged locations of sense and meaning.

## CHAPTER 9

# Modern Citation

I

On New Year's Day, 1918, Ezra Pound had occasion to write a letter to Harriet Monroe, editor of *Poetry*, a magazine to which he had been contributing for a number of years. At one point in this rambling letter, Pound takes up the theme of the folk song: "I liked your comment p. 89, Nov. no. Naturally pleased to see the folk song idea smacked again. Even an eminent London Musical critic has recently got on a platform and said 'all folk songs have authors and the authors are individuals.' The blessing of the 'folk' song is solely in that the 'folk' forget and leave out things. It is a fading and attrition not a creative process" (Pound, 1950, p. 127). The use of *smack* in the second sentence of this paragraph was destined to become, in a way that may well have amused Pound, part of the *Supplement*'s record of the English language. With further corroboration from Dickens, Shaw, and the *Evening Post*, the editors were able to extend the original *OED* entry for *smack* to include a sense of chastisement.

> **smack,** *v.*2 Add: **5. a.** (Earlier and *fig.* examples.) Also *spec.* to chastise (a child) in this manner.
> **1835** DICKENS *Seven Dials* in *Bell's Life* 27 Sept. 1/1 Mrs. A. smacks Mrs. B.'s child for 'making faces'. **1892** G. B. SHAW *Let.* 12 Aug. (1965) I. 359 Smacking Bebel & Singer in the eye for their *dénigrement* of our programme. **1918** E. POUND *Let.* 1 Jan. (1971) 127, I liked your comment p. 89, Nov. no. Naturally pleased to see the folk song idea smacked again. **1976** *Evening Post* (Nottingham) 14 Dec. 18/9 It appeared to have been put there by her two-year-old son, who had been smacked for moving things about the house.

Pound's contribution is figurative; he allows that ideas, in addition to children and eyes, can be smacked. The *Supplement* might be regarded as taking its stand against the "folkful" forgetting that Pound was celebrating. It is determined to attribute changes in the language to individuals, to document the moment of change. Yet inevitably there is still that forgetting, as we might wonder, when we read the citation, what Pound was objecting to. Language—and not only in folk songs—is full of this loss, this continual attenuation of meanings, against which this dictionary takes its stand, locating it in the hands of the proper authorities rather than the "folk," even if it means going through their published correspondence to do it.

It might seem that the private letter, even in publication, is a less-self-conscious and a more folkish realization of English's most immediate patterns. To cite Pound's letters, the lexicographer appears to move that much closer to the "natural language" of the writer, opting to quote not the crafted but the spontaneous word, not the public display of the ideal in words but the more intimate dance of language. The *Supplement* selected 92 citations from Pound's *Letters*, making it the top-cited title among Pound's individual books (although the four different collections of his *Cantos*, published over the course of some fifty years, contribute 174 citations in total). The considerable weight given Pound's letters by the *Supplement* is a continuation of the dictionary's regard for the authority of the writer: the archly literary citation is tempered by the daily traffic of the letter, if that letter, however slapdash, is from the trusted hand of the artist.

Admittedly, the textual status of Pound's letters is, as with most everything about his life, hardly commonplace. Harriet Monroe began publishing his letters to the magazine in 1915, and D. D. Paige, in his introduction to *The Letters of Ezra Pound 1907–1941* (Pound, 1950), describes how these lively letters overshadowed his poetry for a period of years. Even if the letters-for-publication soon dried up, one can still find T. S. Eliot in 1928 commending Pound's "epistolary style" as "masterly," and Margaret Anderson, who had also published Pound's letters, spoke of them fondly as flowing in a torrential fashion while he was living in London (Pound, 1950, p. xvii). A good number of Pound's letters, then, were not of the ordinary sort and the *Supplement* cites far more than his open letters to small magazines. We might ask what it is that the editors of the *Supplement* found in his personal letters that made them the citational equal of poetry. It may well be that they proved to be as much a part of the modern spirit that Pound did so much to promote in literature with his wildly eclectic garnering of common and exotic language, his stark *Imagiste* strictures: "Use no superfluous words. . . . Go in fear of abstraction. . . . Use either no ornament or good ornament" (1935, pp. 4–5).[1]

From among the leading contributors to the *Supplement*, Shaw, Lawrence, Aldous Huxley, and Dickens are also represented with the well-cited letter. As genres go, letters prove a lexicographical favorite for the *Supplement* editors (see table 9.1 in the Appendix). But then for some writers the volumes of collected letters had sheer mass on their side.

George Bernard Shaw, to take a most prolific and long-lived instance, may have sent over 250,000 pieces through the mail (Shaw, 1965, pp. xi–xv). By something of a coincidence, he also had cause to use *smack* in a letter written some years before Pound's. In August 1892, to his dear friend and fellow Fabian, Sydney Webb, he wrote, "I have also, in the letter accompanying my answers, complained of the ignorance of the English among foreigners, smacking Bebel & Singer [a pair of German Social Democrats] in the eye for their *dénigrement* of our programme" (1965, p. 359).

*Letters*, as a generic title, proves to be the single most frequently cited work in the four-volume *Supplement*, with 8,982 citations, attesting to its unmistakable linguistic authority in the dictionary's modern canon. Works with the title *Letters* account for close to 2 percent of the citations gathered for this edition of the dictionary and play an important role in this list of leading authors. Among the most-cited books in the *Supplement*, Aldous Huxley's and Shaw's *Letters* are in twelfth and fifteenth place, respectively (see table 9.2 in the Appendix). While it is tempting to imagine that the *Supplement* reflects a twentieth-century desire for greater intimacy with those whom we trust with the word, we must also recognize the degree to which the published letters of notable authors are the product of the research industry that has grown up around English literature. While certainly playing a less prominent part among the leading authors in the original edition of the *OED*, the current place of letters in the *Supplement* runs only slightly ahead of the original *OED*, suggesting this interest in semiprivate writing was hardly foreign to the Victorian readers of the *OED*.[2]

In calling on the creative writer in this double-barreled way, the dictionary blends the literary masque with the private voice, the deliberative and discriminating diction of *belles lettres* with the quick-draw of the posted note. This lexicographical practice makes something more of writers, giving equal weight to excerpts from their best art and their personal asides. With excerpts from a novel set next to those from the author's letters, distinctions are blurred between the work's narrator or a character's dialogue and what might be understood as the direct voice and views of the writer. The issue is compounded in the *Supplement* by the particular concentration of writers drawn from a single generation or two in the first half of the twentieth century. Many were not only contemporaries but often friends and collaborators, working together to fashion a literature and language within the century's volatile politics of nation, race, and art. I have decided to set this issue of private and literary meanings within the context of the controversy over the definition of *Jew*, discussed in the previous chapter, as it forms a thin thread that draws together a dozen of the *Supplement*'s leading authors. Literary modernism is known for its surprisingly uncharitable moments of elitism, but how those troubled and by no means simple sentiments come to focus on the definition of the Jew as other or outsider becomes another way of seeing how this dictionary filters and amplifies the language:

> 1905 JOYCE *Let.* 29 Oct. (1966) II. 127 For a *Jewman* it's better than having to bathe. 1922—*Ulysses* 336 I'll brain that bloody jewman for using the holy name.

Letter and novel—isolated instances like this cannot help but raise questions about meaning. If there is doubt about a word's status or truth-value, about the author's authorization of meaning with fiction, then how is it further resolved by its earlier use by an author such as Joyce in a personal letter?[3] The *Supplement* further complicates matters by adding a parenthetical note to the sense—"Such expressions now mainly in offensive use but not originally opprobrious." This opens the question of then and now with regard to how the citation is supposed to act as a guide to the use of the language. Does this exonerate the author? Is Joyce's an "original" use; is it fallacious for readers to imagine that there was something opprobrious intended in one or both of the comments? My brief here is with how such controversial instances make vivid the complicated relationship between citation and sense in the *OED*, although I do not want to feign indifference to the instance at hand. There are certainly other prejudices to be found among the citations of the *Supplement*'s leading authors. Yet discussing the contribution that a number of these influential writers made to the meaning of *Jew* seems to require little justification, given the import of the period to its definition, given the difficulties of disentangling the writers' authority as witness and participant in this act of designation.

One way of situating this artistic expression of anti-Semitism is to treat it, as Lionel Trilling did in his literary criticism, as a generalized form of xenophobia connected to the expanding role of imperialism and racism in British and American society. In reviewing T. S. Eliot's collection of Rudyard Kipling's verse (in which Eliot goes some distance in denying Kipling's racism), Trilling insists that Kipling's anti-Semitism is but an element of a larger prejudice tied directly to the elements of nation and empire, culture and class.[4] Kipling represents the language of prejudice in his fiction, but it somehow becomes more than that with, in the nature of the citation, his name clearly attached to it:

> 1891 KIPLING *Life's Handicap* 197 My *Irish American*-Jew boy.

One might compare the sense of such a Kipling citation for readers who (1) know little enough of the writer, (2) share Trilling's understanding, or (3) believe, to put it somewhat unfairly, what Eliot believes of

Kipling. The fact that this citation comes from a bit of dialogue spoken by a soldier to a known traitor does little to alter its sense of life's handicap or the irony of it providing the complete sense for the *OED*'s banal definition, "an American of Irish origin." The particular non-English association struck by the citation's reference to an Irish-American Jew brings out one of the breaking points in the historical development of the language recorded in the *Supplement*. The Bombay-born Kipling comes between the Irishmen, Shaw and Joyce, on the list of the *Supplement*'s top three writers, indicating a complex identification with, and feeling for, the language and culture of the English colonizer, complemented further down the list by the presence of American writers. With the twentieth century, the *Supplement* comes to reflect a decentering of the language, a separation of English from England, in the distribution and definition of the language. Kipling reminds us, in the context of his fictional and turn-of-the-century work, of a resistance to the loss of authority in the face of this expanding circle of dominion for English as language and nation. His sentiment may well be purely colonial in a way that is "pre-fascist," as George Orwell describes it (1968, p. 211). The connection with a fascist racism of identification is not far removed from Kipling's better-known contributions to the language, found under the *Supplement*'s short entry for *burden* (*sb* **2.**):

> **1899** KIPLING *White Man's Burden* vi, Take up the White Man's *burden*— Ye dare not stoop to less. **1911** H. G. WELLS *New Machiavelli* I. iv. 128 We were all . . Imperialists also, and professed a vivid sense of the 'White Man's Burden'.

H. G. Wells, who shares a place with Kipling among the most-cited authors of the *Supplement*, goes on in this passage cited from the *New Machiavelli* to describe the swell of "Kiplingism" that he experienced during his undergraduate days before the turn of the century; it was given to "boyish enthusiasm for effective force" and "the very odours of empire"—Kipling "colored the very idiom of our conversation" (1910, p. 120). Through the abbreviated citation, the *Supplement* is able to offer readers a sense of that particular coloring, not as some final truth about the meaning of the English language, as I have repeatedly stressed, but as it forms part of the published record of an era. By the early years of the twentieth century, Wells was setting Kipling's burden in the past tense, within the irony of inverted commas. The colonial legacy, nonetheless, was no more a thing of the past in 1910, after the bitterly won British victory in the Boer War, than it was in 1991 with the ending of legalized apartheid in South Africa. In fact, what seems to set Wells off from Kipling, in this instance, manages to creep back into Wells's work at other points.[5] Still, the pair of citations illustrates the play of meaning by which one authority rewrites another in a manner that only arises in a dictionary based on historical principles.

On this question of modern prejudice and literature, Ezra Pound is, of course, the key figure from among the *Supplement*'s leading authors. His admiration for fascism, Italian and British, was unequivocal and widely broadcast. Although the *Supplement* avoids the crude anti-Semitism of the pamphleteering Pound, the dictionary does employ the ambiguities of the *Cantos* in its entries on matters Jewish:

> **1930** E. POUND *XXX Cantos* x. 45 Wives, *jew-girls*, nuns.
> **1940** E. POUND *Cantos* lii. ii Sin drawing vengeance, poor *yitts* paying for—.

It seems fair to say that, on the one hand, these citations hardly do justice to what Pound meant by *Jew*, and yet, on the other, they at least begin to suggest how the great poetic series of the *Cantos*, in all of its richly multicultural interests, is fitted with what we might imagine as the pattern of his prejudice. If these isolated lines give little sense of Pound's anti-Semitism, they at the very least add to part of a literary norm that identifies the difference, the Otherness of *Jew*, as it is named at every level of language use in the *Supplement*, with citations from the columns of *Sporting Times* to Pound's *Cantos*.

Again, I hardly imagine that the two *Cantos* citations foster hatred among readers of this dictionary. Even setting the lines back into the larger context of the poem seems beside the point in considering the relation of citation to meaning and bigotry.[6] The relationship of interest here is the more general effect of the dictionary affirming the poet's hold on word and meaning, in return, one might say, for the fair use of the poet's work in support of the dictionary's definition. It is a celebration of the author's powers of discrimination in the language, while leaving the reader ill-equipped to decide precisely what the full meaning of that discrimination is about, at least in controversial cases. Harvey Teres, for one, argues that the use of such terms as *jew-girls* and *yits* in the poetry is not removed from the hatred: "The poetic elements which normally have an illuminating effect function only to enhance the subtlety, sophistication, prestige and ultimately the appeal of anti-Semitism" (1991, p. 72). Isolated like this and clearly declared by the *Supplement* to define what it means to use words related to *Jew*, these two excerpts from the *Cantos* can encourage a critical re-reading of the modernist canon, as our faith in poetry's illuminating effect is put to use in dictionaries and schools around the globe. This does not mean that one is simply missing the point of the poem's aesthetic qualities. No less a critic than Jerome McGann, for example, has little trouble pronouncing the *Cantos* "the greatest achievements of Modern poetry in any language," while declaring it at the same time "a fascist epic in a precise historical sense" (1989, p. 97). Pound's contribution calls for a rethinking of how literature, and the uses to which it is put, can fall between the art and politics of language.[7]

T. S. Eliot was far more reserved on the Jewish question than his friend Pound and yet comes to play much the same role in affirming the poetic identification of "Other." He could defend Kipling and object to both the crudeness of fascism and its common pagan element, while all the while indulging a certain disdain for Jews. While that disdain is explicitly expressed in his *After Strange Gods*, it might also be thought to surface, at times, in the poetry and its representation in the *Supplement*.

> **1920** T. S. ELIOT *Ara Vos Prec* 14 The *jew* is underneath the lot. Money in furs.

Again, we might ask about the function of authority here, about what Eliot's citation represents on behalf of art and language, if not the ease of associated meaning. But for the same reason, this authority needs to be re-read in terms of poetry's other project, as it defines the civilized life both for its readers and the dictionary. This is not merely a matter of citations out of context, as the negative connotation of the line is only exacerbated by returning to the poem, "Burbank with a Baedeker: Bleistein with a Cigar," with its echo of Shakespeare's *The Merchant of Venice*:

> On the Rialto once.
> The rats are underneath the piles.
> The jew is underneath the lot.
> Money in furs. The boatman smiles,

Because every act of inclusion cost precious space, the *Supplement* editor's decision to leave "Money in furs" in the citation might be assumed to carry some part of the meaning of the word under definition. Although we may have been taught that art and artist espouse the universal qualities of humanity, to what do these lines relate, as a citation in the *OED*, if not to the definition of *Jew*? At issue are the complications of sense that arise with citation, rather than conclusions about culpability. Although Eliot, as poet, is both speaking and not speaking this line, it was Eliot who, in editions after 1963, capitalized the spelling of the word *Jew* in this and other poems. In 1940, when challenged by a correspondent about his friendship with the anti-Semitic Pound, he claimed in a rather standoffish way that, "As for Mr. Pound, I do not associate myself with any of his opinions about Jews" (cited in Ricks, 1988, p. 54). It is the *association* of opinion that appears to happen in the columns of the *Supplement*, as the editors search the literature for uses of *Jew*, finding something of a similar note struck in author after author. If this is part of their contribution to what the English language has come to mean by certain words, it reflects how the process of citation, in rare but important cases, serves to deny the sense and experience of those who are defined but barely cited, of those who fall outside the range specified by the *Supplement*'s version of the literary and literate canon.

> **1929** D. H. LAWRENCE *Let.* 10 Oct. (1962) II. 1208, I do hate John's Jewish nasal sort of style—so uglily moral . . Spring doesn't only come for the moral *Jew-boys*—for them perhaps least.

Again, there is that startling immediacy of the letter cited in the *Supplement* which provides the more troubling, less easily disavowed instance of an authority that seems to go beyond a testimonial to the particular use of a given word. Is there a *use* of the word taking place in this citation that can still be separated from the writer's intentions? Do we tell the truth about ourselves, letting the mask drop, in our letters? In the case of Lawrence's letters, this is by no means an isolated instance of virulence. As Eliot himself stressed, in a comment on an edition of Lawrence's letters, there is no easy or necessarily desirable separation of convictions and art:

> Does "culture" require that we make (what Lawrence never did, and I respect him for it) a deliberate effort to put out of mind all convictions and passionate beliefs about life when we sit down to read poetry? If so, so much the worse for culture. Nor, on the other hand, may we distinguish, as people sometimes do, between the occasions on which a particular poet is "being a poet" and the occasions on which he is "being a preacher." That is too facile. (1933, p. 97)

The *Supplement*, as an abbreviated record of the times, affords a whiff of prejudices that shaped the language during this period, although their status is still ambiguous as the opinions that the citations express seem both amplified and deactivated. I do not drag out these citations in order to ask that they be purged and the dictionary rewritten around what are, after all, common enough expressions. But I do ask that we continue to read the work in light of the tension that holds between its descriptive and affirmative functions of citation and definition. This dictionary is more than an unequivocal celebration of English literature for the manner in which it has unfalteringly struck a clean and pure path for the language. The historical element, so important to this record of the language, is the period leading up to the Second World War, from which one is reminded, in spite of considerable efforts in Great Britain to serve as a refuge for European Jews, of the common sense of anti-Semitism. It was simply part of the language and art of the times.

Among the literary citations are also those that carry an especially ambiguous relationship toward intention and prejudice. Take, for example, this long and challenging quotation from an 1883 letter by Gerard Manley Hopkins:

> **1883** G. M. HOPKINS *Let.* 6 Dec. (1938) 195 You will I know say . . that the Jew is a reproach because Jews have corrupted their race and nature, so that it is their vices and their free acts we stigmatise when we call cheating *'jewing'*—and that you mean that Disraeli in 1871 overreached and jewed his constituents.

What is lost in this citation is that Hopkins is trying to discourage Coventry Patmore in his use of *Jew* in his poem, "1867," as a device for attacking Disraeli—"the false English Nobles and their Jew" (Hopkins, 1956, p. 343). The indeterminacy of citation does not totally discourage the association of author and expressed sentiments, and at the very least the citation attests to the ongoing presence and weight of racism as somehow part of the literary tradition. Here the conservative force of the dictionary, in giving weight to the usage of an earlier period, carries forward into the twenty-first century the prejudices that once infused literature and letters and carries them forward with the compounded authority of both the authors cited and the dictionary's own name.

> **1931** W. FAULKNER *Sanctuary* xxvi. 265 A durn *low-life* Jew.[8]

Of course, counter-instances to this case of the anti-Semitic citation can be found from among the leading authors cited in the *Supplement*. Julian Huxley, who shares a place on the list with his one-time collaborator, H. G. Wells, as well as his brother, Aldous, is cited in his efforts at debunking on scientific grounds the very myth of Nordic superiority that underwrote the German racial laws of the 1930s:

> **1939** J. S. HUXLEY *'Race' in Europe* 24 Biologically it is almost as illegitimate to speak of a 'Jewish race' as of an *'Aryan* race'.

The frequent ambiguities of citation emerge, in this case, through the equivocation of "almost" that leaves the racial question in doubt. In another of Huxley's critiques that came to serve the *Supplement*, he states that "the Nazi racial theory is a mere rationalization of Germanic Nationalism on the one hand and anti-Semitism on the other" (1941, p. 50).[9] Working with this sentence to illustrate the entry for *anti-Semitism*, the editors of the *Supplement* oddly abbreviate it for the citation:

> **1941** J. S. HUXLEY *Uniqueness of Man* ii. 50 Germanic nationalism on the one hand and *anti-Semitism* on the other.

What Huxley originally sets together in Nazism, the citation seems to break apart by dropping the crucial opening of the sentence, suggesting that the editors thought this nationalist distinction was important to the definition.[10] It seems to insist that keeping German nationalism and anti-Semitism apart is somehow the point of meaning in this case. The tenuous balance of meaning in this clipped form can ride against the best efforts to represent the language in a disinterested manner.

Huxley's objections to anti-Semitism were scientific, but those of Arthur Koestler, as another of the *Supplement*'s leading authors, arose out of his personal involvement in the fight against fascism. This Hungarian Jew, who wrote originally in German, escaped to England in 1940, after having been jailed in Spain and France for his antifascist writings. Koestler's was the voice of an outsider in English literature, whether in railing first against fascism and then communism, or exploring the metaphysical dimensions of modern science. His contribution to the *Supplement* includes giving postwar expression, in his novel about an Israeli kibbutz, to a slightly off-center parallel that may well speak to his own pattern of commitments.

> 1946 KOESTLER *Thieves in Night* 279, I became a socialist because I hated the poor; and I became a Hebrew because I hated the *Yid*.

The very sense here of *yid* as a hateful term, and thus as grounds for empathetic identification, plays against the more common pattern of writers considered here, who, if they took exception to virulent forms of anti-Semitism, did not call into question the implications of their use of the word *Jew*. Koestler's upbringing "in an assimilated environment without roots in Judaic tradition," as he neatly puts it in his autobiography (1952, p. 110), places a special emphasis on his taking up of Jewish themes after the war and his considerable inclusion in the *Supplement*, which features as his most-cited work the history of Palestine, *Promise and Fulfilment*.

And finally, from the list of leading authors whose reflections on the Jewish experience came to be cited, there is P. G. Wodehouse. In his very remove from politics, he manages to become a farcical figure of a (comical) writer. At the beginning of the war, he was to think it of little consequence to broadcast humorous bits on the radio for the Nazis, after he was captured by them in his Belgian villa (Orwell, 1968, pp. 293–305):

> 1934 WODEHOUSE *Right Ho, Jeeves* xi. 141 A story about a Scotchman, an Irishman, and a Jew . . I said 'Hoots, mon,' 'Begorrah,' and 'Oy, oy.'

For all of the citation's innocence, in this and the other cases, it still draws attention to the ever-so-slight but darker contribution of those authorities on which the dictionary depends. The issue of literal sense and citational inference, denotation and connotation, takes on special importance when it comes to the definition of a people. This, too, is part of the complex matter of taking our lead for meaning from the selected, always partial, excerpt.

I want to conclude this section on the leading authors of the *Supplement* by briefly reviewing the five thoroughly nineteenth-century presences on the *Supplement*'s list. Along with Charles Dickens, who was heavily cited in the first edition, a considerable body of citations in the *Supplement* is drawn from Gerard Manley Hopkins, William James, Mark Twain, and Charlotte Yonge. Hopkins's late inclusion was a matter of posthumous publication, his work forestalled by the religious order to which he belonged. The first edition of this Jesuit scholar's poems appeared in 1918, nearly three decades after his death, followed by his letters in 1935 and notebooks in 1937. Among the Americans on the *Supplement*'s list of leading authors, William James represents the philosopher, turning a brand of American pragmatism into the human science of psychology, becoming a forefather of a productive area of language growth for the twentieth century. Mark Twain joins Faulkner on the list in giving regional and rural America a strong presence in the list. Like Shakespeare and Milton, Twain has earned his place by virtue of a previously published lexicon dedicated to his work (Burchfield, 1973, p. 99).

That Charlotte Mary Yonge, nineteenth-century novelist, editor, and children's writer, is the only woman to appear in the tables thus far may merit some explanation. Why not George Eliot and Elizabeth Barrett Browning, too, as part of the *Supplement*'s catch-up from an earlier era? One very practical reason for Yonge's considerable inclusion in the *Supplement* is that Marghanita Laski, the tireless carder of citations, was a founding member of the Charlotte Yonge Society. Yonge herself was among those whom James Murray thanked in the first fascicle of the dictionary for lending "their services to the work," and her publications were the source of a similar number of citations in the first edition of the OED. The *Supplement* includes citations from her popular novels, *The Pillars of the House* and *The Daisy Chain*, as well as from *Womankind*, a book on improving women's education and creating a better place for single women in society, if from within a fairly traditional stance:

> home-maker. [HOME sb.1 14 h.] A housewife, esp. one in charge of the domestic arrangements (as opp. to a paid housekeeper); also, one who manages a household. So home-making sb. and a.
> 1876 C. M. YONGE *Womankind* xxx. 266 *Home-making* is . . her paramount earthly duty.

Yonge's coining of *home-making* serves as an excellent instance of the meaning of a citation spilling over the given sense. It has a way of making womankind's paramount earthly duty the meaning of *home-making*. The citations bring senses and sensibilities to the dictionary's entries that often run beyond the literal, and sometimes the entries require appended notes declaring that certain meanings are "now considered" opprobrious and sometimes not.

## II

In this and the following section, I offer a far more abbreviated treatment of the top books and periodicals. Many of the titles for both are familiar, and readers will quickly draw their own sense of where the editors and readers have turned for developments in the language. There are only a few patterns to which I want to draw attention, especially in relation to the editing of the first edition. The leading books of the *Supplement* turn out to be principally lexicographical, including dictionaries of musical, technical, mechanical, medical, and occupational terms, along with three works devoted to slang (see table 9.2 in the Appendix). Although these reference books are not typically consulted until work has begun on an entry for the dictionary, they still attest to the increased role of specialized vocabularies that are less likely to emerge out of the reading program. While Murray frowned on this sort of shortcut to citation and sense, a number of these reference books represent a newfound land of linguistic expansion for the *OED* that justified some extra assistance from other lexicographers. Yet in a comparison of the total set of citations, the *Supplement*'s use of reference works for citations is up only slightly over the first edition (see table 9.3 in the Appendix). The far greater presence of these works on the list of leading titles for the *Supplement* does suggest that a few of them have displaced the key literary and sacred works, with the exception of Joyce's *Ulysses* (while the reference books are, in turn, superseded by the plethora of citations drawn from modern periodicals in the *Supplement*).

Certainly, *Webster's* and *Century* dictionaries, which were heavily consulted by the editors, give a ready boost to the representation of standard American English in the *Supplement*.[11] The dictionaries of Eric Partridge, Sydney Baker, Lester Berry, and Melvin Van Bark add to the colloquial and informal reach of language that was to mark literature and other forms of writing in the modern era. But there is still a troubling circularity to this citation of other dictionaries. You can hear it in Partridge's introduction to *A Dictionary of Slang and Unconventional English*, in which he asks that his work be taken as "a humble companion" to the *OED* "from which I am proud to have learned a very great amount" (1984, p. xiii). Partridge drew roughly 45 percent of his words from the *OED* which were, along with his other entries, fed back into the files prepared for the *Supplement*, since Partridge's entire dictionary was carded at Oxford (Burchfield, 1973, p. 99). There are entries that appear in both, such as for *absol-bally-lutely*, to which Partridge adds "With thanks to Mr. R. W. Burchfield" in his dictionary. The *Supplement*, in turn, credits Partridge with the first incidence of such gems as *jowler*, *mocker*, and *shag*, giving an odd twist to the originating landscape of this discourse:

> **1937** PARTRIDGE *Dict. Slang* 748/2 *Shag*, a copulation; also, copulation generically.

This lexicographic reference loop is extended by the encyclopedia and companions on the list. The considerable inclusion of these works seems to challenge Murray's original mapping of the English language, with "Common" vocabulary in the center, buffered by an overarching "Literary" on top and "Colloquial" on the bottom. What this list makes clear is that the *Supplement* is extending the language in scientific, technical, and colloquial directions, and is doing so with considerable support not so much from their general readers or area specialists, but just by looking them up, that is, through the in-house consultation of standard technical reference works. We might still approach this reliance on reference works as indicating a balkanization of the language, an eroding of the idea of a shared, common core, represented by the dictionary of the English language. With the *Supplement*, the editors have assumed responsibility for defining the language of a number of new constituencies, many of which are housed in the university, to return to an earlier theme I introduced on the changes in editorial policy that mark the *Supplement* over the first edition. Among the other language constituencies not previously consulted in lexicographical circles is the republic of childhood, which now finds its record in Iona and Peter Opie's classic, *The Language and Lore of Schoolchildren*, from among those on the list of leading books in the *Supplement*. In a few instances, the children are credited with the earliest cite on words that later appear in the *Times*, the *New Scientist*, and *Daily Telegraph*:

> **1956** in I. & P. OPIE *Lore & Lang. Schoolch.* (1959) vii. 119 Joined the *Teds* when he was only three, Coshed a cop when he was only four.

Given Burchfield's own literary training and his stated commitment to a privileged treatment of literature, the relative absence of literature is notable. Even the letters of two literary figures that are featured on the list must be credited in part to those editors, researchers, scholars, and writers who constitute the reference industry. But then Joyce, too, is known to have quipped, with prophetic accuracy, that his novel would keep the professors busy for a long time. The list of leading book titles might be appreciated as another side to Burchfield's thoroughly modern approach of soliciting the services of consultants to assist in building the twentieth-century dictionary.

III

If the leading books in the *Supplement* are more likely to be consulted than read, the comparable list of periodicals, playing a substantially larger role in the dictionary, constitutes another form of browsing for busy readers (see table 9.4 in the Appendix). Between the two periods, Victorian and modern, only a few of the periodicals from the original *OED*—the *Times*, *Nature*, and the *Westminster Gazette*—retain a position on the *Supplement*'s list. The others have been usurped by the increasing influence of other newspapers (five titles), American sources (five titles), and scientific and technical interests (four titles), with some overlap among them.

A big difference in comparing this modern survey of the periodical with the Victorian list is that the magazines that dominate the list are no longer as closely tied to the culture of the book as were the weeklies, reviews, and quarterlies favored by the first edition of the *OED*. The book-centered weekly is represented by the *Times Literary Supplement* in this list. The other periodicals often feature a book-review section as one of the areas of interest. The magazines that prevail in the modern edition of the dictionary range from the *Listener*, which supports and supplements the BBC broadcast service, to the *New Statesman*, which is, in its own words, "radical, dissenting, enquiring independent of any party or power hungry proprietor." These organs may well serve essentially the same class of readers as the earlier literary reviews and weeklies, providing them with a more generally newsy approach to cultural and political affairs and opinion. In terms of book serialization, the *New Yorker* alone on the *Supplement* list makes a regular feature of running long installments of almost exclusively nonfiction works, in continuity with earlier periodicals.

Taking this matter of currency a step farther is the "newsmagazine," with *Time*'s punchy treatment of news and trends, and the *Economist*'s neat divide, at least in more recent times, between the categories of "World Politics and Current Affairs" and "Business, Finance and Science." The list of leading periodicals features the learned organs of the newsstand, the *New Scientist* and *Scientific American*, as well as mixing in more entertaining vehicles of the leisure-reading classes:

1964 *Economist* 31 Oct. 518/2 Professor Yamey . . has published the first independent assessment of the Resale Prices Act . . for those who love *in-jokes*. 1966 *Punch* 4 May 657/1 The dialogue peppered with British upper-class in-joke slang of the most blatant appeal to Lancashire slum-dwellers and Turkish primary schools.

One difference in the *Supplement*'s approach to periodicals is that the editors made magazines and newspapers a substantial part of the Press's prescribed reading program in a way that their Victorian predecessors did not, while going much farther afield in their systematic coverage of news-stands from around the world than is reflected in the list presented here. Another substantial change is that the *Times* now leads the list of oft-cited periodicals with almost Shakespearean proportions (after placing fifth among Victorian newspapers in the original *OED*). It is clearly the news-paper of choice for the Oxford readers and editors. Among the news-papers, the Baltimore *Sun* has become the *Supplement*'s leading Ameri-can paper, as you may recall from the previous chapter, by virtue of a substantial donation of citations to the Press from Professor Hench.

The list of leading papers reflects a similar mix of Tory and Whig ori-entations, from the *Daily Telegraph* and the *Times* on the one side to the *Manchester Guardian* and the *Observer* on the other. In terms of the record of the language the papers provide, the tendency is to irony rather than the once strident tone of the dailies. Of the top two papers, the *Times* is no longer the "Thunderer" on the side of Tory causes that it was during the mid-nineteenth century, and the *Daily Telegraph* has long ago lost sight of its roots as a radical liberal paper (Brown, 1985, p. 276). The differences between them have grown more subtle; their independence, as sources of news and views, is their governing principle in support of more conservative issues:

> 1984 *Times* 2 July 1/8 Mr Scargill . . said: '. . My facts show to me . . that the people guilty of intimidation and *violence* in this dispute have been the po-lice.' 1984 *Daily Telegraph* 5 Oct. 20/2 [At the Labour Party Conference] Much violence was done to the word violence, which it appears can be used to describe almost anything you do not care for.

The rare identification of a speaker and a conference in these two cita-tions appears necessary, not only to come to the point of their attack, which is typically not of interest to the lexicographer, but to preserve the equally rare elements of irony and judgment that find their way, in this particular case, into the *Supplement*'s particular definition for *violence*:

> Add: **1. d.** Now used in political contexts with varying degrees of appropri-ateness.

Judging by the final figures for the second edition of the *OED*, the *Supplement* introduced close to 50,000 new entries into the language, along with 20,000 additional senses and citations added to existing entries. All told, it adds up to roughly a 15 percent increase in Oxford's estimation of what constitutes the vocabulary of the English language. Yet the *Supplement* amounts to more than an increase in vocabulary and sense. Like the original *OED*, the *Supplement* makes its own peace with the times, cutting a path through an English-speaking culture that stretches out from London, Oxford, and Cambridge. Burchfield brings home to the *Supplement* an English that has found a life abroad, if principally in Ireland and America. Glancing back over the lists of favored sources for this work, it may seem that literature's hold on the language shows signs of waning. This twentieth-century collection of citations represents a modern faith in the authority of periodical and reference books that now fully supplements the literary text and makes up the disappearance of the sacred work. The dictionary's citation program continues to follow the reading habits of the better-educated classes, without falling under the commercial spell of book sales or circulation figures. If there is a striking contrast between the Victorian *OED* and the modern *Supplement*, it is that the *Times*, having become the single-most important source of citations, signals a shift within the tripartite governance of the language—literary, referential, periodical—to the most immediate of forms. The font of language to which the dictionary turns is still the work of a writing profession and publishing trade that is both larger than the literary arts and less than the full extent of the business. As a rule, the dictionary draws on a level of trade in words that imbues it with respectability and authority. The *Supplement* did, however, take stock of underground publishing and some works from far and wide in the world of English. Its penchant for highbrow citations was broken by Burchfield's daring with a couple of taboo words, just as it was permanently altered by the detective-fiction reading habits of Marghanita Laski.

The *OED* does propose a set of writers to preserve meaning and nuance in the language, as well as to move it along to new senses and turns. They articulate the word as they would have the world, no less than the rest of us, yet their writing becomes part of the record of the language. My interest in this chapter has not been to villainize the dictionary's leading lights, but more simply and humanely to examine how each edition of the *OED* carries forward something more than the full triumph of the English language. It is foolish, of course, to expect the dictionary to lead in a reformation of the language, the purging of its imperialist and xenophobic elements. But can we get beyond the way things have been defined up to now if we do not ask how the world has spoken and has been spoken for in ways with which we are no longer comfortable? The editors at Oxford work a selective tradition within the published record, but it is one they have deliberately shifted with the *Supplement* to encompass a greater span of popular writing and a greater reach into world English. Setting a new course for attending to the whole of the English language has to come slowly on the scale of the massive *OED* project. What is determined as desirable for one edition may only begin to show with any appreciable impact in later ones. The *Supplement*'s coverage of Anglo-American publishing activities for the better part of this century reflects an age that many of the dictionary's users still live comfortably within, but that for many more people is already past. In every corner of the former empire, the users of the dictionary need to explore the standards that would be set for them in such works as the dictionary, as they inevitably live within this language and learn to write beyond its defined borders.

# The Second Edition,
# 1984–1989

A MODEST but significant indication that the second edition of *The Oxford English Dictionary* represents a new era of dictionary publishing occurs on the dictionary's title page. It states that the work has been "prepared," rather than edited, by John Simpson and Edmund Weiner. Using newly developed electronic tools, Simpson and Weiner fashioned a seamless union of the original *OED* edited by James Murray's editorial team and Robert Burchfield's extensive *Supplement*. In addition to the integration of the two texts, "new vocabulary has been added," the introduction explains, "certain important general revisions, and numerous local corrections have been made." The result is an *OED* prepared to guide the English language into the twenty-first century which was released, appropriately, in three formats: (1) a twenty-volume set of books in 1989, (2) a single-volume *Compact OED* with magnifying glass in 1991, and (3) a laser CD-ROM (compact disk: read-only-memory) in 1992 for personal computer use.

The electronic restoration of the dictionary began in 1984 under the joint initiative of John Simpson, who figured earlier in this book as director of the Press's reading program, and Edmund Weiner, an Oxford graduate with a B.A. in English language and literature and a member of the *Supplement* team since 1977. Through the five years of preparation, Simpson and Weiner worked on what was termed The New Oxford English Dictionary Project both at Oxford University Press and the University of Waterloo in Canada. However, the resulting dictionary published in 1989 was identified as *The Oxford English Dictionary*, Second Edition, rather than invoking all that might be implied by entitling it once again *New*. On paper at least, it is unmistakably the same dictionary that Richard Trench proposed and James Murray built. Although the work has "an entirely new typographic format," it still resembles, in most facets, Murray's original specimen pages of 1879. The CD-ROM version, on the other hand, does allow the "user" to customize the color and size of the typefaces.

The most substantial structural change in the actual text of the dictionary is the substitution of the International Phonetic Alphabet (IPA) for Murray's own rather idiosyncratic system of phonetic transcription.

Otherwise, the dictionary's general organization of meaning-making has been retained. Yet, in another sense, this multiple-format edition of the dictionary represents a considerable change in what might be termed *lexicographical ontology*, or the state of the dictionary's existence as *text*. The *OED* is now in a position to become a far more responsive instrument to the nuances of language change and advances in scholarship on the history of meaning. The record of the English language is now suspended in an electromagnetic field, its body malleable and plastic. It is no longer fixed in cases of lead type as a permanent tribute to the printed life of the English language and the accomplishment of Victorian lexicography.

Common sense dictated that with the publication of each supplement to the *OED*, even if it incorporated earlier ones, the dictionary was becoming less useful as a reference work. A century's worth of defining and redefining the language had to be consolidated to keep the *OED* viable as a dictionary rather than as a museum of period pieces. If for no other reason, the original lead type set in place for the printing of the *OED*, with the early fascicles dating back to the nineteenth century, was on the point of failing to make a fair copy. At the same time, developments in computer technology, during the 1980s, especially in the areas of text manipulation and electronic publishing, seemed to promise a way of not only resetting the entire work by integrating the original with the supplement, but also as a means of continuing to work with the text, improving its historical coverage and keeping it current with the language. However, as Edmund Weiner pointed out on publication of the integrated work, "No one had ever done a scissors-and-paste job using a computer to integrate two large dictionaries." Not only did it entail a "dialogue between lexicographers on the one hand and computer people on the other," but, as Weiner concludes, "both sides had to be re-educated" (cited in Baum, 1989, p. 12).

As Simpson and Weiner describe the process in their introduction to the second edition, when the project to create an electronic *OED* was considered in 1983, during the work on the final volume of the *Supplement*, it was quickly recognized to be more than the Press could handle in-house. Once again an appeal had to be made to the public, if in a rather different form from the one first sounded by the Philological Society during the Victorian era. The project required a level of financial investment and technological development that was only to be met by the substantial involvement of IBM and the British and Canadian governments. Within a year of drawing up plans and securing partners for this project, the Press formally announced in 1984 the commencement of the New Oxford English Dictionary Project at a gathering of the Royal Society in London. What had been resolved by an amateur society over a century earlier, and initially edited by a part-time schoolteacher in his corrugated-iron Scriptorium, was now fully a prestigious international venture representing university, government, and corporate interests. It was still, as Murray had claimed for his dictionary, infused with the scientific spirit, taking more of its lead, however, from computational linguistics and computer science than the principles of philology. The partnership of IBM's Academic Programme in Great Britain and the Computer Science Department at the University of Waterloo in Canada that was overseen by Oxford University Press resulted in the construction of a remarkable database, with supporting software capable of opening the text to a whole new range of inquiries, turning it into a far more powerful research instrument, while also holding out possibilities for working with other texts in this manner (Berg, Gonnet, and Tompa, 1988).

With the entire text in this electromagnetic state, corrections and revisions to the work can be made directly and easily. Much thought has gone into how the text, as a whole, can now be further refined, standardized, and updated on a continuous basis (Raymond and Warburton, 1987). As it is, the second edition, published in 1989, represents only the preliminary steps in bringing the work up to the level of today's scholarly understanding of the language. The OED can now be far more responsive to developments in the day-to-day (published) life of the word, and to new work being done on its history and literature. In spite of the vast potential for improving the dictionary inherent in this new lexicographical technology, the Press decided to go to print only five years into the project, shortly after the integration of the work was to be completed. Burchfield has expressed regrets about the early publication of the merged text, which has left the overwhelming majority of the dictionary in its Victorian state, blaming the rush on the financial considerations of the Press (Baum, 1989, p. 12). *The Economist*, in its review of the second edition, treated with some irony this unprecedented meeting of both the projected publication date and length of the dictionary with the query, "What went wrong?" ("Dressing Old Words New," 1989, p. 79). They attribute the anomaly to the "Spirit of the Age" in the New Britain of the 1980s, the technology, a grant from the Department of Trade and Industry, and the relatively modest task of assembling the pieces of previous editions of the OED.

Weiner has pointed out that one issue the Press still has to face in proceeding with any revisions is the need to develop a consistent and comprehensive editorial policy for practices that evolved without being specified or standardized. The current inconsistencies of abbreviations, terms of reference, identification of titles, and so on frustrate the efficacy of computer searches, or as Weiner puts it, "Every time one carries out a computer search for anything in the OED one finds that one must use two or three different arguments," showing his own mastery of the requisite Boolean logic for conducting electronic searches (1989, p. 29). Only with this new comprehensive policy in place will the real work of revising the *OED* begin. Not only does each entry have to be brought into line with policy, but there are countless antedatings (consisting of citations for words predating those currently listed in the dictionary) and additional quotations, many of which have already been found by readers. Based on his work on the citations of Shakespeare and Nashe, Schäfer estimated that some 29,000 of the original *OED*'s 240,000 main entries can be antedated by half a century (1980, p. 67). For his part, Schäfer managed to assemble some 5,000 "additions and corrections" from his work with Early Modern English lexicography (1989). As I noted earlier, James Murray had not hesitated to announce to the Philological Society that earlier citations could be found for fully three-quarters of the entries (*TPS*, 1882–84, p. 516). Among the other points for future revision, Simpson and Weiner point out in their preface that there are references to "countries, currency values, institutions, and persons which are now anachronistic," adding that "there are still a few definitions which enshrine social attitudes that are now alien." The publication of the second edition marks only the starting point for a thorough revision of the entire work.

With the newly integrated electronic text, it was relatively easy to insert the 5,000 new words and senses into the second edition that were intended to cover the fourteen-year spread in the publication of the four-volume *Supplement*, as well as the three years that had passed since the last volume was completed. The simultaneous publication of the twenty volumes meant that, for the first time, words that began with *A* were contemporary with those listed under *Z*. The second edition marks the end of serial publication for the dictionary, a Victorian marketing feature that, over its four-decade run, had alphabetically distorted this mirror of the language. To meet this new ability of the dictionary to keep current, as well as to serve the many other dictionaries that it was now publishing, Oxford established the New English Word Series (NEWS) in 1983 under the direction of John Simpson. By 1987, NEWS had prepared entries for a set of 5,000 items, backed by 14,850 citations, for inclusion in the second edition. Simpson has reported that among these items, the language of computing produced the largest number of new words, followed by medicine, politics, and slang (Baum, 1989, p. 12). The figure of 5,000 was chosen by the editorial staff at Oxford in 1984 as a manageable number while still representing a substantial effort to top up the coverage of the *Supplement* and give an additional currency to the second edition. In Burchfield's words, "these are the most obvious words that no one in his right mind could have missed, and not the results of in-depth research"

(Baum, 1989, p. 13). Simpson has called them "the top 5,000" (*ibid.*). Yet a few of them are hardly new at all. Shakespeare, for example, is credited with a new sense to *die v.*1: "To experience sexual orgasm (Most common as a poetical metaphor in the late 16th and 17th cent.)." The citations for this sense begin with *Much Ado about Nothing* and end with songwriter John Denver's "*Annie's Song* (sheet music)" from 1974: "Come let me love you . . . Let me die in your arms." It is, I should add, simply the wrong question to ask whether 5,000 is a number that bears any relationship to the actual growth in the vocabulary of the English language.

My visits to the English Dictionary Division at Oxford University Press, in 1986, 1988, and 1992, allowed me to gain a sense of the evolving organization of the directed-reading program behind the New English Word Series (NEWS). The reading program is worth considering in some detail as it clearly reveals changing attitudes at Oxford over how the great expanse of the English language is to be covered. In terms of the monthly lists of titles in 1986, March consisted of forty-two books to be read for citations and a dozen periodicals. John Simpson, who was directing the program at the time, pointed out to me that while some of the periodical titles on the program's monthly list represented several issues, an effort was generally made to balance the number of periodicals and books that were read for the program. Eleven of the books were fiction, dating back to 1979, and included Anita Brookner's Booker prize-winner *Hotel du Lac* (which had been, a note adds, "previously read only for adverbs") and Jeffery Archer's best-seller, *First Among Equals*. The other categories for this 1986 list included (besides the large one for fiction) squash, opera, computing, and psychiatry. The list also referred to a continued reading of the 1985 *Sears Catalogue*. Among the periodicals consulted during the month were *Modern Railways*, the *New Yorker*, *Barnhart Dictionary Companion*, *Here's Health*, and the *Pennysaver* (from Waterloo, Ontario). An assortment of newspapers was lumped together within the list of periodicals and assigned to a single reader, as opposed to the two readers devoted to British fiction and biography. The Press had, in addition, a full-time reader of the *Times*, but, it was explained to me, she kept falling behind, as one can easily imagine, as even the classified advertisements in the newspapers were read.

On my return visit in 1988, I found that the reading program at Oxford, now under the direction of Sara Tulloch, had extended its reach into publishing activities across the English-speaking world. The titles for the 1987 lists were divided between "General" and "Subjects," with the country of origin serving as a subcategory in each. April featured fiction from Britain, the United States, India, and Nigeria, along with five newspapers from India and one each from Britain and America. The lists for

February and March divided the fiction titles between what were termed "quality" novels, by Julian Barnes (who had worked on the *Supplement*), A. N. Wilson, Ann Tyler, and W. Soyinka, and "popular" titles by Dick Francis, Joseph Heller, and Robert Coover. But such difficult distinctions were dropped from subsequent lists. Poetry made a rather thin showing for 1987, with two collections from Seamus Heany (January), N. Ezekiel's *Latter-day Psalms* from India (June), and *Dread Affair*, listed as a Rastafarian collection by B. Zephaniah (November). There were no plays or movie scripts. By far the biggest difference since my previous visit was the sheer number of magazines on the list: April featured thirty-five magazine and journal titles covering no less than Africa, American football, angling, the armed forces, computing, darts, diving, equestrian, folk music, law, martial arts, music, outdoor pursuits, peace, skiing, and wind surfing. In looking over the Directed Reading Program for 1987, I found between 7 to 16 percent of the titles, on a monthly basis, came from outside North America and Great Britain, while the North American contribution ran between 21 and 54 percent. Titles related to science and technology amounted to roughly a fifth of the titles. As we saw with the leading sources for the *Supplement*, the editors no longer hold the common reader as the ideal target of their work; as they now seek out specialized organs of professional information, with the exception of the securely middle-class news magazines, the *Economist* and *Time*. The master-narrative of a common tongue seems to have been subsumed by the professionals' specialized language communities. Publishers have been developing new markets of what might be termed language and image consumption, and the lexicographers are following their lead.

As I noted earlier, it has also become part of the daily routine of the English Dictionary Division at Oxford to check electronically a series of commercial database services, such as Nexis, Dialog, and World Reporter, for the frequency of occurrence and the earliest use for new items in a series of American and British periodicals dating back to the 1980s and earlier. The Press is also taking advantage of the growing number of electronic concordances of major works in English history and literature prepared by the Oxford Centre for Computing in the Humanities. As the most advanced consultant of electronic source texts in my survey of five dictionary publishers in Britain, America, and Canada, the editorial team at Oxford has realized much of the promise and shortcomings of the electronic database. Oxford's century-old commitment to the full documentation and historical verification of entries made the electronic database especially useful. Yet the search in an overwhelming number of cases for the *OED* still begins with what first catches the reader's eye and is noted on a citation slip. The computer serves as a supplement in ascertaining the earliest use and most frequent form of spelling, which is especially crucial with nominalizations and new compounds. The instance which John Simpson showed me in 1986 was *file management*, for which the database turned up over seven hundred uses versus rather skimpy results for twenty other *file* collocations. However, when it came to making the final decision, even with the computer-generated figures, the editors decided to go with another *file* term:

> **1969** *Computers & Humanities* III. 132 This search (once through the file), whether for a single interrogation or for several, is called a *file-pass*.

Simpson also reported that the electronic search was still severely limited by its inability to make semantic and syntactic distinctions, which prevented the search of specific meanings or uses of a word. Another problem is the tendency of the database companies to promote their own norms in the language by allowing only a single spelling for terms in its word index, which adds a further layer of editing in the still-evolving standardization of the language. Finally, the electronic search remains an expensive service for the Press, especially in light of having to follow up with a check of the original document in the library for such matters as page number, often omitted by the database companies as irrelevant. Yet the lexicographical importance of the commercial database, as it accumulates greater historical depth in its files, can only increase, lending greater weight to its selection of the leading periodicals for professionals.

When compared to the citations gathered for the first edition and the *Supplement*, the second edition's 5,000 NEWS items represent a remarkably small sample. As it is, the majority of the 14,850 citations are drawn from works that had already appeared in the *Supplement*. Yet the importance of the NEWS items for this survey of changing editorial practices is how they serve as the first indication of the editorial tendencies of Simpson and Weiner, as the next generation of *OED* editors. They are also important, on this limited scale, because they more closely represent what will be added to the dictionary in a continuous process of updating its collection of terms. The leading authors and periodicals for this small sample reveal both familiar staples and a considerable shift toward the timely. They represent a growing reliance on both American and periodical literature, while signaling the belated gains made by women writers, as well as indicating a few curious new developments in Oxford's pursuit of the English language.[1]

Five of the authors on the top twenty list for the 5,000 items (see table 10.1 in the Appendix) are familiar literary figures who made strong showings in the *Supplement*—Shaw, Joyce, Faulkner, Lawrence, and Huxley. A number of the other literary figures on this list also appear in the *Supplement*, but have, for this set, risen in standing to the status of the top twenty, all but one of them American—Eugene O'Neill (with a concordance), Joseph Wambaugh, Martin Amis, Saul Bellow, Alison Lurie, Scott Fitzgerald, and Gore Vidal. The other notable change to this list, aside from its increased American coverage, is that women writers have finally been granted more than a toehold on authorizing the language, with the choice showing a good deal of variety—Susan Townsend, Lady Bird Johnson, Ann Barr, Cyra McFadden, Kate Millet, and Alison Lurie. All told, literature still prevails among the callings followed by the authors most often cited by the readers and editors at Oxford, but the strength of the individual author as a factor in setting the language does appear, as far as this slight set indicated, to be declining.

By a certain irreverent twisting of tradition, the language was enriched by Joyce and Shaw, who dominate the author lists for both the *Supplement* and the 5,000 NEWS words, just as the century before Scottish writers proved a powerful influence on the *OED* through both Sir Walter Scott and the sizable Scottish contingency working in the periodical press (Gross, 1991). The appearance of Joyce and Shaw points to a process of antedating or "ante-citing," as it might be called. This is a matter of a more recent citation sending the editors back into the files for earlier and overlooked instances. For example, it appears that the *New York Times*'s use of *anti-feminist* in 1982 proved a turning point for admitting the term that had accumulated earlier citations dating back to Shaw's use of it in 1924 but had failed to be included in the *Supplement* in the mid-1960s. The use of the French, *allons* ("let us go"), by D. H. Lawrence and Wallace Stevens calls forth earlier uses of the term by Dryden, Congreve, Sterne, Mary Mitford, and Trollope. The tide is turned, seemingly by a letter written by Stevens in 1954, and *allons* enters the English language, while its use since the seventeenth century in plays and novels had not been sufficient. Does this suggest a relaxed attitude to importations or a loss of familiarity with French among readers? Similarly, the appearance of *Appalachian*, as part of American geography and culture (as opposed to the strictly geological formation) now appears in the second edition with dozens of cites running back to 1672, with Appalachian notes from Washington Irving, William Faulkner, and Lady Bird Johnson, among others. The door having been fully opened by Oxford on this new American land and language, elements of its history come tumbling out in a complex tapestry of three centuries worth of citations. This belated recognition of what has become the leading postcolonial site/cite in the English language serves as a reminder of just how much catching up might really be at stake in even imagining a dictionary that represented the broader English language on historical principles.

In making sense of the Irish's particular take on the English language, Declan Kiberd has recently pointed to their coming at it from outside: "Equipped by analytic colonial education to write the most rigorous critiques of their masters, Irish writers were enabled to offer witty deconstructions of British imperial culture" (1992, p. 3). He cites Marx's supposition that Ireland is the Achilles' heel of the British empire, although Marx could hardly have foreseen its contribution to this great lexicographical tool of the empire. Judging by its standing as the top literary source of citation in both the *Supplement* and the NEWS collection, Joyce's *Ulysses* appears to be the century's unrelentingly modern work of English literature and language. It is well to recall that it was originally burned in New York and seized in Great Britain, before reaching its final acquittal of obscenity charges by the United States District Court in 1933, due to its purported failure to promote lustful thoughts. Kiberd observes of Joyce that "living like other Irish writers, at a certain angle to the English literary tradition, he could use it without superstition, irreverently, even insolently" (1992, p. 5).[2]

> **1922** JOYCE *Ulysses* 740 Be sure and write soon kind she left out regards to your father also Captain Grove with love yrs *affly*.

The NEWS entry for *affly*, as an abbreviation of *affectionately* that is judged "now *rare*," is also backed by earlier citations from published letters dated 1846 and 1898. It seems another odd instance, this time of updating the dictionary by backdating a now-rare familiarism, in what, according to Oxford's files, may be the last published instance of *affly*. But this, too, is part of Joyce's power in the English language. If he saw himself as, in his words, "a scissors and paste man," then his paste-up of a Greek, Semitic, Gaelic saga, in its own act of postcolonial translation, came to serve the empire and the *OED* (cited by Kiberd, 1992, p. 5). Of course, when it comes to word-play, *Finnegans Wake* would seem by far a greater fount than *Ulysses*. This word-playful work might have been expected to fill the dictionary from its first trick:

> **riverrun** *nonce-wd.* [Cf. Run *sb.*[1] 29 a.] The course which a river shapes and follows through the landscape.
> **1939** JOYCE *Finnegans Wake* (1964) I. 3 Riverrun, past Eve and Adam's, from swerve of shore to bend of bay, brings us by a commodius vicus of recirculation back to Howth Castle and Environs.

However, this most dictionary-challenging work, riven with nonce words, is only cited 186 times in the *OED*, compared to *Ulysses'* 1,319 citations. Simpson explained to me that the *Ulysses'* concordance made all the difference, adding that the great Joyce biographer Richard Ellman suggested *riverrun* and a handful of other Joycisms for inclusion. The *OED* contains fifty-five entries for which Joyce provides the only documentation, and with each of these modern *hapax legomena*, the dictionary continues to build lexicographical tributes to the accomplished writer, as holding a special place in the formation of the English language.

Three of the women on the list—Townsend, Barr, and McFadden—bring a particular kind of currency to the *OED*, collectively raising another issue over the authority on which the dictionary rests its definition of the language. Each of them presents a somewhat satirical regard for the language of a distinct social group. Susan Townsend brings to the dictionary the voice of disaffected youth in the fictional figure of Adrian Mole, who in diary form tells the story of his kindly but disheveled low-income English life in a series of popular books that are not without their political bite and social commentary. This is rather a different voice of the young than captured in the Opies' *Language and Lore of Schoolchildren*, which turns up among the *Supplement*'s top titles. The dictionary's editors recognize that something is happening here with the young and disaffected, and have selected the traditional literary vehicle for importing the linguistic riches of adolescence, as they had with Dickens and the language of nineteenth-century London streets.

> 1984 S. TOWNSEND *Growing Pains A. Mole* 19, I can't go on like this. I have written to Auntie Clara, the *Agony Aunt*.

Adrian Mole, at wits' end and in need of a little authoritative advice—"Pandora has just left my bedroom. I am just about devastated with frustration"—turns to the *agony aunt*. The *OED* glosses the term as "a familiar name for the (female) editor of an agony column." The *agony column*, in turn, is supported in the *OED* by citations dating back to an issue of *Fun* from 1863, which claimed "our own agony column," as if what was then advertisement for missing relatives and friends was already a familiar term and ready to be mocked. The alliterative extension, *agony aunties*, turns up in the 1970s, with Townsend giving it a youthful affirmation and the mark of common usage. The other citations, from the *Daily Telegraph* and a book on the topic by R. Kent—"Perhaps a university should start an agony aunt course"—seem to use the term with the irony of implied inverted commas. If Townsend is gently mocking her Adrian ("I am quite aware" she has him assure Aunt Clara, "of the awesome things about bringing a baby into the world and I would wear a protective dildo"), then this, too, becomes part of the dictionary's regard for those who are not otherwise heard in these lexicographical circles.

This satirical turn toward contemporary language, citing it without having to endorse it, comes up again with *The Official Sloane Ranger Handbook: The First Guide to What Really Matters in Life* by Ann Barr and Peter York. This book takes its play on the cowboy hero in white from the fashionable Sloane Square in London and the Range Rovers parked there. The term *Sloane Ranger* warrants its own entry in the *OED*, with the highly irregular lexicographic practice of having the first five citations drawn from a single article in *Harper & Queens* by Peter York in 1975 ("Sloane Ranger pet hates . . incense, Norman Mailer"). By 1983, the term made the headlines in *The Times*—"Bogus Sloane Ranger lived like a lord." It had clearly caught on, but the citations from the *Handbook* have a different quality to them as the book pretends to speak for those it mocks:

> **1982** BARR & YORK *Official Sloane Ranger Handbk*. 10/1 *Sloane Rangers* hesitate to use the term 'breeding' now (of people not animals) but that's what background means.

A third instance of this ironic form of citation, from among the leading authors of the 5,000 items, is Cyra McFadden's illustrated and spiral-bound *The Serial: A Year in the Life of Marin County*, which had origi-nally been read for the *Supplement*. McFadden adds another of what might be taken as missing voices to the dictionary, with her taste of a new-age California run amok in the 1970s on "this whole high energy trip with all these happening people." What is perhaps more interesting is that the citing of this book may well have been on advice offered by John Ryle's review of it for the *Times Literary Supplement*: "It furnishes an account of changing modes of speech which could be a valuable source of citations for the editors of the *OED*, though the talk is a stale cocktail of social science jargon and the old hippie slang that derives from the superannuated in-talk of Blacks, gays and junkies" (1978, p. 464). This consigning of stale cocktail jargon to the editors of the national diction-ary, if intended as only a slight to the author, perhaps caught the attention of the diligent and responsive reading program at Oxford. While McFad-den's sampling of the sun-dried human-potential movement expands the dialectical reach of the dictionary, it also suggests a rather stale path of inclusion, as the reviewer for the *TLS* recommends to the *OED* a work that plays this language for a giggle. This is as true of the *Official Sloane Ranger Handbook* and Townsend's *Adrian Mole* series. The sense of the lexicographer going farther afield to dip into the life of the language, out to Big Sur or down to Sloane Square, is still limited by the linguistic sensi-bility of the literary supplement. Satire makes for a lesser lexicographical source, throwing into question the accuracy and authenticity of the lan-guage represented, as it seems to set everything into inverted commas. This satirical poke, both up and down the social scale, reasserts the au-thority of the dictionary's standard, while making a questionable contri-bution to the scientific or sociolinguistic spirit of the work.

The Americanization of the leading-author list is continued among the periodicals (see table 10.2 in the Appendix). The *New York Times* and the *Washington Post* make substantial appearances, while the *New Yorker* has improved its standing. Although the *Times* and *Daily Telegraph* still dominate the list, the editors at Oxford have clearly begun to attend to the language emanating out of New York City. The monitoring of the *New York Times*, especially, forms a bond between Oxford and American dictionary publishers, in an Anglo-American meeting of Englishes and dictionaries. Although the paper is not cited as often as the leading British papers in the *OED*, the fact that it is so widely consulted among lexicographers on both sides of the Atlantic makes it that much closer to a universal and authoritative standard for the English language, as a newspaper of record:

> **1983** N. Y. *Times* 20 Nov. VI. 75/3 What Giacomo Casanova *chauvinistically* called 'the Italian style'—and what the Americans call the French kiss.

A further sense of the rising contribution of the *New York Times* and the *Washington Post* can be gained by comparing them with the two leading London papers over the three periods of editorial activity considered in this study (see table 10.3 in the Appendix). One reason for the increasing influence of the American papers is that while the London papers have always been available at the corner shop in Oxford, by the mid-1980s the American ones were wired into the basement of the St. Giles' office of the *OED* through a computer link to the commercial database services that gave the American papers a citational advantage.

Among the other newcomers to the list of the top twenty periodicals is the *Financial Times*, which adds to the influence of the daily paper while reflecting an increase in the contribution of commerce to the language matched by the strong showing of the weekly *Economist*, which was also consulted electronically. Although this business newspaper dates back to the nineteenth century, it had been largely ignored by Oxford until the NEWS program, with 222 cites from it appearing in the *Supplement*. Another new title on the list is *Commentary*, a monthly that had incorporated the *Contemporary Jewish Record*. The relative increase in its contribution is worth noting in relation to my earlier discussion of anti-Semitic citations in the *Supplement* (and there are 912 *Commentary* cites in that work), but it is also worth commenting on the fact that it is the only monthly review of current affairs, a genre with a strong showing on the Victorian list, to appear in table 10.3. The weeklies, including the Sunday papers, have taken over the list, with the *Sunday Times* balancing the liberal leanings of the *Observer*, lending further emphasis to the news format as the vehicle for shaping public thinking. *Publishers' Weekly*, caught up in news about the business of publishing, might be seen as complementing the *Times Literary Supplement* with its interests in the substance of the industry. Finally, the fourth new entry on this list is the

Canadian newspaper, the *Globe and Mail*, the first appearance of a high-ranking source from the British commonwealth, reflecting an interest among the editors at Oxford in moving beyond the Anglo-American circle, although not so far beyond that circle of influence, nor always in a significant fashion.

> 1985 *Globe & Mail* (Toronto) 9 Oct. A9/4 Weather *advisories* were issued for all parts of Manitoba.

In terms of this latest set of additions to the *OED*, the twenty leading periodicals contributed over a quarter of the citations. Clearly, the size of this contribution is warranted, on one level, by the sheer number of words in periodicals produced and consumed on a daily basis. Of course, the editors at Oxford have rarely been persuaded by quantity alone. Within this list of periodical titles, the editors seem to favor an upscale packaging of the news in a variety of formats, daily or weekly, for business or science.

As the *OED* both documents and contributes to our understanding of the primary sources of linguistic authority in the English language, it appears to have increasingly entrusted the journalist with the devolvement of the language. It is a process that was well underway during the Victorian era, although the widely consulted titles were of a far more literary nature. In this century, and especially among the leading periodical titles that contributed to the 5,000 NEWS items, we see the flowering of the journalist and staff writer still working anonymously for the most part in the *OED*. James Murray opened the door for the daily newspaper, the pamphlet, the advertisement, and now it has come to the point where the periodical leads in setting the permanent record of the language. Yet in comparison to other dictionary publishing houses I visited in the course of my preliminary research, the program at Oxford continued to reflect a predilection for literary treatments of the language that far exceed those underwriting other English dictionaries. However, in my final visit to the Press in 1992, I did meet a recently appointed head of the reading program who suggested that poetry presented a problem for lexicographers, as its language was "unrepresentative" and "used willfully" in a way that interfered with its citational qualities, an attitude I had found earlier among more than one American publisher (Willinsky, 1988a).

Whatever the fate of the reading program in the future, the *OED* continues to reflect, as I have been arguing, what amounts to a writers' guild, the language of a profession, albeit one given to working many vocabularies. Yet the representation has not been evenly distributed among those who write professionally in English. Both the periodical press and the sciences, which began to exert a strong influence during the Victorian era, have taken on increasing weight in this century, accompanied by a pronounced shift to a mid-Atlantic, Anglo-Irish-American center of linguistic gravity. The handful of additions to the second edition, representing the work of this new generation of editors, points to a furthering of this process. The technology of lexicography has always defined the scope of the project, from Johnson's penciled passages through the citation slips of voluntary readers and on to the electronic searches of databases that feature periodical literature of a professional bent. No method completely disappears, but the new ones have a way of asserting their own influence, and in this case, with only the 5,000 NEWS items to run with, the computer gives this electronic form of searching the language an exhaustive authority that will only increase the lexicographer's reliance on this approach. Still, the serendipitous citations will continue to play their part as well, even if as they may turn out to reflect one of the editor's efforts to keep up with the news from back home:

> 1976 *Billings* (Montana) *Gaz.* 7 July 9A/2 Miss Jillison, a *libra*, is married to a slim libra, Joseph Gallagher, film-production executive at 20th Century Fox—a marriage that took place after three dates and her reading his chart.

The *OED* has taken up a new sense of World English, not in Richard Trench's original sense, as an expression of empire and an extension of Christianity, but as part of a redefined role for the United Kingdom and its venerable institutions in a postcolonial world. Oxford dictionaries that fit the pocket or fill a shelf are on sale in over one hundred nations; the "Oxford" name has been legally registered in countries around the world to reserve its use for the Press's dictionaries (Shenker, 1989, p. 100). The Oxford family of dictionaries is still about the discriminating use of authority and the authority of a discriminating language. Only now the labor is assisted by the most sophisticated electronic text-manipulation technology developed to date. Simpson and Weiner conclude their preface to the second edition by committing themselves to further improvements for future editions, "so that *The Oxford English Dictionary* may continue to be an accurate and comprehensive register of the whole vocabulary of English" (p. lvi). The irony to such conclusions is that the *OED*'s register, to play on the notion of it as a particular level of language use, has expanded with the *Supplement* and NEWS items, while still holding to the antiquated concept that it remains "an accurate and comprehensive" measure "of the whole vocabulary of English."

## CHAPTER 11.

# The Sense of Omission

"THERE IS no document of civilization," Walter Benjamin has written, "which is not at the same time a document of barbarism" (1968, p. 256). As is commonly known, the origins of the Greek term *barbaric* lie in what the Greeks found foreign and rude, as in a language other than their own. The barbaric falls beyond the bounds of that familiarity which is taken as civilization. By extension, the *barbarian*, as the *OED* specifies among its "historical" definitions, is "one outside the pale of Christian civilization" (**2.c.**). Marking what falls outside the pale of civilized speech is the work of the dictionary. The barbarism might also be construed as lying in the process of exclusion, in closing the gate on the language and lives of certain speakers of the language:

> 1611 BIBLE *I Cor.* xiv. II, I shall be vnto him that speaketh, a *Barbarian*, and he that speaketh shal be a Barbarian vnto me.

It is not the inevitable incompleteness of the dictionary that is at issue here. Murray and Burchfield both readily conceded the limitations of their accomplishment; the *OED* makes no pretense, with the odd exception as we have seen, to being the whole of the English language. While it is not particularly helpful to imagine the English language as a circumscribable mass, a single entity, of which the dictionary only captures a portion, it does seem fair, after considering how the book is defined by those who contributed the most at each editorial stage, to turn an eye to those who go all but uncited.

As the *OED* finds the core of the language in its enormous collection of citations, it represents a trade in words that has ultimately been driven by the play of market forces and curtailed by the exercise of state and clerical interests, censuring some and coaxing others to circumspection in their choice of what and how things were to be said.[1] The published record of the English language is further striated by such textually disruptive events as Henry VIII's dissolution of the monasteries and their magnificent libraries in the sixteenth century (Kerr, 1985); it suffers gaps by virtue of what Aarsleff identifies as a "bibliomania" that has kept more than a few rare books and manuscripts locked away in private collections (1983, p. 265).

However, there are far more systematic elements to what has been omitted from this civilizing document; they occur in its relative marginalization of certain areas of language activity, its more substantial sins of omission. The *OED* turned to literary heroes, the respectable press, and the reference trade as its primary sources of authority, but it also finds part of its power in the exclusion of texts and authors. Holding the line against the barbarian becomes its own source of authority. All told, the *OED*'s literary, prosaic, and omitted citations authorize a definition of the English language that was part of a nation's hegemonic brief in the last century, both abroad and at home. It is currently finding a rich afterlife in a slowly decolonizing world. My work with the citations in this dictionary has hardly been exhaustive, and yet in terms of specific historical periods of publishing activity, along with the slighting of the Romantics, as mentioned in chapter 6, I was struck by the considerable oversight shown toward (a) the highly influential Chancery court of the fifteenth century, which made a substantial contribution to the standardization of English; (b) the working-class press movement that blossomed during the first half of the nineteenth century; and (c) the entire body of women writers, who, in spite of whatever difficulties were placed in their way, did publish, only to find themselves further excluded across the centuries by, in this case, the minuscule degree of representation they receive in the selection of citations for the dictionary.[2]

Now that we have deliberated in some detail about those who have contributed most to the shaping of the *OED*, it seems appropriate to reflect on those who, even while they actively participated in the literate life of the language, failed to receive their due when it came to gathering citations for the dictionary. Their texts were readily available to the members of the Philological Society; their language spoke strongly to the power of public broadcast through official and unsponsored channels. But they were considered marginal figures, not fully a part of the writing profession, of the trade that was seen to give expression to the imaginative life of the nation. These lexicographic lacunas suggest one sense in which the *OED* may have got the language wrong in more serious ways than suggested by the common accusations of literary or journalistic biases. Not wrong in the sense of the *OED* recording what is not really a part of the English language, except perhaps in a few minor Shakespearean instances, but wrong in the editorial team's betrayal of its historical principles at points where it really would not have taken much extra effort, and only a little daring, to get it right. This is, of course, to read their work in light of current concerns with issues such as gender, disenfranchised classes, and power, but these issues were hardly absent from the period in which the dictionary was edited. This reading across time also has to it a certain degree of urgency, I have been arguing, as the principal reference work in the English language moves into the twenty-first century while continuing to reflect Victorian standards in scholarship. So it seems highly appropriate, as the electronic text stands ready for substantial historical revision, briefly to reflect on three areas of substantial omission in the *OED*.

I

The influential use of English by the clerks of the Chancery courts in the middle decades of the fifteenth century poses a different sort of challenge to the *OED*. A number of scholars have argued that these scribes and attorneys, numbering in the hundreds, played a crucial role in the initial development of standards for English as a written language (Fisher, 1977; Richardson, 1980; Christianson, 1989). The period surrounding the arrival of the printing press was bound to be a formative one for the language. When Caxton first set up his press in 1476, he chose Westminster "under the shadow of the government offices," historian John Fisher points out, "where Chancery English was by that time the normal language for all official communications" (1977, p. 899). Fisher is intent on attacking the romantic myth of the English language finding its way into print on the wings of poetry:

> Historians of the English language are agreed that the genesis of the standard language is not literary, even though our predilections as literary scholars lead us to study most closely and to take examples largely from 'literary' materials. The truth of the matter is that *written* literature (poems, plays, tales, sermons, treatises) bulked as small in the lives of most people in the fifteenth century as they do now. . . . The sort of writing most likely to carry a sense of national authority would be bureaucratic (licenses, records, etc.), legal (inheritance, transfer of property), or business (bills, agreements, instructions). (1977, p. 894)

The *OED*'s general exclusion of these clerks, as founders of the standard, lends weight to my hypothesis that admission to the dictionary, as a witness to the language, tends to fall on the company of writers and the publishing industry. Murray actually complains in his Romanes Lecture on the evolution of English lexicography that, unlike the French government, the British authorities failed to publish old documents "illustrating the history of the language, the literature or the science of England" (1970, p. 25). By coincidence, the *OED*'s first editor, Herbert Coleridge, began his short-lived career as a Chancery barrister (Bailey, 1988, p. 155). To its credit, the Philological Society appealed, if unsuccessfully, to the English treasury on two occasions for copies of Record Office publications, although these had been distributed to a good many libraries (Murray, 1970, p. 164). However, examples of Chancery English were not only buried in the archives, but by the latter half of the nineteenth century they had been published in a number of forms. Yet, as far as I have been able to calculate using the principal collections of the period, the Chancery courts contributed only 181 citations to the *OED*.[3] During this period encompassing the invention of movable type and the printing press, what counted as a published work was hardly well defined. It is enough to say that, relatively speaking, the work of the Chancery clerks circulated widely.

In arguing for the contribution of Chancery English to setting a standard, Malcolm Richardson (1980) gives special emphasis to the leadership shown by Henry V (1413–22) in using the vernacular for royal communications. Richardson tells the story of Henry's conversion to the vernacular on the road to his second invasion of France in 1417, after which point he began regularly to correspond and rule in his native language. He was not the first English king to recognize the value of the vernacular, as King Alfred, in the ninth century, had translated Latin works into English. But Henry went a step further and employed English in doing the business of the realm, with those engaged in trade happy to follow suit.[4] Yet after examining the evidence, Richardson concludes that the king's "motive for using the vernacular was undoubtedly to win support for the war" against France (1980, p. 740). The king had won support from Parliament for attacking France by suggesting that the French were set on destroying the English language. While Henry's invasion plans had little to do with spreading English to the continent, his affirmation of English had much to do with maintaining his "first kingdom," as Richardson puts it, as his sovereignty at home (p. 740). To look abroad, with an eye to securing the homeland, remains a reflective theme behind the empire of English that inspired Thomas Carlyle, Richard Trench, and other Victorians during the *OED*'s formative years. Ultimately, Richardson's thesis suggests the centrality of this courtly discourse community in shaping English literacy:

> Bolstered and sustained by the prestige and authority of any documents issued by the Chancery, by the needs for a standardized form of English among lawyers, government officials, legal scribes, and the eternally litigious English gentry, and by the increasing patriotic goodwill toward the vernacular, Chancery English slowly spread throughout England during the middle years of the fifteenth century to the point where it became the most commonly accepted written dialect, and in turn, the ancestor of the modern Standard English. (1980, p. 726)

Official uses of the language are bound to be influential on conventions of spelling and grammar, as well as providing a source of ready metaphors. Edward Philips, who published *The New World of English Words: Or a General Dictionary* in 1658, may stand alone among lexicographers in expressing a concern for clerical influences on the language. In the preface to a dictionary he largely borrowed from Blount's own heavily plagiarized *Glossographia*, Philips does propose that a history of the language should begin with attending to "ancient Records and Manuscripts," followed by "the Works of our ancient poets . . . as also some of more Modern Poets," which include Spenser, Sidney and others (cited in Jones, 1953, p. 276). It does seem as if clerks, taken up with the paperwork and legalities of the royal prerogative, did not fit the Victorian vision of the enterprising writers, translators, or editors who had shaped and given life to the English language. The Chancery clerks possessed a "sense of national authority" that was by no means regarded as a particular point of pride by those who rallied behind the making of the *New English Dictionary* during the nineteenth century. The larger question it raises is the degree to which the standard language has been and continues to be shaped by such institutional forces, and how much the choice of the publishing industry as the source-point of the language is a matter of constructing a particular image of the nation's community of discourse. There is more to these omissions than the fact that the *OED* does not yet do justice to Romantic poets and ancient attorneys. Nonetheless, these are specific historical failings that catch the dictionary short within its mandate of fairly representing the language's literary and historical origins.

II

During the first half of the nineteenth century, the industrial classes came into their own through a struggle that utilized, among other things, the development of a press dedicated to giving voice to the disenfranchised. The government was not long in responding to this display of literate desire by escalating its repressive stamp tax, which provoked, in turn, an unstamped press that led to a good number of pressmen and women, as well as street hawkers of the papers, appearing before the courts (Altick, 1957). Tory forces, especially, were not inclined to support educational efforts among the working classes. Some time later, a liberal James Murray came to attack these still-lingering fears, commending the Americans at one point for their concern with universal literacy: "They have no dread of 'over-educating the masses,' and making them 'unfit for their position'" (*TPS*, 1880–81, p. 146). Yet the *OED*, in building its history around close to a millennium's worth of English published expression, was to give only cursory treatment to the contemporary developments in working-class publishing activities. The dictionary did include a number of instances that can be taken as articulations of working-class interests and language. A pamphlet such as the *Poor Man's Plea Against the Extravagant Price of Corn* (1699), or a collection such as the *Black-letter Ballads and Broadsides* (1557–1597), filled in historical gaps in the dictionary's coverage of the language, while the contemporary *Mechanics Magazine* (1823–1871), which was written by and for artisans about their trades, offered the editors of the *OED* support for technical vocabulary. The dictionary also takes instances from earlier underground-press activity, such as the Puritan tracts by Martin Malprelate that had been printed in secret locations and surreptitiously distributed during 1588 and 1589. It also found a substantial place for William Cobbett, the nineteenth century's leading radical journalist, though he was somewhat middle class himself and equally successful at writing a popular guide to English grammar. In 1810 Cobbett did receive a sentence of two years in jail and a substantial fine for suggesting that flogging had no place in the military, in another reminder of the state's hand in the free market of words and ideas. His *Political Register*, in all of its indignant vituperation, was selling 40–50,000 copies an issue, compared to a far more polite *Blackwood's* that, as I noted earlier, did not exceed 10,000 copies (Altick, 1957, p. 392). Without suggesting that circulation figures should dictate citation level, it is still interesting to note that the *Register* is cited 154 times out of Cobbett's total of 607 citations; *Blackwood's* accounts for 5,772 citations in the second edition of the *OED*.

In fact, the missing chapter in the *OED*'s life of the language, represented by working-class newspapers of the early nineteenth century, becomes apparent only when one considers their substantial circulation. The figures suggest the degree to which they have a claim to representing a common (written) vocabulary for a good part of the nation that was intent on participating in the articulation of the nation. Among the Sunday papers for sale in 1830, Altick reports, "the radical papers outsold the conservative ones at a ratio of almost ten to one" (1957, p. 329). But their presence in the *OED* is decidedly skimpy: *The Poor Man's Guardian*, with a circulation in 1833 of 16,000, is cited seven times; *The Northern Star*, at 60,000 copies in 1838–39, is cited once; and *The Black Dwarf*, with 12,000 copies in 1819, is not cited at all.[5] Although the delegates of Oxford University Press, as well as some of the dictionary's reviewers, had objected to the citing of newspapers of any sort, Murray had won the battle for *The Times* and *Daily News*. Neither Murray nor the readers of the *OED* appear to have been ready to make these other, widely distributed papers part of the heroic literacy celebrated within the historical principles of the dictionary. Yet it was not just the journalistic genre that was at issue. The dictionary's far more careful representation of poetry was also not to be evenly distributed among practicing poets, paying considerably less attention to the writing poor, leaving out, for example, any citation of the seven poets modestly acclaimed by Robert Southey in his 1831 collection, *The Lives and Works of the Uneducated Poets* (1925).

Earlier in this book, I referred to Disraeli's theme of the two nations, rich and poor, that had begun to inhabit Great Britain in ways that were all too acceptable to the governing classes. During the period of the *OED*'s preparation, there was a certain trepidation among the governing classes of intercultural influences, as the lower classes were felt to be exerting an undue and degrading influence over the English language as indicative of unfortunate democratic tendencies. Late in the century, George Gissing portrays the perceived threat posed by this all-too-common language in his novel, *Born in Exile*, as Godwin Peak seeks to assert, "from the depths of his conviction," the extent of his natural nobility in spite of his lowly birth:

> "My own experience" pursued Godwin, "has been among the lower classes of London. I don't mean the very poorest. . . . But the people who earn enough for their needs, and whose spiritual guide is the Sunday newspaper. . . . And *these* are the people who really direct the democratic movement. They set the tone in politics; they are debasing art and literature; even in the homes of wealthy people begin to show the effects of their influence. One hears men and women of gentle birth using phrases which originate with shopboys; one sees them reading print which is addressed to the coarsest million. . . . When commercial interest is supreme, how can the tastes of the majority fail to lead and control?" (1985, pp. 269–270)

By 1892, when Gissing published *Born in Exile*, the earlier torrent of radical opinion from the working-class press had settled into a gentler mix of democratic and commercial interests—a market populism that was to make the literary interests of the majority seem to fall within the scope of the English language represented in the *OED*. As Gissing's Godwin despairingly notes, it is the commercial interests of the press that finally managed to grant the majority a voice that was widely heard, although the relation between a popular press and its readership is by no means a straightforward one. This contested arena of expression, cast here disparagingly between democracy and quality, does come to be represented in the *OED* through its choices of Victorian citations. The *OED*'s decidedly liberal tenor, making it a progressive force compared to many English dictionaries, has its limits, which fall short of fairly representing the literate tastes of the majority in more ways than one, as will become apparent in the final section of this chapter.

## III

Otto Jespersen's *Growth and Structure of the English Language* (1982), as one of the first works to draw heavily on the *OED* in its scholarship, opens with a preliminary sketch of the "chief peculiarities of the English language," allowing that no one characterization will do a language justice, before launching into just such a formula: "Nevertheless, there is one expression that continually comes to mind whenever I think of the English language and compare it to others: it seems positively and expressly *masculine*, it is the language of a grown-up man and has very little childish or feminine about it" (1982, p. 2, original emphasis). Unfortunately, this alarming and disheartening view, expressed in a text still common to undergraduate classes, is borne out by the *OED*. In investigating the sex-role stereotyping in the *OED* using the electronic resources at the Centre for the New OED at the University of Waterloo, Hannah Fournier and Delbert Russell uncovered a number of measures in the wording of definitions and citations that reflected the diminished regard paid to women in the language, noting that the wording of the definitions is decidedly less denigrating than the language cited (1992). They found instances of disparagement in the definitions of such terms as "strong-minded" and a consistent "social stereotyping of women in roles limited to appearance, and the domestic and affective spheres" (p. 19). I want to complement this work with an examination of the ways in which women were called upon to define the English language through the selection of citations. The expressly masculine citational authority of the *OED* makes a good case for how the selective traditions of canons and dictionaries, especially citational dictionaries, can exacerbate prejudices, giving these prejudices a greater veracity by further restricting access to what is already an uneven playing field. For his part, James Murray not only managed to reduce the misogyny reflected in the definitions, but applauded the admittance of women into universities leading to the formation of a school of English language and Literature at Oxford. In his history of lexicography, he credited the preparation of early seventeenth-century English dictionaries "to a consideration of the educational wants of women," although it was to grant women very little, as Robert Cawdrey's *Table Alphabetical* from that period declares itself "for the benefit and help of Ladies, Gentlewomen, or any other unskillful persons" (Murray, 1970, p. 31).

Assessing the masculine imbalance among cited authors has been greatly facilitated by the *OED*'s use of honorifics, such as Miss and Mrs., as well as Lady and Lord (see table 11.1 in the Appendix). As it turns out, the *OED*'s exclusive interest in published instances was stacked against both women and aristocrats. If women lacked the same opportunity as men to publish, a good number of the titled peerage were steered away from it, as it might indeed be thought to resemble a trade. I realize that it is somewhat perverse to link the historical situations of women and titled aristocracy, especially where they do not overlap. Yet in considering the historical economy of the writer in English society, there has long been a connection between women and aristocracy in supporting the arts. Matrimonial dutifulness and aristocratic patronage ultimately afforded a great deal of writing and publication by their respective benefactors. While my interest here is in the representation of gender, and having dealt with social class at another level, I do want to consider how this combined deterrence worked with Lady Mary Wortley Montagu. Montagu's contribution to the *OED* is principally through her letters, as one of the few vehicles for lively and sustained intellectual activity available to her. And she did not hesitate to put it to good use, engaging in epistolary discussions and debates with Pope and Swift among others. Her correspondence from abroad also took up other issues in an equally acerbic and not less consequential manner, as she wrote, for example, to Sarah Criswell in 1717 about successful inoculations against smallpox in Turkey: "I am patriot enough to take pains to bring this useful invention into fashion in England; and I should not fail to write to some of our doctors very particularly about it, if I knew any one of them that I thought had virtue enough to destroy such a considerable branch of their income for the good of mankind" (1909, p. 65). But when she decided to campaign publicly for smallpox inoculations after returning from her travels abroad, she had to work anonymously through the publication of her short-lived self-published journal, *The Nonsense of Common-Sense* (1737–38) and through the personal network of her letters:

> 1722 LADY M. W. MONTAGU *Lett., to C'tess Mar* (1887) I. 338 Accounts of the growth and spreading of the *inoculation* of the small-pox, which is become almost a general practice, attended with great success.

These widely admired letters tell a publishing tale about class, gender, commerce, and medicine, that is, about the unseemliness of publication for a titled woman about scientific topics. As Robert Halsband explains in his biography of Mary Montagu, when one of the letters she had sent from Constantinople fell into the hands of a printer, it was published "(without her authority), its title page calling her 'an English Lady, who was lately in Turkey, and who is no less distinguish'd by her wit than by her Quality'" (1956, p. 100). Although her friend, the early feminist

Mary Astell, encouraged her to publish her letters, the single pirated one from Turkey was to be the extent of it during her lifetime. When Montagu turned her travel correspondence into the semifictional manuscript "Embassy Letters," it was strictly for private circulation. On Montagu's death, her family took steps to prevent this degrading lapse into authordom, but the letters were stolen, appearing in 1763 as *Letters of the Right Honourable Lady M——y W——y M——e*. Halsband reports on their instant success; they were praised by Smollett, Voltaire, Johnson, and Gibbon for their wit and knowledge of Europe and Asia, and it was not long before fabricated Montagu letters began to appear. Her family burned other bits of her writing, seemingly to protect her name, and it was not until well into the nineteenth century that the family felt forced financially to sell the rights to what remained of her writing. The path into print was difficult in the best of circumstances for women, and the story could be told in a dozen different ways for those women whose work was to be a source of citations for the *OED*.

"Thus, towards the end of the eighteenth century," Virginia Woolf asserts, "a change came about which, if I were re-writing history, I should describe more fully and think of greater importance than the Crusades or the War of the Roses. The middle-class woman began to write" (1929, p. 112). The impact of this historical event on the *OED*'s positioning of women in relation to the making of the language is most clearly demonstrated in a list of the leading women cited in the second edition of the dictionary (see table 11.2 in the Appendix). The list includes those women who could be said to have earned a place in the canon of English literature, such as George Eliot, Browning, Burney, Austen, Stowe, Gaskell, and Brontë. And then there are those detective novelists who I imagine were favorites of Marghanita Laski, including Ngaio Marsh, Agatha Christie, and Dorothy Sayers. Recalling her substantial insertion of detective-novel prose into the *Supplement* and her role in founding a Charlotte Yonge Society, discussed earlier, it seems that Laski's relentless "carding" for the *OED* may well be responsible for a good part of what is still the remarkably slight citational space awarded to the writing of women in the dictionary. I might add that Laski certainly read far more widely than the detective novel, even as detective-novel writers wrote beyond that genre.

> **1941** D. L. SAYERS *Mind of Maker* iii. 33 We may say . . that *Einsteinian* physics has superseded Newtonian physics.

Harriet Martineau presents a special instance on the list, as a popular journalist and intellectual from the Victorian era who had a part in the operation of such journals as *The Westminster Review*. She was well covered by readers for the *OED*, with no less than eight of them, by Murray's

1884 list, claiming to cite from aspects of such work as the nine volumes of her *Illustrations of Political Economy*. The top women contributors to the *OED* also contain a coterie of highly productive and popular nineteenth-century novelists that includes Braddon, Yonge, Oliphant, and Whitney.

> 1879 MISS BRADDON *Vixen* III. 168 This . . must end in darkness, desolation, despair—everything dreadful beginning with *d*.

Briefly, Mary Braddon, author of more than seventy novels, was never to escape critical censure—including from Oliphant—for the liberal morality of her themes; Margaret Oliphant contributed to *Blackwood's* and *Cornhill* and also published more than one hundred novels, along with biographies, histories, and two partial autobiographies; and Adeline Whitney was an American author who wrote serialized books for young women. Among the others, Mary Russell Mitford, whose principal contribution to the *OED* is the five-volume *Our Village*, which consists of gentle sketches depicting the humor and humanity of village life. The women represented in this table played a vital part in the life of publishing and language, and yet their contribution, and that of women generally, to the record of the language reflected in the *OED* appears to be the dictionary's largest sin of omission. This exclusion has its roots in the general regard of the masculine hold over artistic creation, philosophical speculation, scientific inquiry, political theory, and so on, in a concept that reached something of a pinnacle during the last century (Gilbert and Gubar, 1979). But even in areas in which women came to dominate publishing activity, such as in the eighteenth-century novel, their work was to be overshadowed in literature courses and dictionary citations by a few male writers.

And if this general underrepresentation by citation were not enough of a lexicographical slight, there is a loss experienced in the very definitions concerning women, where the meaning of gender, from citation to sense, can be lost, as in this entry, in its entirety, for *journeywoman*:

> **journeywoman**. *rare*. [f. as prec.] A woman working at a trade for daily wages.
> 1732 FIELDING *Miser* I. ii, No journeywoman sempstress is half so much a slave as I am. 1843 C. Elizabeth *Wrongs Wom*. I. 99 The journeywomen . . . receive very poor wages.

It is not just to work for wages, as the definition has it, but, as the citations assert, to work for less than one might imagine is the case for a journeyman. Charlotte Elizabeth is the pen name for C. E. Tonna, who was an evangelical writer and editor, whose work contributed to the success of the 1844 Factory Bill that limited the working day for women to twelve hours.

One might also take this small set of citations drawn from among the literary lights who serve the first sense of *woman*, which reads in the *OED*, "an adult female human being. (The context may or may not have special reference to sex or to adult age: cf. man *sb*.1 4 a, c, d.)." Against this banality of definition, there remains an unsettling sense of reference, to dip into the citations from Congreve to Byron, that do something more than define *woman* with special reference to sex or adult age:

> **1697** CONGREVE *Mourn. Bride* III. ad fin., Heav'n has no Rage, like Love to Hatred turn'd, Nor Hell a Fury, like a Woman scorn'd. **1735** POPE *Ep. Lady* 216 Men, some to Bus'ness, some to Pleasure take; But every Woman is at heart a Rake. **1780** J. BROWN *Toleration* (1803) 81 No ecclesiastical power can reside in a heathen, a woman, or a child. **1804** WORDSW. '*She was a Phantom*' 27 A perfect Woman, nobly planned, To warn, to comfort, and command. **1818** BYRON *Juan* i. lxi, Her stature tall—I hate a dumpy woman.

This is again, as we saw with Shakespeare and the citing of *The Shrew*, the gap that can fall between citation and definition, as the editor of the dictionary comes between implied meaning and literal sense. I would hesitate to refer to this entry's citations (extending back to the year 893 and continuing to 1889) as simply a matter of misrepresentation. The question is rather one of what precisely is on display with these excerpts, what is exemplified or defined by this *use* of the word *woman*, and who is defined by whom—"*She was a Phantom.*"

Here may be the best lesson in reading the *OED*, not just in this entry's perfect record of jaundiced literary and theological viewpoints, but more importantly in the filtering process of what is, after all, the editor's choice of defining tributes to womankind. One is left to wonder about the eighteenth-century omission of Mary Astell, Fanny Burney, Hester Chapone, Catherine Macaulay, Mary Wortley Montagu, Hester Lynch Thrale, Charlotte Smith, Phyllis Weatley, and, by all means, Mary Wollstonecraft who pointedly asked that she "may be allowed to doubt whether woman were created for man" (1975, p. 174). Certainly the English language, as defined by the *OED*, appears to be. With this identification of woman, we can see how the dictionary lends its weight to creating a natural history of the English language, a natural history constituted by the inequity and exclusionary nature of the citations. Dictionaries "give the values they select stability and authority," in the words of lexicographer Sidney Landau, and in doing so, he optimistically states, they can "be a progressive influence . . . faithfully reflecting the values of their time" (1985, p. 269).

This progressive influence can only be felt, I would think, if the dictionary is read critically, in ways that reflect an interest in "furthering social change" (ibid.). The *OED* dates its citations as reflections of a language past, as it describes what the writing profession in large part has, for example, made of gender and race. But whether those citations reflect a sacred heritage, an authorized view of the language and the culture, depends in large part on how one approaches a work such as the dictionary. Does the meaning and use of the word *woman* have to stay this way because the word is so defined in the *OED*, as some might argue, or do they have to change, as others would hold, because, as the dictionary makes so apparent, the concept (and person) have indeed been defined this way for far too long?

It may seem incumbent upon me to demonstrate precisely how the dictionary would be different if these civil servants, working-class journalists, and women had been more fairly cited. Just how different would the vocabulary list and the meanings be? Would it be the same dictionary? While John Simpson, after reading an earlier draft of this chapter, has indicated that the plans for the historical revisions of the *OED* will include the areas indicated here, I want to make clear that what is at stake with these omissions is not simply the size of the vocabulary. Undoubtedly, only a relatively small number of additional words and senses will be located through a consultation of these additional sources. On the other hand, many citations from these previously overlooked works will be added to existing entries. My argument has been that the citations, which give the *OED* its distinctive character and scholarly claim, often carry a greater sense of the language than the definitions provided, both in who is authorized to define the language and in the nuances they bring to the accretion of meaning. The new mix of citations would suggest a slightly different take on the nature of the English language proposed by the dictionary. As it stands now, the *OED* possesses a somewhat more masculine and middle-class complexion than is warranted by published instances in the language, and a somewhat less bureaucratic reflection than is justified by current understandings of linguistic influence. The arguments in favor of a greater inclusiveness of sampling are divided between Murray's claim of a scientific pursuit of the language that privileges no one segment of linguistic activity, and the moral terms of a democracy of the English tongue that calls for an equality of enfranchisement and an extension of the community of discourse.

This is not simply a matter of the *OED* accurately reflecting a historical social structure that extends far beyond the making of dictionaries in English society. The dictionary is more than a mirror of the times—would that it had been that easy, Murray might have exclaimed—but is itself among the largest and most concrete of the social structures that encode the language. The Philological Society embarked on assembling a structure that set in place the who and the what of the English language. My primary purpose has been to identify something more of how the resulting dictionary has structured the language, while capturing a sense of how that structure has evolved up to this point. As a result of discussions such as this, the *OED* can continue to advance its original project of fairly representing the extent of activity in the English language. The current editors of the dictionary, John Simpson and Edmund Weiner, continue to welcome the suggestions of readers. They are also consulting with linguists and other scholars in pursuing the historical revision of the *OED* that lies ahead. The starting point for these revisions has been to look critically at how the editors and readers originally put the language together, with an eye to both re-reading important works, as Laski suggests, as well as returning to areas that did not receive serious consideration in the first instance. Instances of overlooked citations, especially of the earliest sort, have already begun to be assembled—some systematically, for example by Jürgen Schäfer (1989), and others found incidentally and submitted to the Press or published elsewhere. There has been, I should note, another form of response to the dictionary's sins of omission that reads against the grain of this work's own history, to adopt Benjamin's response to the barbarism of civilizing documents (1968, p. 257). It is perhaps best conveyed by citing the appropriate entry from *A Feminist Dictionary* (Kramarae and Treichler, 1985), one of a series of wordbooks that women have written as a means of reauthorizing their own participation in the language:

**dictionary**
A dictionary is a word-book which collects somebody's words into somebody's book. Whose words are collected, how they are collected, and who collects them all influence what kind of book a given dictionary turns out to be and, in turn, whose purpose it can best serve. Though thousands of dictionaries exist for many different purposes, men have edited or written virtually all of them; and the words they have collected have, in large part, been from the speech or writing of men. Women's invisibility as language producers is closely bound to the scholarly practices of dictionary-producers.[6]

## CHAPTER 12

# A Source of Authority

At a moment, therefore, when it is agreed that we
want a source of authority, and what seems
probable is that the right source is our best self,
it becomes of vast importance to see whether or
not the things around us are, in general, such as
help and elicit our best self, and if they are not,
to see why they are not, and the most promising
way of mending them.
(*Matthew Arnold*, Culture and Anarchy)

ENGLAND has a long history of calls for an academy to govern its language, but they have all come to naught in the face of what might be taken as the spirit of English liberty. It had been Philip Sidney's proud Elizabethan claim that "nay truly, [English] hath that praise that it wanteth not grammar," pointing to how it was free of Latinate rules and strictures (1970, p. 85). Still, a century later, Daniel Defoe decided that only if a rule-issuing academy were established, "I dare say the true Glory of our English stile wou'd appear" (1961, p. 59). Proposals for an English-language academy continued to appear, only to be summarily dismissed by those who reminded readers of how a rather unruly Anglo-Saxon had found its native eloquence through the literary arts while losing nothing of its energetic, copious, and seemingly self-regulating qualities. When, in the latter half of the nineteenth century, Matthew Arnold came to commend the French Academy for its salutary influence on, among other things, the quality of reference works in France, he allowed that the pride of English "energy and inventive genius" would not profit by the collective deliberations of such an academy (1906, pp. 35, 32).[1] This was not to deny, as he noted in *Culture and Anarchy*, that there was a widely felt desire in Victorian Britain for "a source of authority" in such cultural matters as the English language. If an academy was not to be enacted by royal decree among such a liberty-loving people, then this need had to be met in another symbolic form to which the English could turn for that otherwise missing authorization.

As Arnold wrote in the 1860s of the search for authority among the English, the Philological Society of London was already engaged in the formulation of the *New English Dictionary*. This dictionary might well be regarded as, in Arnold's terms, one of the "things around us . . . such as help and elicit our best self." Educated citizens can find in its pages the assurance that they are participating in no less than the language of Chaucer and Shakespeare. In its extensive literary citation, the *OED* realized Arnold's dream that such talented writers, as "spirits of an excellence almost ideal in certain lines," would be adopted as "spokesmen" for the human race (1900, p. 165). Through the pages of the *OED*, as much as in any single work in the language, literary genius does speak for humanity in its English-speaking guise; where genius is silent, lesser members of the writing profession are found to cover the gap. Coming out of a humanist tradition, with its interests in philological detail and historical accuracy, and an Enlightenment feeling for bringing a system to the knowledge of the world, with a Victorian ambition for scale, the Philological Society willingly took up the largest and most scholarly project in the language. It made Shakespeare, in his Carleyean standing as heroic and national Poet, the principal authorizer of the language in the dictionary. In this Shakespearean turn, the society was drawing on what Leo Bersani refers to as a "culture of redemption," which cultivated in writers and readers a belief "that the work of art has the authority to master the presumed raw material of experience in a manner that gives value to, perhaps even redeems, that material" (1990, p. 1).[2] Against whatever problems Shakespeare might pose for the scientific methods of the dictionary, there remained within nineteenth-century positivism this certain faith in art's insight into language and the world at large.

On one level, the *OED* was to garner its authority from two of Arnold's touchstones—literature and Oxford University—as each had come to symbolize a moral, aesthetic, and intellectual center for the nation. Of course, it should now be clear that poets, playwrights, and novelists form only one among a number of leading citational sources that extend to the less-celebrated members of the reference trade and periodical press. It should also be apparent that the great university was little involved in the original editing and had only begun to lend itself, somewhat reluctantly, to the scholarly claim of English language and literature during the production of the first edition. The Philological Society had been fortunate to find support from Oxford University Press for its lexicographical project in 1879, even if it was through the back door, as a hired editor/tradesman might be called to work. However, by the time the work on the *New English Dictionary* was completed, the university was only too happy to have it take on the Oxford name to match the university's seal on the spine—three crowns surrounding an open book that reads from Psalms, *Dominus illuminatio mea* (the Lord is my light).

What has come of this light that has grown from a glimmer in Richard

Trench's eye to the language's most authoritative dictionary? The principal issue for me is no longer, as it once was and I assume still is for Roy Harris (1988), that Murray and *OED* are major contributors to the false idea of an incontrovertible standard in the English language. This dictionary may well contribute to "the language myth" of a standard English, but one that is far more the work of, as Harris (1981) has argued, the grammar books and dictionaries of the classroom. Those works are backed, I would add, by a society of anxious teachers, parents, and others (myself included) who hold that "the doctrine of correctness," which Sterling Leonard (1962) identified as emerging in the eighteenth century, is now a necessary function of modern communication (Willinsky, 1988b). It now seems to me that such correctness is by far a secondary aspect of the *OED*. A close examination of this dictionary suggests that, as Trench had originally proposed in 1857, the *OED* is far more a record than a rule book—it is simply too vast in its historical coverage to play a strong prescriptive role. The Victorians had taken issue, first with Trench and then with Murray, on the project's failure to propose a standard of inclusion, or as one contemporary critic put it, "to throw down all barriers and rules, and to declare that every form of expression which may have been devised by the humour, the ignorance, of the affectation of any writer is at once to take the rank in the national vocabulary" (cited by Dowling, 1986, p. 97). The *OED* is not as open to "any writer" as all that, but it is inclined to record the exceptions and counter-instances to any given norm in particular aspects of usage. It may resemble, as at least one Victorian noted, the Crystal Palace exhibition of 1851, so oppressively full of exhibits that it inevitably seems incomplete (Dowling, 1986, p. 99). Yet within its midst are to be found a series of intersecting themes on the nature of language and authority that have influenced this work's definition of the language . While the *OED* does label some four hundred entries with "spurious," "error," or "misreading" and does on occasion use ¶ to designate "catachrestic and erroneous usage," the dictionary is surely given to a far larger project than establishing the myth or substance of a single standard for the English language.

The members of the Philological Society were far more intent on setting out the scope and claim of their language in what amounted to an expression of the nation's writing class and vital publishing trade. Through the record of the citations they gathered, they created a dictionary which above all invested a certain body of writers with the power to define the history and substance of the English language. By that proud act, they did far more than pronounce on a standard to establish the nature of the nation's cultural and linguistic enterprise. The repeatedly cited writers and works testify to the linguistic centers of authority in the language, just as those who were not called upon also have a way of testifying to what often goes unsaid in the life of this language. Through its authorizing citations, the *OED* represents the contribution of a class and trade that has profited by the word and especially the technology and commerce of print. I think it worthwhile to examine how this dictionary encodes the nation's faith in these language practices, as something more than setting a standard of usage. The dictionary's history of writing is about who will speak for a nation and in what terms, as this assembly came to be projected on the Victorian stage, in the first instance, and since then throughout the English-speaking world. The *OED* was originally a nineteenth-century monument to the mixture of positivism and aestheticism that Dale (1989) identifies as marking the scientific spirit of this earlier time. Now, moving toward the end of this century, it has shown signs of attuning itself, in defining the English language on a global scale, to an Anglo-American professionalism.

The passage I cited above from *Culture and Anarchy* (1896) ends with Matthew Arnold emphasizing "the vast importance" of finding "a most promising way of mending" those things that wanted "a source of authority." "Mending" may seem too strong a word to use for the work that currently faces the *OED*. Yet the original edifice, in its foundations, is well past the century mark. A mending of the text, by way of supplementing it, has been underway for some time, while the historical revision of existing entries has become, with the text now in its electronic state, one of the principal editorial projects of the years ahead. This includes correcting minor oversights and errors among the works originally covered and reading for citations in areas largely overlooked. This work has to be guided not simply by a sense that the editors failed to be comprehensive, failed to cover *"every word occurring in the literature of the language it professes to illustrate,"* as the original proposal emphasized (*TPS*, 1857, p. 2). I have tried to suggest how areas of omission were as often systematic as they were a matter of oversight due to the necessarily limited resources for scouring the literature of the language. Which is to say that efforts to mend this thing that elicits "our best self" also means redefining the nature of that self, of coming to grips with how that self has been defined through a skein of cited authors and works, and how to go about changing that definition within what will always remain a limited ability to monitor and represent the life of the language. A second dimension of particular challenge for this mending process is to extend the dictionary's coverage of world English in a manner that repositions the dictionary. The challenge is to recognize the imperial patterns in the *OED*'s construction of the language as it gradually moved out from London and has now begun to develop a basis for a postcolonial lexicography. The indications from Oxford's reading program are that the reading program is expanding its attention to voices from around the globe, if only in a slowly widening circle that is still very much centered on Anglo-American cultural concerns.[3]

The mending arises out of a critical reading of this dictionary's definition of the language. As the dictionary carries its own house on its back, its self-constructed family estate, it brings a particular focus to the cultural interests that have marked a certain class of English society since the last century. The *OED* has a great deal to tell us about the intertextuality that flows among different genres and the social construction of literate discourse communities. The issues are conceptual and material; they invoke ideas of a natural standard constructed out of the political economy of the publishing trade, with the mediating influences of church and state. The dictionary offers a complicated record of who has come to govern the words of others. It speaks to a particular history of national self-definition during a remarkable period in the expansion and collapse of the British empire and the development of a far more democratic state at home.

At the center of this process is the act of citation, which is fundamental to a literate culture's circle of reference. To *recite* the words of others, to use the anthropological parallel with oral cultures, is to be a vehicle for those who came before, to extend their line through this act. But in citing others for illustrative purposes, or as warrants for conclusions drawn, one turns their words to one's own use. In the case of this dictionary, citation manages to dramatically transform the status of a text as books that were once banned become the very points of authorization and propriety in the *OED*. Whatever troubling despair might infest a poet's work is transformed, in the context of a dictionary citation (or a classroom lesson, for that matter), into a moment of affirmation and participation, if only for those who find themselves successfully reflected within such devices. The alchemy that occurs through textual processes of citation and referentiality transforms the authority, adding to the potency of both the cited text and the one that cites it.

By way of two concluding measures of the citational structure of the *OED*, I offer a final graph (fig. 12.1) and table. The graph profiles the number of citations culled from each decade between the years 1200 and 1980 in the second edition of the dictionary, providing the figures for the total citations, earliest citations, and *hapax legomena*. It reveals a relatively consistent relationship among the three sorts of citations, giving some indication that the pattern of invention in the language has been consistent in terms of how many new coinages were identified in relation to how many were cited, with some decline in this relationship during this century. The great anomaly revealed by the graph—and one widely acknowledged by the editors of the dictionary—is the relative poverty of the dictionary's reading of the eighteenth century, a period that had origi-

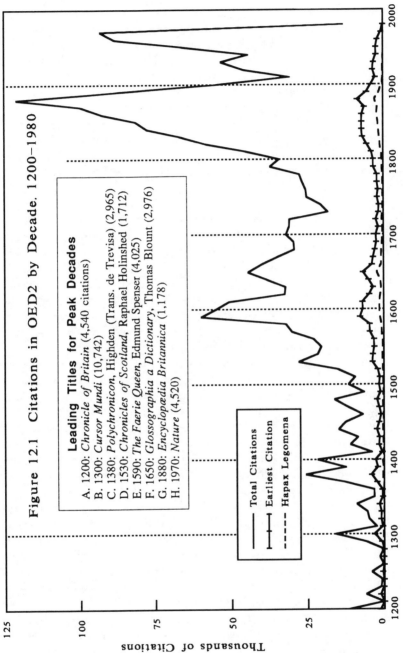

Figure 12.1  Citations in OED2 by Decade. 1200–1980

**Leading Titles for Peak Decades**
A. 1200: *Chronicle of Britain* (4,540 citations)
B. 1300: *Cursor Mundi* (10,742)
C. 1380: *Polychronicon,* Highden (Trans. de Trevisa) (2,965)
D. 1530: *Chronicles of Scotland,* Raphael Holinshed (1,712)
E. 1590: *The Faerie Queen,* Edmund Spenser (4,025)
F. 1650: *Glossographia a Dictionary,* Thomas Blount (2,976)
G. 1880: *Encyclopædia Britannica* (1,178)
H. 1970: *Nature* (4,520)

Total Citations
Earliest Citation
Hapax Legomena

Thousands of Citations

nally been assigned by Herbert Coleridge to American readers but was badly administered (*CWW*, p. 184). The high point for citations came in the years immediately after James Murray took over the editorship and issued his *Appeal to the English-Speaking and English-Reading Public to Read Books and Make Extracts for the Philological Society's New English Dictionary*. There was, it suggests, a great deal of contemporary citation gathering among the public drawn to the project, both for the original edition in the latter half of the nineteenth century and the *Supplement* in the 1960s and 1970s. The titles that made the largest contribution to the graph's various peaks, including the Golden Age of Chaucer and the Elizabethan period, reflect once more the mixture of literary and referential works, as well as indicating, in the final instance, the shift to periodical and professional sources.

In table 12.1 (see Appendix) I rank the authors and works that provided the greatest number of "earliest citations" in the second edition of the *OED*. This list reveals that, indeed, Chaucer coins more new words in English than any other author, although his most productive work in this "creative" regard was his translation of Boethius. He is followed by John Wyclif, the sermonizing translator of the sacred. The list goes on in this fashion, revealing a shared responsibility for earliest citations among poets, scholars, editors, lexicographers, translators, and the anonymous contributors to the periodical press. This is also the case with the figures for *hapax legomena* which, as entries based on a single citation, serve as another indicator of lexicographical status. Caxton, Shakespeare, Carlyle, and Coleridge are among those who received over one hundred of these minor lexicographic monuments scattered throughout the pages of the dictionary. They can be taken as part of the *OED*'s tribute to the literary merits of an English culture in which the truly artful writer moves beyond the normal reaches of the vocabulary, so far beyond that no one has reason to follow them. This dictionary credits their use of a word with an entry, if only to keep the door open to this national treasure for subsequent readers.

Yet, the single-citation entry was not reserved solely for literary texts. In fact, lexicographer Thomas Blount has the greatest number of *hapax legomena* and his colleague Nathan Bailey is not far behind. Against Murray's very principles, dictionary editors do remarkably well on these measures of inventiveness. In addition to lexicographers Blount and Bailey, there is a strong showing from Randle Cotgrave, John Florio, and Geoffrey the Grammarian. One explanation for the *OED*'s seemingly unhealthy dependence on early editors is that they were not given to discriminating against the spoken word in their lexicons, recording words that had yet to reach the page and, in a number of cases, were not going to otherwise. The result was that this small set of lexicographers provided the only published source of citation for more than one thousand words. It does suggest another accredited manner by which this other, spoken life of the language reached the *OED*. It also raises the possibility—and this was Murray's principal concern—that the *OED* is perpetuating a series of words whose life, according to the evidence assembled, appears to be restricted to dictionaries. Here, for example, is the thoroughly lexicographic if admittedly obscure entry for *agonism*:

> **agonism** ? *Obs.*
> 1. A combat, an athletic match.
> **1742** BAILEY, *Agonism*, a Combat or Trial of Skill. **1755** JOHNSON and **1775** ASH, *Agonism*, contention for a prize.
> 2. The prize of a contest.
> **1656** BLOUNT *Glossogr.*, *Agonism*, the reward or prize won by activities; the reward of victory.

Readers are left to wonder if *agonism*, a colorful enough term, has actually been used anywhere outside of the dictionary. The inclusion of *agonism* as indicative of the attention paid to past dictionaries can be compared to the exhaustive coverage of Shakespeare, from his nonsensical *pulsidge* to the five citations for *bold* from his plays. Such instances suggest the play of ultra- and extra-lexicographical interests. In some ways, these entries defy the project of the *OED*, suggesting not only an inevitable confounding of the aesthetic and scientific sensibilities of the Victorian era, but also a realistic limiting of the dictionary's ability to order the often unregulated inventiveness of the word. There is bound to be something less than absolute fidelity to the empirically grounded citations in deducing the history of meaning for each word and sense.

Yet however imperfect the process, the authority taken from these works by the dictionary is paid back to them as part of a canonization process that, in this case, establishes the contribution of a given piece of writing to the formation of the English language. Through this process of citation, the *OED* both establishes the canon and puts it to work in the service of a national culture and character. A comparison can be made with the use of citation in jurisprudence as an authorizing practice in which the decisions made in earlier cases become a precedent for guiding later ones. As legal scholars note, what is lost to sight in ruling by precedents is both the manner in which citations are selected as well as the complex process that guided the thinking in the original case, because it is cited as a clear-cut decision.[4] Yet through this process, the past is no longer a foreign country but a persistent source of contemporary meaning and authority. The cited precedents have come to constitute a warrant for ruling on such matters as guilt before the law and meaning in the dictionary. The citation constitutes a prima facie case.

**citation**

. . . .

3. The action of citing or quoting any words or written passage, quotation; in *Law*, a reference to decided cases or books of authority.
1651 BAXTER *Inf. Bapt.* 248 A vain citation of a passage out of my Book of Rest. . . . 1863 GEO. ELIOT *Romola* i. xii, Impudent falsities of citation.

From first to last citation in this entry, Richard Baxter and George Eliot stand behind the third sense of *citation*, and reciprocally the dictionary stands behind them, if somewhat less often in Eliot's case than might be expected. It is, of course, only after we know to what *citation* refers that the Baxter and Eliot quotations begin to make sense in their unsettling ways. As I tried to make clear with *The Shrew* citations, the definitive element of the abbreviated testimony is often the writer and/or work cited rather than the meaning of the citation. The elements of meaning arising from the excerpted text are suspended within a web of words that cannot be cited completely. This forms its own justification for the abbreviated citation that Murray defended as a matter of the distinctive character of the dictionary: "I fear . . . that we cannot dream of giving to the book this *literary* interest of being a readable collection of pithy sentences or elegant extracts, without abandoning altogether our distinctive character—that of actually showing . . . the history of each word" (*CWW*, p. 207). The history of the word's use is found in the dates given in the entry, with its meaning at any given point only suggested by the citation. In one sense, then, the authority falls to the one who cites, to "the action of citing," whatever aspersions are cast on that act by the Baxter and Eliot citations. The citation drags the weight of a work into a new genre, representing a complex and diffuse intertextuality that can level the differences between sacred and profane, literary and prosaic, acts of writing.

A second theme this book raises, after the micronuances of citation, is the technological future of meaning-making. That is, my computer-assisted Trenchean analysis—on some deficiencies (and strengths) in the *OED*—may seem to suggest a postdictionary era in which writers and readers act as their own lexicographers, electronically checking preselected databases to see how a certain word is being used or has been used within a defined set of publications. Speculations currently abound of the possibilities offered by new forms of "lexicomputing" (Dodd, 1989).[5] Darrell Raymond and Yvonne Warburton (1987), Waterloo computer scientist and Oxford lexicographer, have considered the ways in which the computer can also assist in a more efficient handling of citation and definition, verification and sorting, all of which show promise that the Press will be able to survey much more of the language to arrive at new entries. Given the capabilities of the new technologies, one can imagine, for example, an automated citation process that would monitor a series of periodicals through online services, bringing to the screen new candidates for the dictionary, with each one appearing only after it had been spotted at least, say, five times in assorted publications. The computer could provide a frequency count for the item, a sample of citations with chronological and geographical distribution, as well as a definition, part of speech, pronunciation, and etymology roughed in, ready for polishing and insertion into the giant database known as the *OED*. And just as Oxford University Press now subscribes to commercial database services, such as Nexis and World Reporter to keep its currency, so we might imagine a similar lexicographical service that makes the *OED* available online to individual computers on a subscription basis. That the computer means a different kind of dictionary and perhaps a different direction for the language may seem to overstate the matter. Still, we find Edmund Weiner, the *OED*'s co-editor for this new lexicographical age, turning to the Bible for an image to cover the changes that lie ahead—"'Fresh skins for new wine!' I shall take that as my text" (1989, p. 30).

We do not know yet what the limits are in these new electronic formats. The cyber-era appears to offer a search for meaning that need only stop short somewhere of a Borgean library of endless citation, in what amounts to the ultimate hypertext, linking each word to all of its uses in texts that span the English language and related root languages. The more pressing danger raised by electro-lex editorial practices is that the constant consultation of the current online periodicals tends to narrow the dictionary's "reading program" to the subscription list of society's most powerful readers. Fortunately, there are few signs at Oxford's English Dictionary Department that the reading program will be replaced by machines. It should not be forgotten that, as Marghanita Laski noted some years before, and she was in a position to know, public participation in recording the language means as much to the life of the readers as it does to the dictionary: "Those who have worked for the new *Supplement*, like those who worked for the original *OED*, have had so much delight from doing it that to computerize the reading would provide the clearest possible case of mechanization eroding the quality of life" (Laski, 1972, p. 1226).

There are, however, other electronically assisted changes going on at Oxford University Press that also suggest a shift in the body of the language that lexicographers monitor. The Press's English Language Teaching Department has become involved in the recent development of the British National Corpus, joining forces with Longman, Oxford University Computing Service, University of Lancaster, and the British Library and Chambers (Rundell and Stock, 1992). With financial support from the Department of Trade and Industry, the Corpus has a target of one hundred-million words representing a broad cross section of vocabulary and usage drawn from the daily life of the English language. It is inspired, in part, by a desire to make the common patterns of English more readily ascertainable and available for the growing industry in teaching English as a second language. In this aspect, it represents another element in the Press's postcolonial take on the language, as the Oxford dictionaries continue to respond to a world that is no longer the one that originally gave rise to the OED. Those responsible for this massive word-hoard are reaching well beyond traditional textual sources and taking samples from such helpful areas for learners of the language as telephone calls, pub-talk, and pop-radio announcing, with ten million words set aside for un-scripted speech. My understanding is that the British National Corpus will not supplant, but only supplement, the OED's reading program. It promises to expand the dictionary's coverage in new directions without compromising its desire to historically locate and authenticate its citational sources. It does not appear that the end of the dictionary has been dictated by the age of gigabyte textbases and auto-spellcheckers. As it stands, there are few signs that this lexical artifact of print technology is diminishing as a point of reference for standards of usage and sense in the language. It will continue to be transformed, as the computer incorporates the spelling and grammar functions of the dictionary into its own electro-formats.

A third theme of this book concerns the larger context of meaning and history in which the OED works. The Philological Society set out to assemble a history of the nation's language as a beacon to the moral, intellectual, and aesthetic state of the English people as they were intently given to civilizing the globe. The project for a new English dictionary, to be built on historical principles, was begun shortly after the Great Exhibition set before London the spoils of the British empire in the form of civilization's primitive beginnings. The project was buoyed by Richard Trench's moralizing etymologies that highlighted the divine progress and temptations of English society; it was supported by Max Müller's popular philological Aryanism. Language was "the great universal conscience of men," Trench declared, and the dictionary of the English language he inspired was to become the conscience of the English language. If Trench launched the mission of the dictionary heavenward, it soon found itself, in passing through the hands of editors Coleridge, Furnivall, and Murray, pursuing an evolutionary path through the archaeological record of the language that ultimately demonstrated, once more, the survival of the fittest (phrase and language). It was as if this new dictionary cut a path through the middle of the age's great debate, "as the Great Chain of Being evolved," as Zohreh Sullivan describes it, "into the ladder of Darwinian Evolution" (1989, p. 22). Not only are the evolutionary forces of nature posited here, but so is the unifying moment of language, literature, and lexicography that needs no outside body or academy to authorize it as it takes its imprint from the cultural project of Great Britain.

There has been a recent interest expressed in the relationship among print, poetry, and nation that throws some further light on the dictionary's mediation between language and state. Benedict Anderson's work on the origins of nationalism emphasizes that "the most important thing about language is its capacity for generating imagined communities, building in effect particular solidarities"; he has little doubt that "print-language is what invents nationalism" (1991, p. 133). Complementing this point is Richard Helgerson's contention that this inventive process began in earnest during Elizabethan times, as English was coming into its own as a print-language: "The culturally uprooted young men . . . began writing England in the last decades of the sixteenth century" (1992, p. 201). Similarly, John Lucas describes how more than a few of the English poets who lived between 1700 and 1900 "felt a special responsibility to identify nationhood in a manner that was new" (1990, p. 1). Both Helgerson and Lucas treat this poetic nation-making as a function of art, a function that integrated it into the making of the modern state. Long before football became a national sport, the poet served as a recreational hero, removed from the city, courts, factory, kitchen, that is, from the many halls of power and oppression. The poet could be a source of meaning and history—of national identity—in which to place one's faith in troubled times. The poet could guide a dictionary that assured a certain class of reader of its place within that history of accomplishment. Yet by the nineteenth century, this poetic nation-writing had accumulated a number of ironies—all the more so, as Lucas notes, in the context of poetry's contribution to the *OED*: "With the exception of Kipling, that odd, special case, poets typically made the voices of English people inaudible. They also made the England of city life invisible. . . . To be English was not to be English" (1990, p. 9).

Anderson sees the nineteenth-century "philological-lexicographic revolution" as given to investing these newly imagined communities with a meaningful tradition (p. 83). A good part of the achievement of the *OED* is in its systematic marshaling of English as the center of this nation's history and culture, in which, as Anderson delights in pointing out, the king of England did not always speak English. *The New English Dictionary* was undertaken at a time when the queen most certainly did speak it, and the governing classes, along with what Thomas Nairn calls the "new middle-class intellegentsia of nationalism" (1977, p. 340), were looking abroad to find the unspoken definition of themselves as the white, male, property-owning center of a British empire.[6]

The dictionary contributed to Rule Britannia by equipping the conquering language with a coherent history that ran back through the nation's best writers, with considerable support from its more prosaic authors, serving like the skilled shipbuilders behind Drake's daring voyages. It was not long before an educational version of this virtuous literary heritage was used to arm the "colonial spiritual policemen," as Ngugi wa Thiong'o has termed those who brought English education with a vengeance to the outreaches of the empire (1981, p. 34).[7] By 1847 the missionary Hope Waddell felt assured that with "the aid of missionaries and schools [English] may be made the common medium of communication, yea, the literary and learned language of all Negro tribes as the Roman language was to the modern nations of Europe while yet the modern European languages were in an infantine and unwritten state" (cited in Batsleer et al., 1985, p. 23). As readers assembled the citations for the dictionary, Great Britain and other European nations were parceling up the African subcontinent, extending, in effect, the aftermarket for European cultural artifacts. The OED was but one of many vehicles that formalized aspects of English culture in preparation for advancing the Anglicizing mission.[8] It served to justify, in some small part, England's particular burden of bringing order to an increasingly large part of the globe. The dictionary was a record of civilizing and artful influences on the English language that had already taken place over the centuries, creating a civilizing tongue that could now be used to elevate others, if only to a limited degree, elsewhere. As it turned out, the actual editing of the OED spanned the last great gasp of British imperialism. With the gradual demise of the empire throughout this century, however, the OED has continued to thrive as a cultural authority that serves the farthest reaches of the collapsed empire no less than at home.

This call to distant empires may seem to set too grand a stage for the humble labors of James Murray and his assistants who worked to assemble the dictionary in the Scriptorium. Yet Murray was no less aware of the providence of this imperial turn. He cast it in linguistic terms, pointing out with a nonplused ethnocentrism that for those possessing "the language of a civilized nation," the empire offered no less than "the subject matter of new *ideas*, and the theme of new discourse" (*TPS*, 1880, p. 132). The prevailing spirits of a muscular Christianity and Social Darwinism must have played a part in mobilizing the many remarkable readers at home and abroad who rallied to the cause of the English language with five million citation slips attesting to its unrelenting development as a civilizing force. Following Ngugi's lead, we must consider how during those imperial years "the weapon of language [was] added to that of the Bible and the sword in pursuit of what David Livingstone, in the case of nineteenth-century imperialism, called 'Christianity plus 5 percent'" (1990, p. 284). One result, Ngugi points out, was that "English was made to look as if it were the language spoken by God" (p. 286). In his own case of Kenya, he learned English through the "Oxford Readers for Africa" series: "Before I knew the names of any other towns in Kenya, I already knew about a town called Oxford" (p. 287). As we now begin to consider English as a world language, Ngugi insists that "we must avoid the destruction that English has wrought on other languages and cultures in its march to the position it now occupies in the world" (p. 291). He, for one, has moved from writing in English to Gikuyu, while calling for a greater recognition of the art of translation. The *OED*, on the other hand, has only begun to examine the considerable literature written in English from outside the former white colonies, as the empire artfully strikes back in the language of the colonizer.

1965 W. SOYINKA *Road* 17 The bishop sermonized his *head* off.

This expansion of the tongue has not always been a welcomed sound in the mother country. With the first signs of the crumbling of the empire and the shifting of power in the English-speaking world to the United States, the Society of Pure English was formed in 1915 with a mission to protect the language from "the obnoxious condition" of British colonials engaged in "habitual intercourse" with "other-speaking races"—"It would seem that no other language can ever have had its central force so dissipated" (cited by Dodd, 1986, p. 15). For such xenophobia, as with the spirit of imperialism that ran before it, the *OED* was no less a unifying monument to what was pure, to what had to be preserved. The Society of Pure English was obviously fighting a rear-guard action. With successive supplements to the *OED*, Oxford's record of the English language was destined to give increasing notice to the accents of other voices, especially within literary circles. As Hugh Kenner notes, "since Chaucer, the domain of English literature has been a country, England," while "early in the 20th century its domain commenced to be a language, English" (1983, p. 366). This shift in focus from country to language during this century, as Shaw, Joyce, Pound, and Eliot took the decided lead in shaping literary modernism, was not lost on the new generation of *OED* editors. This great dictionary, with the burnishing of the *Supplement,* was to survive the dissipation of the British Empire as a relatively untarnished protector of a language larger than its native land. Meanwhile, around the world, an education in English remains the last outpost of a colonial legacy that many once-colonized people are still trying to turn to their own advantage.

The challenge that lies head for this dictionary is as much ideological between art and politics as it is about finding the right technology for monitoring and carrying the definition of the language. In the range of its citations, the second edition of the *OED* moves from the golden age of Chaucer to the postmodernism of Thomas Pynchon, from the first recorded awakenings of an artfulness in the English language to an age that calls for an end to art's higher authority as part of that scientific spirit invoked by Murray:

> **1977** *N. Y. Rev. Bks.* 28 Apr. 30/3 A process that culminates, by a curious but inexorable logic, in the *postmodernist* demand for the abolition of art and its assimilation to 'reality'.

As the *OED* has begun to record such concepts as *postmodernism*, the category of "art" as a privileged set of artifacts, as a canon that defines the official culture of the society, is under a postmodernist indictment. This assault is now being felt on many university campuses in which the traditional reading lists, those great canon builders, are condemned for their Eurocentric, patriarchal stance. The postmodernist reading of the *OED* is also engaged in the dictionary's "assimilation to 'reality,'" complete within the citation's ironic "reality" of inverted commas. It seeks to establish how a dictionary comes authoritatively to construct a particular reality of language as the coherent and sustained project of English writing. The postmodernist demand, if you will, is that this insistent act of representing the truth of the language become the subject of inquiry as we seek to understand what this dictionary has made of the language in its development from Victorian through modern times. The investigations reported here should temper the categorical hold that art may have been assumed to have on the formation of language. The dictionary is the work of a diffuse set of authoritative and canonical authors who more often today write for *The Times* or the *Britannica* than for art's sake. But if the makeup of the canon has shifted, the *OED* is nonetheless a canonical work in its authorizing assembly of the principal sources, in its selective consultation, which, however far afield it ranges, still remains heavily concentrated along a London/New York axis.

"Within every society the production of discourse," Michel Foucault has written, "is at once controlled, selected, organized and redistributed according to a certain number of procedures, whose role it is to avert its powers and its dangers, to cope with chance events, to evade its ponderous, awesome materiality" (1972, p. 216). Foucault's own entry in the *OED* comes with his conception of *episteme*, a term the dictionary defines, complete with an untranslated citation from his *Les mots et les choses*, as "Foucault's term for the body of ideas which shape the perception of knowledge at a particular period." The *OED* is a particular realization of a governing episteme; it is the embodied artifact of perception-shaping ideas about language, carried forward from the Victorian era to sit all too comfortably on our bookshelves. This book has been about the awesome materiality of dictionary and citation in its powers and dangers as a body of ideas. It has sought to make apparent just how the *OED* testifies on occasion against the principle of a "fixed code" of meaning. Citations can and do blur denotative and connotative lines, opening the word to a host of meaningful associations even in the excerpt's truncated form. The *OED* does claim to be only describing the state of the language. Its use of the citation in the dictionary has a strange way of affirming Foucault's equally overstated claim that "the function of the author is to characterize the existence, circulation, and operation of certain discourses within a society" (1977, p. 124). In the context of the *OED*, the cited author does approach the role of functionary, as the dictionary itself runs in the background of certain powerful discourses in the society. To bring the workings of the dictionary to the fore, to explore the intricacies of its construction, is to expose the mechanisms behind a naturalized, controlled and selected, production of discourse. It is to open this great work to an Arnoldian mending process that, without walking away from its inextricable and inherent complicity in the organization of power, can press it to do better at representing our best self.

That prospect of improvement begins with the expansion of *our* self, extending this collective sensibility and thus the dictionary's inclusiveness; it means no less than finding a basis for representing the English of a decolonizing world in which the seventy million Indians using English on the Asian subcontinent outnumber the population of Great Britain, while citations from Indian publications make up less than one percent of the total gathered for the Oxford reading program between 1989 and 1992. The challenge is to rethink the nature of a language that need no longer be imagined as secured by its original white center, as it increasingly forms a network of communication across a richly colored global community. To what degree, we need to ask in examining the *OED*'s sources of authority, is the principal record of the English language tracking a linguistic phenomenon while preserving a cultural heritage? How does one work with and against this tradition of scholarship and prejudice within that impossible goal, the full definition of the language? It might well begin once more, as it did with the Philological Society, in the conception of a reading program. A good deal of thought and discussion still needs to go into what it might mean to cover developments in English on a global scale: what should be read, what demographics and publishing figures should be used, what are the markets and uses of the dictionary? From my discussions with the Press, it does seem apparent that, to take a simple point of entry, far more could be done in attending to the English language used in the seventeen countries in which the multinational Oxford University Press has offices.

However, my aim with this book has not simply been to suggest a realignment in the attention the dictionary's editors pay to various parts of the globe or to different genres in the language. I am not sure what percentage of poetry should be cited, although I appreciate why John Simpson, at one point, could not resist posing the question to me. Rather, this book has been about turning to the *OED* with a greater sense of interest in its accomplishments and limits, its inclusions and omissions, while it is also about how the authority of citation is constituted out of a necessarily selective reading and editorial program. Citations reflect both the times in which they are written and the times in which they are selected, just as they carry to the dictionary page the intentions of the author overlaid by those of the editor. The citation can spell out the sense and use of a given word; it can fall short of conveying much sense at all; it can be the site of many more layers of meaning than definitions can convey; and it can capture the very indeterminacy of sense. In all of this, the citation process actively undermines the very assuredness of definition. Certainly, many citations carry far more than the editors would dare to define about what it has meant and continues to mean, for example, to be a *woman* (and thus what it means to be a *man*) or a *black* (and thus what it means to be a *white*). At another level, to attend to the patterns of citation in this dictionary is to catch Oxford University Press filtering and sorting the language, to see, frankly, who gets to define whom and what within the citations, as the language becomes differentially authorized through this editorial process. The citation authorizes the use of a language that stretches worldwide. It seems incumbent upon a dictionary of scholarly and historical principles to make the pattern of its coverage— the favored sources, the national distributions—better known to its readers. If it goes without saying that the *OED* cannot cover all of the English language, the marketing and editorial staff of the dictionary not only need to resist the temptation of suggesting as much, they need to support a more accurate reading of what the dictionary does represent. Part of what might contribute to a postcolonial education for readers around the globe, I imagine, is learning how the Oxford dictionaries work on the world, how they authorize a complex perspective on what was and will be the English language.

The great tension between British interests in liberty and authority in the language are reflected in the editors' curtailing of the dictionary's prescriptive force, even as they continue to forge the language out of an alloy that currently favors the most powerful newspapers and magazines, leading reference works, and, somewhat farther down the list than in previous editions, celebrated literature. To spell out the principal influences on "the most authoritative and comprehensive dictionary of English in the world," as Oxford University Press rightfully describes it, is to gain some insight into the community and culture that has taken hold of the language in the past and for the years ahead. To consider the complex relationship between citation and the sense given is to appreciate the fluidity of meaning that marks a language we want to have defined and authorized. James Murray made a convincing case for the *OED* as the culminating moment in a history of English dictionaries. Today, it represents the best efforts of more than one era in capturing and enhancing a definition of language by which those who use the English language are asked to find their words and themselves. It seems more than a little worthwhile to attend to how, going into its third edition and a new millennium, it continues to take stock of the English language. The generations of editors behind this empire of words would be the first to claim that *The Oxford English Dictionary* is not meant to be the final or redemptive keeper of the word; it is only an extensive instance of what each of us does in attending to the passing meaning of the world.

# Appendix of Tables

**TABLE 1.1**
Summary Figures for Oxford English Dictionary Project, 1879–1989

| | OED1[a] | "Supplement"[b] | OEDS | NEWS | OED2 |
|---|---|---|---|---|---|
| Editor(s) | J. Murray et al. | C. Onions | R. Burchfield | J. Simpson | J. Simpson & E. Weiner |
| Volumes | 10, 12 | In OED1 | 4 | In OED2 | 20 |
| Publication | 1888–1928, 1933 | 1933 | 1972–86 | 1989 | 1989 |
| Editing | 1858–1927 | 1928–32 | 1957–85 | 1983–87 | 1985–88 |
| Period cited[c] | 888–1918 | 1880–1930 | 1750–1985 | 1965–88 | 888–1988 |
| Citations | 1,827,306 | 73,260 | 560,415 | 14,850 | 2,412,400 |
| Entries | 240,165 | 28,722 | 69,372 | 5,000 | 290,500 |
| Citations/ entry | 7.6 | 2.6 | 8.1 | 3.0 | 8.3 |
| Word forms | 414,825 | — | — | — | 616,500 |

[a] From the publication of the first fascicle in 1884 to the tenth and final volume in 1928, the dictionary was entitled *The New English Dictionary*; the Oxford title was introduced with the complete re-publication of the first edition in 1933.

[b] The citation and entry figures for the 1933 "Supplement," appended to the first complete edition of the *OED1*, are based on a sampling of the text; the "Supplement" entries were incorporated in the *OEDS*.

[c] The years indicate the general period, with exceptions typically found in each case.

*Abbreviations:*

OED1  *The Oxford English Dictionary*, 1st ed., 12 vols., edited by James A. H. Murray, Henry Bradley, W. A. Craigie, and C. T. Onions (Oxford: Oxford University Press, 1933).

OEDS  *A Supplement to the Oxford English Dictionary*, edited by Robert Burchfield (Oxford: Oxford University Press, 1972–86).

OED2  *The Oxford English Dictionary*, 2d ed., 20 vols., prepared by John Simpson and Edmund Weiner (1989).

NEWS  New English Word Series, directed by John Simpson for in-house use at Oxford University Press, 1984–88.

### TABLE 4.1
Top Five Authors by Citation in Johnson's *Dictionary* and in *OED1*

| Johnson's *Dictionary* (Vol. I)[a] | | |
|---|---|---|
| *Author* | *Citations* | *Leading Title, Publication Date (Citations)* |
| 1. William Shakespeare | 8,694 | *King Lear*, 1605 (584) |
| 2. John Dryden | 5,627 | *Virgil's Aeneid* (tr.), 1697 (568) |
| 3. John Milton | 2,733 | *Paradise Lost*, 1667 (1,661) |
| 4. Francis Bacon | 2,483 | *History Naturall and Experimentall*, 1638 (878) |
| 5. Joseph Addison | 2,439 | *The Spectator*, 1711–14 (789) |
| **Total** | 21,976 | or 39.3% of citations in Vol. I (55,932) |

| *OED1* | | |
|---|---|---|
| *Author* | *Citations*[b] | *Leading Title, Publication Date (Citations)* |
| 1. William Shakespeare | 32,868 | *Hamlet*, 1597 (1,580) |
| 2. Walter Scott | 15,877 | *The Heart of Midlothian*, 1818 (941) |
| 3. John Milton | 12,293 | *Paradise Lost*, 1667 (5,760) |
| 4. John Wyclif | 11,921 | Bible, 1382 (8,000) |
| 5. Geoffrey Chaucer | 11,696 | *Troilus and Criesyde*, 1374 (1,258)[c] |
| **Total** | 84,655 | or 4.6% of citations in *OED1* (1,827,306) |

[a] Compiled from Lewis Freed's *The Sources of Johnson's Dictionary* (1939) which includes figures for only the first of Johnson's two volumes; note that Johnson did not consistently list the title with citations.

[b] These figures benefit here and in table 6.2 from J. C. Gray's (1988) tracking of variations in authors' names in the dictionary; the figures do not reflect the *OED*'s use of *ibid.* or a dash for consecutive citations by a single author which, to take the most extreme instance, would add 165 citations to the figure for Shakespeare.

[c] The *OED1* uses the titles of the individual books that make up the well-cited *Canterbury Tales*.

## TABLE 6.1
Top Twenty Authors by Citation in *OED1*

| Author | Citations | Leading Title, Publication Date (Citations) |
| --- | --- | --- |
| 1. William Shakespeare | 32,868 | *Hamlet*, 1597 (1,580 citations) |
| 2. Walter Scott | 15,877 | *The Heart of Midlothian*, 1818 (941) |
| 3. John Milton | 12,293 | *Paradise Lost*, 1667 (5,760) |
| 4. John Wyclif | 11,921 | Bible (tr.), 1382, 1388 (8,000) |
| 5. Geoffrey Chaucer | 11,696 | *Troilus and Criseyde, c*1374 (1,258) |
| 6. William Caxton | 10,172 | *The Golden Legende* (tr.), 1483 (1,369) |
| 7. John Dryden | 8,987 | *Virgil's Georgics* (tr.), 1697 (2,023) |
| 8. Philemon Holland | 8,095 | *Pliny's Historie of the World* (tr.), 1601 (3,034) |
| 9. Charles Dickens | 7,490 | *Our Mutual Friend*, 1865 (808) |
| 10. Alfred Tennyson | 6,827 | *In Memoriam*, 1850 (688) |
| 11. John de Trevisa | 6,408 | *Bartholomeus De proprietatibus rerum* (tr.), 1398 (3,914) |
| 12. Thomas Carlyle | 6,370 | *The French Revolution*, 1837 (1,468) |
| 13. Edmund Spenser | 5,988 | *The Faerie Queene*, 1596 (4,025) |
| 14. Alexander Pope | 5,860 | *Homer's Odyssey* (tr.), 1726 (1,443) |
| 15. William Langland | 5,855 | *Piers Plowman*, 1362–93 (5,513) |
| 16. William Cowper | 5,843 | *The Task*, 1784 (1,753) |
| 17. Thomas Macaulay | 5,444 | *The History of England*, 1849 (4,375) |
| 18. Jehan Palsgrave | 5,402 | *Lesclarcissement de la langue françoyse*, 1530 (5,211) |
| 19. Samuel Johnson | 5,292 | *The Rambler*, 1750–52 (1,223) |
| 20. Miles Coverdale | 5,263 | Bible (tr.), 1535 |
| **Total** | 183,951 | or 10.1% of citations for *OED1* (1,827,306) |

*Note*: In this and subsequent tables, *author* includes translators but not editors; edited works are included in top twenty book tables.

## TABLE 6.2

Top Twenty Authors by Citation in Vol. I of Johnson's *Dictionary* (2 Vols., 1755)

| Author | Citations | Leading Title, Publication Date (Citations) |
|---|---|---|
| 1. William Shakespeare | 8,694 | *King Lear*, 1605 (584) |
| 2. John Dryden | 5,627 | *Virgil's Aeneid* (tr.), 1697 (568) |
| 3. John Milton | 2,733 | *Paradise Lost*, 1667 (1,661) |
| 4. Francis Bacon | 2,483 | *History Naturall and Experimentall*, 1638 (878) |
| 5. Joseph Addison | 2,439 | *The Spectator*, 1711–14 (789) |
| 6. Alexander Pope | 2,108 | *The Odyssey* (tr.), 1725 (335) |
| 7. Jonathan Swift | 1,761 | *Gulliver's Travels*, 1726 (47) |
| 8. John Locke | 1,674 | *Some Thoughts Concerning Education*, 1693 (60) |
| 9. Edmund Spenser | 1,546 | *The Fairie Queen*, 1590 (841) |
| 10. Richard Hooker | 1,216 | *Of the Lawes of Ecc. Politie*, 1594 (1,114) |
| 11. Robert South | 1,092 | *Sermons*, 1679–98 |
| 12. Sir Thomas Browne | 1,070 | *Vulgar Errors*, 1646 (884) |
| 13. John Arbuthnot | 1,029 | *The Nature of Aliments*, 1731 (310) |
| 14. Philip Sidney | 762 | *The Arcadia*, 1586 |
| 15. Matthew Prior | 706 | *Solomon on the Vanity of World*, 1718 (3) |
| 16. Sir Roger L'Estrange | 654 | *The Fables of Aesop and other . . . Mythologists*, 1692 (132) |
| 17. Robert Boyle | 592 | *The Experimental History of Colours*, 1663 (51) |
| 18. Thomas Wallace | 554 | *A Farrier's and Horseman's Dict.*, 1726 (554) |
| 19. Issac Watts | 509 | *Logick*, 1725 (193) |
| 20. Edward Clarendon | 482 | *The History of the Rebellion & Civil Wars*, a1647 (482) |
| **Total** | **37,731** | or 67.5% of citations in Vol. I (55,932) |

*Note*: Compiled from Lewis Freed's *The Sources of Johnson's Dictionary* (1939), which includes figures for only the first of Johnson's two volumes; note that Johnson did not consistently list the title with citations.

## TABLE 7.1
Top Twenty Books by Citation in *OED1*

| Title | Citations | Date | Author/Editor/Translator |
|---|---|---|---|
| 1. Bible | 20,160 | 1382–1894 | Various translations[a] |
| 2. *Cursor Mundi* | 12,747 | c1300–1400 | Anon. |
| 3. *Encyclopædia Britannica* | 6,134 | 1768–1926 | A. Bell et al. |
| 4. *Piers Plowman* | 5,855 | 1362, 1393 | William Langland |
| 5. *Paradise Lost* | 5,760 | 1667 | John Milton |
| 6. *Promptorium parvulorum* | 5,657 | 1499 | Geoffrey the Grammarian |
| 7. *A Dict. of French and English* | 5,344 | 1611 | Randle Cotgrave |
| 8. *Cyclopaedia of Eng. Lit.* | 5,147 | 1844 | William C. Chambers |
| 9. *Dictionarium Britannicum* | 4,960 | 1730, 1736 | Nathan Bailey |
| 10. *The Aeneid* | 4,913 | 1513 | Virgil (tr. Gavin Douglas: 3,469)[b] |
| 11. *The History of England* | 4,375 | 1849 | Thomas Macaulay |
| 12. *Polychronicon* | 4,204 | 1387 | Ranulf Higden (tr. John de Trevisa: 2,808) |
| 13. *The Faerie Queen* | 4,025 | 1596 | Edmund Spenser |
| 14. *De proprietatibus rerum* | 3,914 | 1398 | Bartholomeus Anglicus (tr. John de Trevisa) |
| 15. *Ancrene Riwle* | 3,864 | a1225 | Anon. |
| 16. *Confessio Amantis* | 3,819 | 1390 | John Gower |
| 17. *Pract. Dict. of Mechanics* | 3,813 | 1874, 1877 | Edward Knight |
| 18. *A System of Medicine* | 3,629 | 1896, 1899 | Thomas C. Allbut |
| 19. *Destruction of Troy* | 3,513 | c1400 | Guido de Colonna (tr. anonymous) |
| 20. *Glossographia . . . A Dict.* | 3,275 | 1656–74 | Thomas Blount |
| **Total** | 115,108 | or 6.3% of citations in *OED1* (1,827,306) | |

[a] The number of citations for the Bible, drawn in part from Tompa and Raymond (1989), is an approximation based on fourteen translations, with the leading contributions from John Wyclif (1382, 1384 editions: 8,000 citations), Authorized Version (1611: 4,800), Miles Coverdale (1535: 4,200), and William Tindale (1526: 2,000).

[b] The dates for translated works refer to their principal English publication.

**TABLE 7.2**

Top Twenty Periodicals by Citation in *OED1*

| Title | Citations | Dates |
|-------|-----------|-------|
| 1. *Phil. Trans. of the Royal Society* | 9,546 | 1665– |
| 2. *Daily News* | 8,832 | 1846– |
| 3. *London Gazette* | 6,614 | 1665– |
| 4. *Pall Mall Gazette* | 5,468 | 1885–1923 |
| 5. *Blackwood's Edinburgh Magazine* | 4,752 | 1817– |
| 6. *Westminster Gazette* | 4,646 | 1893–1927 |
| 7. *Spectator* | 4,585 | 1711–14, 1784–86, 1828– |
| 8. *Times* | 4,085 | 1788– |
| 9. *Athenæum* | 4,036 | 1828–1921 |
| 10. *Penny Cyclopaedia (S.D.U.K.)* | 3,748 | 1833–46 |
| 11. *Lex. of Medicine & Allied Sciences* | 2,668 | 1877–99 |
| 12. *Harper's New Monthly Magazine* | 2,603 | 1850– |
| 13. *Saturday Review* | 2,557 | 1855– |
| 14. *Rolls of Parliament* | 2,510 | 1278–1503 |
| 15. *Annual Register* | 2,507 | 1758– |
| 16. *Gentleman's Magazine* | 2,188 | 1731–1868 |
| 17. *Fraser's Magazine* | 2,185 | 1830–82 |
| 18. *Tatler* | 2,112 | 1701–11 |
| 19. *Nature* | 1,996 | 1869– |
| 20. *Sporting Magazine* | 1,906 | 1793–1870 |
| **Total** | 79,544 | or 4.4% of citations in *OED1* (1,827,306) |

**TABLE 9.1**

Top Twenty Authors by Citation in *OEDS*

| Author | Citations | Leading Title, Publication Date (Citations) |
|---|---|---|
| 1. George Bernard Shaw | 1,999 | *Collected Letters*, 1965 (316) |
| 2. Rudyard Kipling | 1,731 | *Limits and Renewals*, 1932 (102) |
| 3. James Joyce | 1,667 | *Ulysses*, 1922 (1,251) |
| 4. P. G. Wodehouse | 1,600 | *Laughing Gas*, 1936 (96) |
| 5. D. H. Lawrence | 1,528 | *Letters*, 1932 (157) |
| 6. Mark Twain | 1,513 | *The Adventures of Huckleberry Finn*, 1884 (147) |
| 7. Aldous Huxley | 1,362 | *Letters*, 1969 (482) |
| 8. William James | 1,004 | *The Principles of Psychology*, 1890 (258) |
| 9. Charles Dickens | 963 | *Letters*, 1880–82 (195) |
| 10. H. G. Wells | 910 | *Experiment in Autobiography*, 1934 (86) |
| 11. W. H. Auden | 754 | *The Age of Anxiety*, 1948 (65) |
| 12. Julian Huxley | 683 | *Essays in Popular Science*, 1926 (111) |
| 13. Charlotte M. Yonge | 676 | *The Pillars of the House*, 1873 (62) |
| 14. William Faulkner | 657 | *The Hamlet*, 1940 (98) |
| 15. Arthur Koestler | 603 | *Promise and Fulfillment: Palestine, 1917–1949*, 1949 (101) |
| 16. Graham Greene | 545 | *Brighton Rock*, 1938 (87) |
| 17. T. S. Eliot | 539 | *The Rock*, 1934 (52) |
| 18. Ezra Pound | 533 | *Selected Letters, 1907–1941*, 1971 (92) |
| 19. J. B. Priestly | 532 | *Angel Pavement*, 1930 (76) |
| 20. G. M. Hopkins | 519 | *Poems*, 1918, 1948, 1967 (200) |
| **Total** | 20,318 | or 3.6% of citations in *OEDS* (560,415) |

**TABLE 9.2**
Top Twenty Books by Citation in *OEDS*

| Title | Citations | Dates | Author/Editor |
|---|---|---|---|
| 1. *Encyclopædia Britannica* | 5,461 | 1768– | Andrew Bell et al. |
| 2. *Ulysses* | 1,302 | 1922 | James Joyce |
| 3. *Webster's Dictionary* | 1,138 | 1909–61 | W. T. Harris et al. |
| 4. *The Century Dictionary* | 818 | 1989, 1991 | William Dwight Whitney |
| 5. *A Dictionary of Music* | 800 | 1890, 1993 | Sir George Grove |
| 6. *A Companion to Medical Studies* | 735 | 1968, 1974 | Reginald Passmore & James S. Robinson |
| 7. *Chambers's Encyclopædia* | 609 | 1860– | Andrew Findlater et al. |
| 8. *The American Thesaurus of Slang* | 600 | 1942, 1954 | Lester Berry & Melvin Van Den Bark |
| 9. *Chambers's Technical Dictionary* | 589 | 1940– | C. F. Tweney & L. Hughes |
| 10. *McGraw-Hill Encycl. Sci. & Tech.* | 547 | 1960, 1966 | Sybil P. Parker |
| 11. *The Illus. Medical Dictionary* | 516 | 1901–18 | W. A. Newman Dorland |
| 12. *Letters* | 482 | 1969 | Aldous Huxley |
| 13. *The Practical Dict. of Mechanics* | 379 | 1874, 1877 | Edward Knight |
| 14. *A Dictionary of Slang* | 342 | 1937 | Eric Partidge |
| 15. *Collected Letters* | 316 | 1965 | George Bernard Shaw |
| 16. *Technique of the Sound Studio* | 316 | 1962 | Alex Nisbett |
| 17. *Dictionary of Occupational Terms* | 290 | 1921, 1927 | United Kingdom Ministry of Labour |
| 18. *Lang. & Lore of Schoolchildren* | 279 | 1959 | Iona and Peter Opie |
| 19. *The Principles of Psychology* | 258 | 1890 | William James |
| 20. *A Pop. Dict. of Australian Slang* | 255 | 1941 | Sidney Baker |

**Total** 16,032 or 2.9% of citations in *OEDS* (560,415)

**TABLE 9.3**

Reference Works by Citation in *OED1* and *OEDS*

| | OED1 | | | OEDS | | |
|---|---|---|---|---|---|---|
| | Titles[a] | Citations | % of Total[b] | Titles | Citations | % of Total[c] |
| 1. Dictionaries | 831 | 35,094 | 1.9 | 1,019 | 13,340 | 2.4 |
| 2. Encyclopedias | 282 | 24,363 | 1.3 | 413 | 10,331 | 1.8 |
| 3. Glossaries | 467 | 14,807 | 0.8 | 359 | 2,297 | 0.4 |
| **Total** | 1,580 | 74,264 | 4.0 | 1,791 | 25,968 | 4.6 |

[a] Figures are for titles that include some variation of "dict," "cyclo," and "gloss" (with the exclusion of spurious instances).
[b] Total citations for *OED1* = 1,827,306.
[c] Total citations for *OEDS* = 560,415.

**TABLE 9.4**

Top Twenty Periodicals by Citation in *OEDS*

| Title | Citations | Dates | Country |
|---|---|---|---|
| 1. *Times* | 14,832 | 1788– | U.K. |
| 2. *Nature* | 7,495 | 1869– | U.K. |
| 3. *Listener* | 7,276 | 1929– | U.K. |
| 4. *Daily Telegraph* | 4,888 | 1855– | U.K. |
| 5. *Manchester Guardian* | 4,303 | 1821– | U.K. |
| 6. *Times Literary Supplement* | 3,467 | 1902– | U.K. |
| 7. *Westminster Gazette* | 3,383 | 1893–1927 | U.K. |
| 8. *Scientific American* | 2,967 | 1845– | U.S.A. |
| 9. *Economist* | 2,920 | 1843– | U.K. |
| 10. *Daily Chronicle* | 2,570 | 1872– | U.K. |
| 11. *Observer* | 2,511 | 1792– | U.K. |
| 12. *American Speech* | 2,470 | 1925– | U.S.A. |
| 13. *Lancet* | 2,282 | 1828– | U.K. |
| 14. *New Yorker* | 2,267 | 1925– | U.S.A. |
| 15. *New Scientist* | 2,205 | 1956– | U.K. |
| 16. *Punch* | 2,195 | 1840– | U.K. |
| 17. *Time* | 2,040 | 1923– | U.S.A. |
| 18. *Sun* (Baltimore) | 1,765 | 1837– | U.S.A. |
| 19. *Discovery* | 1,741 | 1920–66 | U.K. |
| 20. *New Statesman* | 1,494 | 1913– | U.K. |
| **Total** | 75,071 | or 13.4% of citations in *OED1* (560,415) | |

## TABLE 10.1
Top Twenty-Two Authors by Citation for 5,000 NEWS Items Added to *OED2*

| Author | Citations | Leading Title, Publication Date |
|---|---|---|
| 1. George Bernard Shaw | 37 | *On Rocks*, 1934 |
| 2. James Joyce | 26 | *Ulysses*, 1922 |
| 3. William Faulkner | 22 | *Light in August*, 1932; *Requiem for a Nun*, 1951; *Fable*, 1954 |
| 4. Susan Townsend | 19 | *The Growing Pains of Adrian Mole*, 1982 |
| 5. Eugene O'Neill | 17 | *The Iceman Cometh*, 1946 |
| 6. Olle Dopping | 15 | *Computers and Data Processing*, 1970 |
| 7. Joseph Wambaugh | 15 | *The Black Marble*, 1978 |
| 8. C. S. French | 14 | *Computer Science*, 1984 |
| 9. Jonathan Hilton | 14 | *Choosing and Using Your Computer*, 1985 |
| 10. Mrs. Lyndon Johnson | 14 | *A White House Diary*, 1970 |
| 11. Ann Barr & Peter York | 13 | *The Official Sloane Ranger Handbook*, 1982 |
| 12. D. H. Lawrence | 13 | *Reflections on the Death of a Porcupine*, 1925 |
| 13. Cyra McFadden | 13 | *The Serial: A Year in the Life of Marin County*, 1977 |
| 14. Michael C. Gerald | 12 | *Nursing Pharmocology and Therapeutics*, 1981 |
| 15. H. L. Mencken | 12 | *The American Language*, 1945–48 |
| 16. Kate Millett | 12 | *Flying*, 1974 |
| 17. Martin Amis | 11 | *Rachel Papers*, 1973 |
| 18. Saul Bellow | 11 | *The Dean's December*, 1982 |
| 19. Aldous Huxley | 11 | *Ends and Means*, 1937 |
| 20. Alison Lurie | 11 | *War between the Tates*, 1974 |
| 21. Scott Fitzgerald | 11 | *The Great Gatsby*, 1925 |
| 22. Gore Vidal | 11 | *Kalki*, 1978 |

**Total** 334 or 2.3% of citations in NEWS items (14,850)

**TABLE 10.2**

Top Twenty Periodicals by Citation for 5,000 NEWS Items
Added to OED2

| Title | Citations | Dates | Country |
|---|---|---|---|
| 1. Times | 616 | 1788– | U.K. |
| 2. Daily Telegraph | 357 | 1855– | U.K. |
| 3. New York Times | 310 | 1857– | U.S.A. |
| 4. New Yorker | 283 | 1925– | U.S.A. |
| 5. Listener | 264 | 1929– | U.K. |
| 6. Economist | 246 | 1843– | U.K. |
| 7. Nature | 242 | 1869– | U.K. |
| 8. New Scientist | 231 | 1956– | U.K. |
| 9. Washington Post | 222 | 1877– | U.S.A. |
| 10. Scientific American | 183 | 1845– | U.S.A. |
| 11. Time | 178 | 1923– | U.S.A. |
| 12. Observer | 146 | 1892– | U.K. |
| 13. Financial Times | 140 | 1888– | U.K. |
| 14. Guardian | 128 | 1821– | U.K. |
| 15. Commentary | 121 | 1945– | U.S.A. |
| 16. Sunday Times | 121 | 1822– | U.K. |
| 17. Publishers' Weekly | 111 | 1873– | U.S.A. |
| 18. American Speech | 97 | 1925– | U.S.A. |
| 19. Globe and Mail | 81 | 1844– | CAN. |
| 20. Times Literary Supplement | 71 | 1902– | U.K. |

Total 4,148 or 27.9% of citations
in NEWS items (14,850)

**TABLE 10.3**

Comparison of Leading British and American Newspapers by Citation

| | | OED1 | | | OEDS | | NEWS | |
|---|---|---|---|---|---|---|---|---|
| | Date | Citations | % of Total[a] | 1788–1927[b] | Citations | % of Total[c] | Citations | % of Total[d] |
| Times | 1788– | 4,085 | 0.2 | 2.0 | 14,832 | 2.6 | 616 | 4.1 |
| Daily Telegraph | 1855– | 1,577 | 0.1 | 0.8 | 4,888 | 0.9 | 357 | 2.4 |
| New York Times | 1857– | 9 | 0.0 | 0.0 | 1,352 | 0.2 | 310 | 2.1 |
| Washington Post | 1877– | – | – | – | 482 | 0.1 | 222 | 1.5 |
| | Total | 5,671 | 0.3 | 2.8 | 21,554 | 3.8 | 1,505 | 10.1 |

[a] Total citations for OED1 is 1,827,306.

[b] Percentage of 779,976 citations included in the dictionary from the founding of *The Times* in 1788 to the completion of the OED1 in 1927 (calculated from OED2).

[c] Total citations for OEDS is 560,415.

[d] Total citations for New English Words Series added to 2d ed. is 14,850.

### TABLE 11.1
Top Six Honorifics among Authors by Citation in *OED1*

| Title | Citations | Top Author (Citations), Leading Title, Date |
|---|---|---|
| 1. Sir | 17,400 | Thomas Browne (3,851), *Pseudodoxia Epidemica* (Vulgar Errors), 1646 |
| 2. Mrs | 14,942 | Elizabeth Barrett Browning (1,439), *Aurora Leigh*, 1856 |
| 3. Bishop | 7,403 | Joseph Hall (3,340), *Satan's Fiery Darts Quenched*, 1647 |
| 4. Miss | 7,400 | Mary E. Braddon (1,467), *Mount Royal*, 1882 |
| 5. Lord | 6,891 | John Bouchier Berners (3,331), *Froissart's Cronycles of Englande . . .*, 1812 |
| 6. Lady | 2,796 | Mary Wortley Montagu (812), *Letters*, 1763–1893 |
| Total | 56,832 | or 3.1% of citations in *OED1* (1,827,306) |

### TABLE 11.2
Top Twenty Women Authors by Citation in *OED2*

| Author | Citations | Leading Title, Publication Date (Citations) |
|---|---|---|
| 1. George Eliot | 3,310 | *Daniel Deronda*, 1876 (489) |
| 2. Harriet Martineau | 1,604 | *Society in America*, 1837 (211) |
| 3. Mrs Elizabeth Barrett Browning | 1,493 | *Aurora Leigh*, 1856 (309) |
| 4. Miss Mary E. Braddon | 1,467 | *Mount Royal*, 1882 (190) |
| 5. Miss Charlotte Mary Yonge | 1,349 | *The Pillars of the House*, 1872 (62) |
| 6. Miss Frances Burney | 1,252 | *Cecila*, 1782 (399) |
| 7. Jane Austen | 1,091 | *Emma*, 1816 (212) |
| 8. Miss Mary Russell Mitford | 1,090 | *Our Village*, 1824–32 (781) |
| 9. Mrs Harriet Stowe | 884 | *Uncle Tom's Cabin*, 1852 (569) |
| 10. Mrs Elizabeth Gaskell | 826 | *Letters*, 1966 (103) |
| 11. Lady Mary Wortley Montagu | 812 | *Letters*, 1763–1893 (445) |
| 12. Charlotte Brontë | 698 | *Jane Eyre*, 1847 (214) |
| 13. Mrs Jane Carlyle | 689 | *Letters*, 1883–89 (640) |
| 14. Ngaio Edith Marsh | 478 | *Artists in Crime*, 1938 (37) |
| 15. Mrs Margaret O. Oliphant | 454 | *The Makers of Florence*, 1876 (144) |
| 16. Agatha Christie | 449 | *An Autobiography*, 1977 (23) |
| 17. Miss Anne Pratt | 448 | *The Flowering Plants & Ferns of Gt. Britain*, 1865 (360) |
| 18. Dorothy Sayers | 434 | *Murder Must Advertise*, 1933 (74) |
| 19. Mrs Adeline Whitney | 433 | *The Gayworthys*, 1865 (101) |
| 20. Mrs Mary Delany | 415 | *Autobiography & Correspondence*, 1779–88 (146) |
| Total | 19,676 | or 0.8% of citations in *OED2* (2,412,400) |

*Note:* Honorifics are as per *OED2*.

**TABLE 12.1**

Top Twenty Sources for Earliest Citations in *OED2*
with *Hapax Legomena* and Total Citations

| Author | E.C. | H.L. | Total | Leading E.C. Title or Author/Editor, Date |
|---|---|---|---|---|
| 1. Geoffrey Chaucer | 2,012 | 132 | 11,906 | *Boethius De consolatione philosophiae* (tr.), *c*1374 |
| 2. John Wyclif | 1,986 | 149 | 11,972 | Bible (tr.), 1382, 1388 |
| 3. William Shakespeare | 1,969 | 284 | 33,205 | *Loves Labor's Lost*, 1588 |
| 4. *Cursor Mundi* | 1,926 | 142 | 12,772 | Anon., *c*1300 |
| 5. *Trans. Royal Society* | 1,543 | 237 | 9,943 | 1665– |
| 6. Thomas Blount | 1,450 | 388 | 3,728 | *Glossographia . . . A Dictionary*, 1656–74 |
| 7. Randle Cotgrave | 1,436 | 198 | 5,530 | *Dictionarie of the French & English Tongues*, 1611 |
| 8. William Caxton | 1,396 | 328 | 10,320 | *The Golden Legende* (tr.), 1483 |
| 9. John de Trevisa | 1,315 | 123 | 6,750 | *Bartholomeus De proprietatibus rerum* (tr.), 1398 |
| 10. Nathan Bailey | 1,174 | 343 | 4,994 | *Dictionarium Britannicum*, 1730, 1736 |
| 11. John Florio | 1,149 | 173 | 3,517 | *Dictionarie in Italian & English*, 1598 |
| 12. Geoffrey the Grammarian | 1,193 | 181 | 5,645 | *Promptorium parvulorum*, *c*1440, *c*1460 |
| 13. Philemon Holland | 1,095 | 170 | 8,392 | *Pliny's Historie of the World* (tr.), 1601 |
| 14. *Acrene Riwle* | 913 | 81 | 3,843 | Anon., *a*1225 |
| 15. *Encyclopædia Britannica* | 889 | 169 | 11,746 | Andrew Bell et al., 1768– |
| 16. Ælfred | 883 | 2 | 2,966 | *Boethius De consolatione philosophiae* (tr.), *c*888 |
| 17. Robert Brunne | 849 | 77 | 4,470 | *The Story of England*, *c*1330 |
| 18. Sir Thomas Browne | 832 | 146 | 3,941 | *Pseudodoxia Epidemica*, 1646 |
| 19. Ælfric | 832 | 5 | 3,461 | *Homilies*, *c*1000 |
| 20. *Blackwood's Magazine* | 793 | 230 | 5,772 | 1817– |
| Totals | 25,635 | 3,558 | 164,873 | |
| Percent of N | 11.2%[a] | 8.1%[b] | 6.8%[c] | |

[a] Total for E.C., N = 230,767 citations.
[b] Total for H.L., N = 41,941 citations.
[c] Total for *OED2*, N = 2,412,400 citations.

# Notes

## Chapter 1
## Introduction

1. This claim is taken from the promotional brochure, *Announcing the Second Edition of the Most Authoritative and Comprehensive Dictionary of English in the World* (Oxford: Oxford University Press, 1989, 12 pp.), which cites a number of similar accolades from the press, to which I would add this line from the *Time* magazine review of the second edition: "Since its completion in 1928, exactly 71 years after it was proposed at a meeting of the Philological Society in London, the OED has stood as the ultimate authority on the tongue of Shakespeare and the King James Bible, not to mention the language of tradespeople and the slang of the streets" (Gray, 1989, p. 64).

2. Burchfield's first complaint is a common theme with editors of the *OED*, as Murray, too, felt that his work had been academically slighted. Certainly linguists have tended to favor oral language as the object of study, and yet the *OED* has formed the center of famous works by language scholars Otto Jespersen (1982) and Owen Barfield (1926), as well as Harris's (1988) treatment of the dictionary and James Murray. Oxford's own research (Benbow et al., 1990) shows that use of the *OED* is heavier among literary scholars than linguists. The distance maintained between commercial and academic ventures seems to have been reduced in recent years, as certainly has been the case with the *Supplement* when compared to the original work on the *OED*.

3. *Announcing the Second Edition of the Most Authoritative and Comprehensive Dictionary of English in the World.* See note 1.

4. The total sales figure is from John Simpson, personal correspondence, June 27, 1986. Israel Shenker reports that in 1987 the top three nonfiction hardcover bestsellers in Britain were the *Pocket Oxford Dictionary*, *Little Oxford Dictionary*, and *Concise Oxford Dictionary*, while the *Advanced Learner's Dictionary* has sold fourteen million copies since 1948 (1989, p. 95). He points out that in 1988, Oxford University Press was able to turn over 1.3 million pounds to the university out of a profit margin of 11 million pounds (p. 86).

## Chapter 2
## At Trench's Suggestion, 1858–1878

1. In *English Past and Present*, to take another example from his history work, Trench holds "that great things are in store for the one language of Europe" which "serves as a connecting link between the North and South" (cited in Dowling, 1986, p. 44). Trench had met with Coleridge and was a great admirer of the man who was largely responsible for kindling an English enthusiasm for German philology and who shared his regard that words are moral acts. Trench felt he was part of Coleridge's intellectual *clerisy* (a "permanent, nationalized,

learned order") that would guide the nation forward, finding its *lingua communis* in the written language and in English literature, in particular, a belief that Linda Dowling has identified as the origins of "the Victorian vision of English as a world language, the conviction, in an age of empire and imperial ambition, that the tongue of Shakespeare and Milton was destined to carry the values of an advanced English civilization to the remote corners of the globe" (1986, p. xiv).

2. The widespread use of Trench's *On the Study of Words*, which went through fourteen editions in its first two decades, can be ascertained from a look at its twenty-second edition, from 1892, in which Theodore Hunt added sixteen pages of questions to the work, turning it into something of a textbook for students of the language: "Show that words contain a witness for moral truth, as in 'pastime,' &c." (1856, p. 349).

3. Kenneth Cmiel (1990), in the context of "the fight over popular speech in nineteenth-century America," points out how new translations of the Bible were created in an effort to forestall its decline as a linguistic force, specifically in relation to the rise of the dictionary as part of the age's scientific spirit. Cmiel does point out that Richard Trench, only a year before he addressed the Philological Society on English dictionaries, published an influential work on biblical revision that advocated tentative scholarly translation, which does not seem out of line with his later lexicographical recommendations (1990, p. 207).

4. In his introduction to a 1925 edition of Trench's work, George Sampson gives some sense of the staying power of the archbishop's sense of, in Sampson's terms, "the truth that words have a genuine life of their own, and that our recognition of that life is a measure of our understanding" (cited in Bromley, 1959, p. 233).

5. Richardson's dictionary held to Tooke's notion that each word's meaning had only contained, as Richardson described it, "the thing, the sensible object . . . the sensation caused by the thing or object (for language cannot sever them), of which that word is the name" (cited in Aarsleff, 1988, p. 42). James McKusick argues that Samuel Coleridge in fact originated the plan as, in the poet's terms, a "philosophical Romance to explain the whole growth of Language," which McKusick concludes eventually "fell into the less capable hands of Charles Richardson," where "it fell short of the high goals that Coleridge set for his own project especially in its almost total ignorance of the new German philology" (1992, pp. 8–9). McKusick also claims Coleridge "played a crucial role in the origins of the *OED*" principally by advocating the study of English texts in light of the German philology that he had brought to the attention of English readers (p. 5).

6. In his careful account of Johnson's work on the *Dictionary*, Allen Reddick finds that no account can be given of which sources Pope approved or how Johnson managed to get hold of the list (1990, p. 22). Did Johnson perhaps turn Pope to his purpose with a posthumous endorsement?

7. Faced with the space restrictions that haunt all dictionary editors, Johnson found himself forced at times to reduce many of his citations to "clusters of words," as he put it in the preface, with only a few gems retained to "intersperse with verdure and flowers the dusty deserts of philology." Yet Johnson appears just as happy to trim and fit his citations to meet his intended meanings, even if it meant that "the divine may desert his tenets, or the philosopher his system." This

was only the beginning of Johnson's manipulation in *editing* this Dictionary of the English Language. As Allen Reddick (1990) establishes through a thorough analysis of the manuscripts for the fourth and final revision of the *Dictionary*, Johnson did not hesitate, in Reddick's terms, to "flood" the work with citations from Milton and the Bible as part of his contribution to the larger theological and political debate of the latter half of the eighteenth century.

8. Passow's statement, in his 1812 pamphlet, *On the Aim, Plan, and Completion of Greek Dictionaries,* does seem in accord with Murray's stress on an evolving rather than an etymologically deduced meaning: "The dictionary should set forth the life history of each single word . . . in which ways it developed, what changes it had undergone with regard to its form and in the development of meaning" (cited in Aarsleff, 1988, p. 43).

9. Robert Burchfield, editor of *A Supplement to the Oxford English Dictionary*, has offered this helpful explanation of the uneven boundary of the early period: "The *OED* excluded some well-defined areas of vocabulary, among them Anglo-Saxon words that were not attested after 1150. . . . this particular exclusion left perhaps three-quarters of all surviving Old English words unrecorded in the dictionary" (1989, p. 169).

## Chapter 3
## Murray's Editorship, 1879–1915

1. As Martin Bernal (1987) has begun retelling this period of German classicism in *Black Athena*, it amounted to, in his polemical terms, "a fabrication of Ancient Greece," with the explicit and anti-Semitic intention of severing its admitted connections with Semitic and Egyptian influences. The climate of Aryanism surrounding the project was to receive affirmation later from Owen Barfield's *History in English Words*, a work based on the almost-completed *OED*, which in its opening chapter, "Philology and the Aryans," describes "the spirit which the Aryans were to bring into the world": "Strengthening their physique through the generations by stricter notions of matrimony, working by exogamy on their blood, and theory that perhaps upon some quality of brightness and sharpness in their thought, the Aryan became—Aryans," to which was later appended a footnote claiming that "race" is used in the book without "intending political or ethnological implications" as it was written before the Nazis adopted the word "Aryan" as a "racial shibboleth" (1926, p. 27). For the historical significance of the myth to European nationalism, see Poliakov (1974).

2. Although I find Darwin's work consistently less ethnocentric than the work of many of his Victorian counterparts, Patrick Brantlinger has argued, using among other sources the man's letters, that he demonstrated his own form of Social Darwinism, as he wrote in 1881 to W. Graham: "The more civilized Caucasian races have beaten the Turks hollow in the struggle for existence. Looking to the world at no very distant date, what an endless number of lower races will have been eliminated by the higher civilized races throughout the world" (Brantlinger, 1990, p. 3).

3. In a related issue, Elisabeth Murray duly notes that the "agreement with James Murray [for royalties] was never canceled, but neither he nor his heirs ever

received any profits from a work costing some 300,000 pounds to produce" (*CWW*, p. 165).

4. For a comparison of the continuities and the break between John Locke and John Horne Tooke on issues of language and politics, see Taylor (1990). Both Locke and Tooke were indeed interested in reducing the philosophical and political abuse of language. Insofar as their work was to serve Johnson, Richardson, Trench, and Murray, it does suggest that something of the liberal reform agenda crept into the writing of English dictionaries, beginning in at least the eighteenth century. On the other hand, Aarsleff points out the fundamental break between those "committed to the moral view of language" that revealed "divine and natural content," a position held by such Victorian sages as Trench and Carlyle, and those embracing "a functional view," based on the "conventional and human origin" of language, as found in Locke and Murray (1982, pp. 37–38).

5. Clarence Barnhart puts the current expense of citations at roughly three to five dollars each, based on the fact that "it would take seven hours or more for a reader to mark the twenty or thirty new words in a single issue of the *New York Times* at an estimated cost of sixty dollars" (1987, p. v). If nothing else, this suggests the degree to which the voluntary readers of this earlier era, in avoiding the outlay of some $20 million for citations (in 1987 terms), made the project possible.

6. This degree of "literary perfection" in the eighteenth century was considered by some to be the very cause of Johnson's *Dictionary*: "It was imagined by men of letters—among them Alexander Pope—that the English language had then attained such perfection that further improvement was hardly possible, and it was feared that if it were not fixed by lexicographic authority deterioration would soon begin. Since there was no English 'Academy,' it was necessary that the task should fall to some one whose judgment would command respect, and the man who undertook it was Samuel Johnson" (Lyons, 1900, p. 187). It was, of course, far more of a commercial arrangement for Johnson than is described here, and one with nationalist overtones as a pointed response to French scholarship, for example, rather than complacently assuming its perfection.

7. A recent skirmish over the question of propriety and plagiarism can be found with Robert Burchfield (1984), editor of the *Supplement*, pointing the finger at a host of offending dictionaries. Burchfield traces the "use" of the *OED* by different editions of *Webster's*, with acknowledgment in some cases, as well as tracking the flow of definitions from the 1947 *American College Dictionary* to the British *Hamlyn's Encyclopedic World Dictionary* published in 1971, before making its way to the Australian *Macquarie Dictionary* of 1981. Fortunately for the integrity of lexicographers, Laurence Urdang (1984), editor of the unabridged *Random House Dictionary*, responded by pointing to the history of "acquired rights to use materials" in a number of Burchfield's cases, including the America to Australia instance. This mitigates the plagiarism charge but it adds to the commercial and scholarly complexity of these textual questions, especially amid the claims of "a completely new and original English dictionary" made on behalf of Urdang's *Collins Dictionary* (Burchfield, 1984, p. 14).

8. Later in the same address, Murray was also not above criticizing "'classical' studies" for its "general failure" and "impotent manner." In the context of re-

porting to the Philological Society the rise of the movement for spelling reform, which he supported, Murray launched a sweeping attack on the claims of a classical education: "Nothing could afford a stronger proof of the general failure of the what are in England called 'classical' studies, to train men's minds, either to observe facts, weigh evidence, or draw deductions, than the impotent manner in which the Head Masters of the Public Schools of England have treated the appeal made to them to read the Latin language as the Romans read it" (*TPS*, 1880–81, p. 141).

9. Samuel Johnson, too, had been deeply disturbed by Oxford's refusal to grant him an honorary A.M. degree, with the university relenting only weeks before the publication of the *Dictionary*, which permitted Johnson to appear properly "degreed" on the work's title page (Reddick, 1990, p. 78).

## Chapter 4
## Shakespeare's Dictionary

1. The point seems to have escaped the attention of Robert Burchfield, at least on one occasion, when he suggests that Shakespeare was "more thoroughly excerpted by the contributors (quotation-gatherers) than the works of some others" (1989, p. 169).

2. For the 1963 edition of the Oxford *Learner's Dictionary of Current English*, Marvin Spevack calculates that "10,357 of Shakespeare's words account for some 35 per cent of the total of 30,000" (1988, p. 155), and while that represents a larger percentage than in the *OED*, it does fall short by roughly 9,000 words of the playwright's basic vocabulary.

3. Robert Crawford (1992) has pointed out that it was the Scottish universities that first began to use excerpts from English literature during the eighteenth century as part of their program in rhetoric and belles lettres, reaffirming the common theme of the margins' contribution to a realization of the center, which comes up more than once in thinking about this dictionary. Linda Dowling identifies how this Aesthetic movement, or literary decadence, as she terms it, drew from the new comparative philology, which equated literature itself as a sign of linguistic decay (1986).

4. Elizabethan playwrights typically sold all claims to a play when an acting company purchased the manuscript, typically it seems for six to ten pounds; the company might sell it in turn to a printer after it had exhausted the play on the stage for another two pounds (Lowenstein, 1988, p. 266). Ben Jonson was somewhat ahead of his times as an enterprising author, bringing out a revised edition of his *Works* in 1616, the year of Shakespeare's death.

5. Coleridge went a step further, elevating Shakespeare's art above that of the Greeks: "Contrast the stage of the ancients with that of the time of Shakspere, and we shall be struck by his genius; with them, it had the trappings of royal and religious ceremony; with him, it was a naked room, a blanket for a curtain; but with his vivid appeals the imagination figured it out 'A field for monarchs'" (Coleridge, 1914, p. 463).

6. It is Tim William Machan's more recent point, relevant to this issue of national prestige, that "England lagged behind other cultures in recognizing

[English's literary] value, inasmuch as grammatical and stylistic discussions of English were preceded by similar discussions of several other vernaculars" (1991, p. 234).

7. See figure 12.1 for a graphic demonstration of this fact. A number of years ago, this was shown to be the case, not surprisingly, for the *Shorter Oxford English Dictionary* as assessed by Finkenstaedt and Wolf (1973).

8. In the latter half of the eighteenth century, Shakespeare did no better, Gary Taylor reports, in literary anthologies of the day than placing fourth in the frequency of inclusion, behind the contemporary poets, Alexander Pope, James Thompson, and William Cowper (1989, p. 150). Yet in his singular promotion of Shakespeare, Johnson was working from an important critical measure that he made apparent in a preface to his edition of Shakespeare's plays in 1765; for a work not yet assured of its greatness, "no other test can be applied than length of duration and continuance of esteem" (Johnson, 1968, p. 261). He allowed that a mix of prejudice and reason could be thought to sustain a writer's reputation, with the safeguard being ongoing comparisons "with other works of the same kind" (p. 262).

9. The subsequent lectures go on to the hero as priest (with Luther and Knox), man of letters (Johnson and Rousseau), and finally, the hero as king, with the rather modern instances of Cromwell and Napoleon. It is worth noting that while there are no classical figures in Carlyle's heroic panoply (although allusions abound to Homer and the classical tradition), Jesus Christ seems conspicuous by his absence.

10. Carlyle and Mill corresponded on the role of poet and critic, and as Ian Small (1991) has argued, the ethical place they established for art did not meet a serious challenge until the 1870s, when proponents of Aestheticism, such as Pater and Wilde, began to suggest that art did not invariably pay homage to a society's need for moral guidance.

11. Riede is led to the rather cynical conclusion that "the church of literature fostered by Carlyle, Arnold, and others in their different ways has worked all too well to replace Christianity—society can pay lip service to the works of high culture enshrined in the universities [and the *OED*?], and go its own way" (1989, p. 118).

12. This element of national formation was hardly exclusive to Great Britain. In *Literary France: The Making of a Culture*, Priscilla Clark has written about the writer's identification with the country: "The prominence of those whom I call public writers is a function of their ability to articulate a sense of country that both comprehends and transcends politics. . . . The writers in the Panthéon— Voltaire, Rousseau, Victor Hugo, Emile Zola—fused the public world of country with the private word of belief" (1987, pp. 4–5).

## Chapter 5
## Citing *The Shrew*

1. One of the primary lessons taught to young readers in school is that on coming across an unknown word, good readers first try to work out its meaning using such "context clues" as contrast or difference. On yet another level, the play of difference was made into the organizing principle of meaning in language

among structuralists beginning with Ferdinand de Saussure (1959) and followed by more recent elaborations on the theme by poststructuralist Jacques Derrida (1974). Language is nothing, we are reminded by linguist and philosopher, but the striking of differences—dog from cat, speech from writing, modesty from passion, man from woman.

2. With the *Supplement* a sense 5. was added in the form of the combination *smackwarm*, a nonce-word creation of James Joyce in *Ulysses* from 1922—"She let free . . her nipped elastic garter smackwarm against her smackable woman's warmhosed thigh."

3. Marvin Spevack points out that interjections closely associated with Shakespeare, including *faugh, hallo, hist, hollo, pah, pish, pooh, whoa, wo, zounds*, have been retained in Oxford's *Advanced Learner's Dictionary*, which has a special interest in the spoken language if not necessarily of a Elizabethan nature (1988, p. 159).

4. The *Supplement to the OED*, I might add, introduces the British form of baby napkins (from a Mrs. Gaskell citation, 1845) and the baby nappy (1927), although it still fails to find an instance in the literature of the diapered baby. The moment may have almost passed as the overwhelming majority of Canadian and American babies find their bottoms wrapped in *disposables*, one of the many lexical gifts from corporate marketing departments.

5. Those with an interest in the philosophical school known as speech act theory may wish to note that publishing the banns before a wedding is a perfect instance of a *performative*, or language that performs an action by its very pronouncement. Speech act theory has mounted an analysis of the language on the basis of the different sorts of things that could be done with words (Austin, 1967).

6. John Ruskin was happy to tell adoring audiences of men and women in the 1860s that a woman's "intellect is not for invention or creation, but for sweet ordering, arrangement, and decision" (n.d., p. 117). The issue of "originality," with its close association with both "origins," "genius," and "Shakespeare," has been exposed for the ways that those who champion it tend to deny women's participation in the concept, stealing from them their powers of creativity, imagination, and reason (Gilbert and Gubar, 1979; Battersby, 1989). Berenice Carroll has set out the careful construction of originality as the work of a particularly narrow class system: "This system assigns most men and almost all women to positions in the lower classes and reserves for a small group of self-recruiting males both hegemony over received knowledge and control of a variety of rewards and privileges" (1990, p. 136).

## Chapter 6
## A Victorian Canon: The Authors

1. Michael Bennett, for example, is convinced that John Gower, who had written only in Latin and French up to that point, was moved by Richard II to write in English on the theme of love, as described in the original prologue to his *Confessio Amatis* (1992, pp. 11–12).

2. It did not take the church long to discern that, as the vicar of Croydon, Roland Philips, pointed out at the turn of the sixteenth century, "we must root

out printing or printing will root out us" (cited in Bennett, 1969, I, p. 73). In the years that followed, more than a few printers were sent to prison by the order of the Privy Council "for printing books thought to be unlawful" (cited in Bennett, 1969, I, p. 37). The Act of 1543 "for the advancement of true religion" forbade the reading of the Bible in English by women, artificers, apprentices, journeymen, servingmen of the rank of yeomen, and under husbandmen and laborers (Bennett, 1969, I, p. 27). Yet only a few years before, Henry VIII ordered copies of Coverdale's translation of the Bible to be placed in every church for all to read (Altick, 1957, p. 24).

3. As one indication of that popularity, his long poem *Marmion* had sold 50,000 copies by 1836, matching the sales for a number of Scott's novels (Altick, 1957, p. 386). David Brown notes how far Scott's reputation had plunged by the beginning of this century: "Scott was not only largely unread, but simply dismissed by the British reading public in the same way educated Scots had dismissed Wordsworth a century earlier. Only Scott's inferior, medieval novels remained in classrooms, supposedly to entertain the young, but more often encouraging them to avoid the Waverly Novels later in life" (Brown, 1979, p. 1).

4. On the other hand, Goethe celebrated Scott—"I discover in him a wholly new art which has its own laws" (Eckermann, 1984, p. 394), and in this century the Marxist critic Georg Lukacs praised his work for its introduction of the "specifically historical" in the form of a social history missing from previous fiction (1962, p. 19).

5. In the first note of chapter 3, I noted Bernal's (1987) work on the German science of philology that emerged during the nineteenth century. It gradually rewrote the history of ancient Greece, cutting it off from its Semitic and Egyptian roots in favor of a racially and linguistically superior Aryan (Indo-European) model that better served the ideological development of European nationalism. The theme is also taken up in Olender's study of nineteenth-century philology (1992).

6. See Niranjana (1992) for an extended critical discussion of William Jones's motives in translating Sanskrit legal and sacred texts which were to preserve them against what was felt to be the historical degradation of the Indian people. The significance of translation has also been tragically marked during the writing of this chapter by the assassination of Hitsohi Igarahi, the Japanese translator of Salman Rushdie's *Satanic Verses*, and the critical wounding of the Italian translator of the novel.

7. Linda Dowling's analysis of Romantic philology provides a very helpful guide to the linguistic debate between Wordsworth, who rejected literary artifice as undermining the basis of human equality, and Coleridge, who saw in it a common basis of communication as well as a claim on civilization and who, it is worth recalling , was a substantial influence on Trench (1986, pp. 15–27).

## Chapter 7
### A Victorian Canon: The Titles

1. The Early English Text Society also produced an edition of John Lydgate's *The Hystorye, Sege and Destruction of Troye* from the Golden Age of the late fourteenth century. In his version, Lydgate offers an apologetic note, giving his

view of English as failing in poetry, for it "stumbleth aye for faute of eloquence" (cited in Jones, 1953, p. 3). Another source of citations for this title is a translation by Sir John Denham of the second book of *The Aeneas*, which he completed in 1656 during his enforced confinement by Oliver Cromwell.

2. The number of Johnsonian senses cited was ascertained by isolating the number of attributions to J. or T. within the *OED* entry (see p. 51). There was also cause to cite Johnson's *Dictionary* as a supporting quotation, with most of the seventy instances drawn from its famous preface, as with *admitted* in this perfect statement of the literary principle of the *OED*—"Obsolete words are *admitted*, when they are found in authors not obsolete"—as well as when Johnson runs contrary to the *OED*: "Every language has likewise its improprieties and absurdities, which it is the duty of the lexicographer to correct or proscribe." And then, too, Johnson's definitions did on occasion serve as citations, as per *Flasher*: "a man of more appearance of wit than reality."

3. An announcement from Oxford University Press in 1894 assured concerned readers about delays in publication that "for the convenience of the original subscribers, therefore the new issue will begin on November 15 with two sections of unequal length:—(1) D-Deceit, of 88 pages, at three shillings and sixpence; (2) F-Fang, of 64 pages, at half-a-crown."

4. David Riede, in a footnote accompanying his discussion of Carlyle and "the church of literature," discusses the technological innovations that came to favor the journal over the book as a business venture, with the result that "the large audience reached by the reviews and the inherent respect commanded by their prestige tended to elevate the authority of reviewers above the poets and philosophers" (1989, p. 119, n.18).

5. There were, for example, those among the best intentioned of the middle class who fought the introduction of newspapers of any sort into the Mechanic's Institutes for fear of diluting the "useful arts" to be gained therein (Altick, 1957, p. 201).

6. Frederick Engels, in *Condition of the Working-Class in England* (1844), took issue with the middle class for failing to have "done so much as compile from those rotting Blue-Books a single readable book which everybody might easily get some information on the condition of the great majority of 'free born Britons'" (cited in Ashforth, 1990, p. 8). Of course, middle-class readable is what that information was transformed into by journalist, essayist, and novelist, in a circulation of meaning that moved the lives of the poor from the commission's report and Ashforth's "reckoning of legitimation" to the artful and middle-class reckoning of a good story, to which the *OED* attended.

7. But then how could it miss, as the *Gentleman's Magazine* offered essays of a moral and biographical nature, poetry, contemporary news, gardening advice, births, marriages, and deaths, as well as a listing of new books. It was also willing to publish submissions from both its gentlemen and gentlewomen readers (Shevelow, 1989, p. 175). By 1732, it was regularly publishing what were at the time illegal reports of proceedings in Parliament, with Samuel Johnson serving as reporter at one point. It escaped criminal charges by disguising the Members' names through anagrams and, in one further irreverent jab, used variations on "Proceedings of the Senate of Lilliput" as the title for the feature (Feather, 1988, p. 111).

8. It was more of a philanthropic venture than originally planned, and it ended up costing Charles Knight, superintendent of publications, £30,788 (Altick, 1957, p. 282). It was also a work of questionable value. Although Altick compares it, at one point, to the *Britannica* in quality, he also reports on rumors of hacks lifting the material from the British Library and gives an anecdote of mistreated authors drawn from the autobiography of contributor Harriet Martineau (1957, p. 272). The S.D.U.K.'s *Penny Magazine* reached a million readers in the first half of the nineteenth century, and so did such imitators and successors as the *London Journal* (1845–1906), *Reynold's Miscellany* (1846–65), and *Cassell's Illustrated Family Paper* (1853–1932). Yet none of this "revolutionary" and popular set was to make the *OED*'s bibliography, suggesting subscription levels were little consulted in gathering up the language for recording in the *OED*.

## Chapter 8
### *A Supplement to the OED, 1957–1986*

1. One of them, Yvonne Warburton, tells firsthand the story behind the "network of research" responsible for tracking down the trickiest of citations in her article, "Finding the Right Words" (1986).

2. The small-print note accompanying *fuck* suggest how the word still defines the coarseness of language and user: "For centuries, and still by the great majority, regarded as a taboo-word; until recent times not often recorded in print but frequent in coarse speech." (The note accompanying *cunt* says: "Its currency is restricted in the manner of other taboo words; see the small-type note s.v. \**fuck*".) What is unlocked here is the back door of propriety's great house of language; the door on the world that uses *fuck* as common not coarse, the world that Lawrence was trying to usher in the front door for what he imagined as the sake of our sanity and humanity.

## Chapter 9
### Modern Citation

1. As it is, the *Supplement*'s definitions of *Imagism* and *Imagist* are supported in the first instance by four of Pound's letters of 1912, with further examples taken from his correspondence of 1915 and 1916. The immediacy of this literary school, which was to have such force in the early decades of this century, has about it some of the imagined directness of the letter—"An 'Image' is that which presents an intellectual and emotional complex in an instant of time" (Pound, 1935, p. 4).

2. The book title *Letters* accounts for 22,107 citations in the first edition, comprising just over one percent of the total (far exceeding *Sermons*, with 10,431 citations, and *Essays*, with 9,158). However, the letter was not the only private/public form on which the editors drew. Published *Journals* account for 6,241 citations in the original *OED*, with the recollections and notes of Sir Walter Scott, for example, cited 348 times. *Diaries* provide another 6,000 quotations, most notably Samuel Pepys's record of life in London dating from 1660, with 1,807 citations. While these lesser forms of literature do reflect the editors' ef-

forts to capture the daily life of the language, the majority of these *edited* works come from the hands of those who have already earned some form of public recognition.

3. Joyce's sympathetic portrait of the twice-baptized and yet still self-regarded Jew, Leopold Bloom, occupies the very center of *Ulysses*, which in all of its inventiveness is the most-cited piece of literature in the *Supplement*. There is something to Vladimir Nabokov's remarks, made while teaching *Ulysses* to undergraduates at Cornell University, that "Joyce is sometimes crude in the way he accumulates and stresses so-called racial traits" (1980, p. 287). The novel carries within it the constant presence of a prepossessing race-consciousness, in all of its prejudicial accents, suggesting a link forged between Jewish and Irish fates made to suffer subjugation amid desires for an independent homeland. But the crudeness of this stress seems to be the very thing that lies deep within the art and language of the age.

4. T. S. Eliot's 1941 introduction to "a choice of Kipling's verse" includes the claim that he is unable to "find any justification for the charge that [Kipling] held a doctrine of race superiority" (Eliot, 1963, p. 29). Yet Eliot goes on blithely to add that Kipling "believed that the British have a greater aptitude for ruling than other people, and that they include a greater number of kindly, incorruptible and unselfseeking men capable of administration" (pp. 29–30). One must wonder about such a defense of Kipling—when is a genetic description of an imperial destiny not a doctrine of race superiority? In reviewing the Kipling collection, Lionel Trilling took aim at the only slightly disguised anti-Semitism in the poem, "Waster," and Eliot shot back that he "was not aware that [Kipling] cherished any particularly anti-Semitic feelings" (cited in Ricks, 1988, p. 26). In turn, Trilling insisted anti-Semitism was, in Kipling's case, "one aspect of a complex xenophobia, his queasy resentful feelings about Jews" (cited in Ricks, 1988, p. 27). This queasiness had not been altogether absent from Eliot's introduction to the Kipling book, as he speaks of how "even those who admire Disraeli most may find themselves more at ease with Gladstone," pointing out that "Disraeli's foreignness was a comparatively simple matter" (p. 28).

5. Wells went on to promote an ardently scientific spirit in the service of a world federalist liberalism that—again Orwell's perceptive point—virtually blinded him to the dangers of a rising fascism in Europe (Orwell, 1968, pp. 194–198). Not only did Wells speculate, in such works as *The Fate of Homo Sapiens*, that Nazi anti-Semitism was brought by the Judaic concept of the chosen people, but he also spoke against what he felt was an untoward Jewish exclusivity (Kushner, 1989, p. 93).

6. The complete line from the tenth Canto runs "Wives, jew-girls, nuns, necrophiliast, *fornicarium ac sicarium*," while the fifty-second Cantos moves from "sin drawing vengeance, poor yitts paying for / paying for a few big jews' vendetta on goyim," and on to "Remarked Ben: better keep out the jews / or yr/grandchildren will curse you / jews, real jews, chazims and *neschek*" (Pound, 1956). On the other hand, the *Supplement*'s citation for *Christer* is from the sixty-first Canto, "You Christers wanna have foot on two boats."

7. One model for a return to the modernist canon is the work of Chinua Achebe, who has reexamined Joseph Conrad's *Heart of Darkness*: "And the

question is whether a novel which celebrates that dehumanization, which depersonalizes a portion of the human race, can be called a great work of art. My answer is: No, it cannot. . . . The time is long overdue for taking a hard look at the work of creative artists who apply their talents, alas often considerable as in the case of Conrad, to set people against people" (1977, pp. 788–789).

8. The *Supplement* defines *low-life* (**B. sb.**) "a course, vulgar, or no-good person," adding an ambiguous parenthetical "(esp. in Jewish use)."

9. Huxley bolstered his case against Aryanism by referring to Max Müller's "recantation" of this racial position in 1888, after Müller had done much to introduce it into England as a well-respected philologist at Oxford. As you might recall, Müller was a delegate of the University Press, overseeing the Press's sponsorship of the dictionary and trying to bring his influence to bear on James Murray's editorship. In the entry for **Aryan** (**B.** *sb*), Max Müller is quoted from the 1873 edition of the *Science of Language*: "The state of civilization attained by the Aryans before they left their common home."

10. At the same time, Huxley was promoting a program of human eugenics intent on preventing humanity from, in his view, destroying itself. His language has a haunting tone for us today: "We must pick out the genetically inferior stock with more certainty and we must set in motion counter forces making for faster reproduction of superior stock" (1941, p. 81).

11. It should be noted that Burchfield originally had access to Merriam-Webster's extensive citation files, which were naturally very rich in American English; when Merriam-Webster suspended this service, Oxford was forced to rely more heavily on the American publisher's dictionary entries as themselves published instances of the language used in America.

## Chapter 10
## The Second Edition, 1984–1989

1. Before the NEWS items were electronically folded into the second edition, I unfortunately missed gathering complete figures for the leading book titles beyond the first two—*Britannica* (109 citations) and *Webster's* (79 citations).

2. Yet *Ulysses* suffers something of the same textual status that a good part of Shakespeare's work bears. The 1980s have been marked by bibliographical scandals over the editing of Joyce's book as it has become apparent that with this work, too, notions of the fixed and authentic text do not hold. Hans Walter Gaber's 1984 definitive edition, with some 5,000 emendations, has been pillaged in turn by John Kidd, whose corrected edition of the work has yet to appear ("Ulysses," 1992, p. D2). Once more, the text that plays such a leading role in underwriting the language betrays something of an ill-defined nature itself.

## Chapter 11
## The Sense of Omission

1. In discussing the literary issues raised by this history of censorship, Annabel Patterson advocates that works such as *King Lear* be read with the "cultural

ed., *Foedora, conventiones, litterae, et cujuscunque gneris acta publica etc.*, 10 vols. (1739), is cited sixty-eight times; Henry Ellis, ed., *Original Letters Illustrative of English History*, 3 series (1824–46), is not cited; Sir Harris Nicolas, ed., *Proceedings and Ordinances of the Privy Council of England*, 7 vols. (1834), is cited fifty-four times; George Williams Saunders, *Orders of the High Court of Chancery* (1845), is cited forty-three times. Of these, the bibliography of the OED lists only the works by Rymer and Ellis.

4. Richardson cites a resolution from the Brewer's Guild that applauds the king's use of the "common idiom," meaning English, as a move to be emulated: "For that our most excellent lord king Henry the Fifth hath, in his letters missive, and divers affairs touching his own person, more willingly chosen to declare the secrets of his will [in it]; and hath for the better understanding of his people hath, with a diligent mind procured the common idiom" (cited by Richardson, 1980, p. 739). Richardson, through a close comparison of linguistic styles, points out that King Henry's writing "was a blend of different dialectical forms which, as far as is known corresponds to no known contemporary spoken dialect" (1980, p. 734). Granting Richardson's reminder that the relationship between oral and written language is hotly debated, it still seems worth contemplating whether, at a formative moment in the development of standard English, writing broke with the spoken language at many points due to its close association with the written forms of Latin or in an effort to give it a distinct formality in this permanent medium.

5. One needs to add to these circulation figures the likelihood of the sturdy newspapers of the day passing through perhaps thirty hands as well as being read out loud in public houses (Webb, 1955, pp. 33–34, 47).

6. In addition, one might note the lexicographical efforts of Daly's *Wickedary of the English Language* (1987) and Mills's *Womanwords* (1989).

## Chapter 12
## A Source of Authority

1. William Mackey has observed that "in France, such dictionaries as Littré, Larousse and later Robert were more heeded than the works of the *Académie*" (1991, p. 60, n. 26).

2. Bersani goes on to point out that this redemptive aesthetic "*depends on a misreading of art as philosophy*" (p. 2, original emphasis). He calls upon Plato, who argued against the dependability of art as it lacked "the unity, the identity, the stability of truth; it does not belong to world of perfectly intelligible ideas" (p. 3), suggesting not everyone believes it a bedrock of meaning on which to define the language with precision.

3. The electronic database now used to store the "bundles" of citations for each item reveals that of the 327,897 citations stored between 1989 and 1991, 63 percent were of American and 33 percent of British origin, with the remainder distributed among Canada, India, Australia, the West Indies, Nigeria, New Zealand, South Africa, among other places.

4. Peter Clinch describes how the power of the cited instance in court cases appreciates with each reference to it: "Judges select from the authorities [presented by counsel] those which are considered applicable and legitimate to the resolution of the case to be decided, and so, in turn, legitimize the source of authority used, making the citation of it in the future more likely and its authority increased" (1990, p. 288). Another legal scholar, John Merryman, goes a step farther and specifies how cited authorities are typically utilized, ranging from direct applicability, which leave judges little choice in selecting authorities, to freely selecting those that "support the position the judge wishes to take and therefore lend weight to it" (1953–54, p. 614, n. 1). He concludes, on a point of striking relevance to the case at hand, "that the great bulk of the published works available to judges in book form—the encyclopedias, texts, treatises, and Restatements—are written in such a way as to overemphasize the role of stated authoritative doctrine and submerge the role of process of decision in the solution of social problems in the courts" (p. 673). Merryman wisely recommends that such authorities not be taken as deciding cases—"they are at best data" (ibid.). For a discussion of the legal and linguistic ramifications of citing a dictionary in court, see Harris (1981, pp. 190–193) and Robinson (1982).

5. For speculations on the electronic dimensions of improving the historical coverage of the *OED*, see Schäfer (1987); and of facilitating the connection among semantic elements, see Bailey (1987).

6. I take this self-definitional process from Edward Said, who has written extensively about how "the Orient has helped to define Europe (or the West) as its contrasting image, idea, personality, experience" (1978, pp. 1–2).

7. The most famous of these is Macaulay's Minute of 1835 in which, with no knowledge of the languages at issue, the historian was to declare that "a single shelf of a good European library was worth the whole of native literature of India and Arabia," from which point he moved on to defy those members of his committee who favored "the oriental plan for education," recommending a colonial education in English literature and science (cited by Said, 1983, p. 12).

8.  As part of this imperial effort during the middle decades of the nineteenth century, a part of England's common law was codified to facilitate its use in India (Baker, 1979, p. 190), and candidates for the civil service of the East Indian Company were examined in English language and literature, a topic given equal weight to mathematics (Taylor, 1989, p. 194).

# References

Aarsleff, Hans. 1982. Introduction. In *From Locke to Saussure: Essays on the Study of Language and Intellectual History*, pp. 3–41. Minneapolis: University of Minnesota Press.

Aarsleff, Hans. 1983. *The Study of Language in England, 1760–1860*. 2d ed. Minneapolis: University of Minnesota Press.

Aarsleff, Hans. 1988. The Original Plan for the *OED* and Its Background. In Robert Burchfield and Hans Aarsleff, *The Oxford English Dictionary and the State of the Language*, pp. 33–42. Washington, D.C.: Library of Congress.

Achebe, Chinua. 1977. An Image of Africa. *Massachusetts Review* 4, 782–794.

Ackerman, Robert W., and Dahood, Roger, eds. 1984. *Ancrene Riwle: Introduction and Part I*. Binghamton, N.Y.: State University of New York Press.

Altick, R. D. 1957. *The English Common Reader: A Social History of the Mass Reading Public, 1800–1900*. Chicago: University of Chicago Press.

Anderson, Benedict. 1991. *Imagined Communities: Reflections on the Origin and Spread of Nationalism*. Rev. ed. London: Verso.

Arnold, Matthew. 1895. *On the Study of Celtic Literature and on Translating Homer*. New York: Macmillan.

Arnold, Matthew. 1896 (orig. 1869). *Culture and Anarchy: An Essay in Social and Political and Social Criticism*. New York: Macmillan.

Arnold, Matthew. 1900. Saint-Beuve. In *The Encyclopædia Britannica*. 9th ed. New York: Werner.

Arnold, Matthew. 1906. The Literary Influence of Academies. In *Essays Literary and Critical*, pp. 27–50. London: Dent.

Ashforth, Adam. 1990. Reckoning Schemes of Legitimation: On Commissions of Inquiry as Power/Knowledge Forms. *Journal of Historical Sociology* 3(1), 1–22.

Austin, John. 1967. *How to Do Things with Words*. Cambridge, Mass.: Harvard University Press.

Bailey, Richard W. 1987. On Some Discontinuities in Our English Dictionaries. In Richard W. Bailey, ed., *Dictionaries of English: Prospects for the Record of Our Language*, pp. 136–149. Ann Arbor: University of Michigan Press.

Bailey, Richard. 1988. A Letter to the Very Rev. The Dean of Westminister: Coleridge, Hebert, Esq. *Dictionaries* 10, 115–124.

Bailey, Richard W. 1991. *Images of English: A Cultural History of the Language*. Ann Arbor: University of Michigan Press.

Baker, J. H. 1979. *An Introduction to English Legal History*. 2d ed. London: Butterworth.

Barfield, Owen. 1926. *History in English Words*. London: Faber & Faber.

Barker, Nicholas. 1978. *The Oxford University Press and the Spread of Learning, 1478–1978: An Illustrated History*. Oxford: Oxford University Press.

Barnhart, Clarence. 1987. Foreword. In Richard W. Bailey, ed., *Dictionaries of*

*English: Prospects for the Record of Our Language*, pp. v–vi. Ann Arbor: University of Michigan Press.

Bartlett, John. 1962. *A Complete Concordance . . . of Shakespeare*. London: Macmillan.

Bassnett-McGuire, Susan. 1980. *Translation Studies*. London: Methuen.

Batsleer, Janet, Tony Davies, Rebecca O'Rourke, and Chris Weedon. 1985. *Rewriting English: Cultural Politics of Gender and Class*. London: Methuen.

Battersby, Christine. 1989. *Gender and Genius: Towards a Feminist Aesthetics*. Bloomington: Indiana University Press.

Baum, Julian. 1989, April 14. The Definitive Word on English. *Christian Science Monitor*, p. 12.

Baylen, J. O. 1987. Politics and the "New Journalism": Lord Esher's Use of the *Pall Mall Gazette*. *Victorian Periodical* 20(4), 126–140.

Benbow, Timothy, Peter Carrington, Gayle Johannesen, Frank Tompa, and Edmund Weiner. 1990. Report on the New Oxford English User Survey. *International Journal of Lexicography* 3(3), 155–203.

Benjamin, Walter. 1968. Theses on the Philosophy of History. In H. Arendt, ed., *Illuminations*, pp. 253–264. Trans. Harry Zohn. New York: Schocken.

Bennett, H. S. 1969–1970. *English Books and Readers, 1475–1640*. 3 vols. Cambridge: Cambridge University Press.

Bennett, Michael J. 1992. The Court of Richard II and the Promotion of Literature. In Barbara A. Hanawalt, ed., *Chaucer's England: Literature in Historical Context*, pp. 3–20. Minneapolis: University of Minnesota Press.

Berg, Donna Lee, Gaston Gonnet, and Frank Tompa. 1988. *The New Oxford English Dictionary Project at the University of Waterloo*. Waterloo, Ontario: University of Waterloo Centre for the New OED.

Bernal, Martin. 1987. *Black Athena: The Afroasiatic Roots of Classical Civilization*. Vol. I, *The Fabrication of Ancient Greece*. New Brunswick, N.J.: Rutgers University Press.

Bersani, Leo. 1990. *The Culture of Redemption*. Cambridge, Mass.: Harvard University Press.

Bradley, Henry. 1904. *The Making of English*. London: Macmillan.

Brantlinger, Patrick. 1990. Pensée Sauvage at the MLA: Victorian Cultural Imperialism Then and Now. *The Victorian Newsletter* 77, 1–5.

Bromley, J. 1959. *The Man of Ten Talents: A Portrait of Richard Chevenix Trench, 1807–86, Philologist, Poet, Theologian, Archbishop*. London: S.P.C.K.

Brown, David. 1979. *Walter Scott and the Historical Imagination*. London: Routledge & Kegan Paul.

Brown, Lucy. 1985. *Victorian News and Newspapers*. Oxford: Oxford University Press.

Burchfield, Robert W. 1972, October 13. Four-Letter Words and the OED. *The Times Literay Supplement*, p. 1233.

Burchfield, Robert W. 1973. Data Collecting and Research. In Raven McDavid and Audrey Duckert, eds., *Lexicography in English*, pp. 99–103. New York: Annals of the New York Academy of Sciences.

Burchfield, Robert W. 1982, September 10. Letter. *The Times Literary Supplement*, p. 973.

Burchfield, Robert W. 1984, July/August. Dictionaries, New and Old: Who Plagiarises Whom. *Encounter*, pp. 10–19.

Burchfield, Robert W. 1986. The Oxford English Dictionary. In Robert Ilson, ed., *Lexicography: An Emerging International Profession*, pp. 17–27. Manchester, U.K.: Manchester University Press.

Burchfield, Robert W. 1988. Editing a Supplement to the *OED*, 1976–1986. In Robert Burchfield and Hans Aarsleff, *The Oxford English Dictionary and the State of the Language*, pp. 45–56. Washington, D.C.: Library of Congress.

Burchfield, Robert W. 1989. *Unlocking the English Language*. London: Faber & Faber.

Bush, Douglas. 1945. *English Literature in the Earlier Seventeenth Century, 1600–1660*. New York: Oxford University Press.

Carlyle, Thomas. No date (orig. 1841). *On Heroes, Hero-Worship and the Heroic in History*. London: Collins.

Carlyle, Thomas. No date (orig. 1838). Sir Walter Scott. *Soottish and Other Miscellanies*, pp. 54–111. London: Dent.

Carlyle, Thomas. 1912 (orig. 1843). *Past and Present*. London: Dent.

Carpenter, Humphrey. 1985. *Secret Gardens: A Study of the Golden Age of Children's Literature*. Boston: Houghton Mifflin.

Carroll, Berenice. 1990. The Politics of "Originality": Women and the Class System of the Intellect. *Journal of Women's History* 2(2), 136–163.

Casey, Ellen. 1985. In the Pages of *The Athenæum*: Fiction in 1883. *Victorian Periodical Review* 18(2), 57–72.

Chandos, John. 1982, September 17. Letter. *The Times Literary Supplement*, p. 1010.

Chaucer, Geoffrey. 1958. *Chaucer's Poetry: An Anthology for the Modern Reader*. Ed. E. T. Donaldson. New York: Ronald.

Christianson, C. Paul. 1989. Chancery Standard and the Records of Old English Bridge. In Joseph Trahern, Jr., ed., *Standardizing English: Essays in the History of Language Change*, pp. 82–112. Knoxville: University of Tennessee Press.

Clark, Priscilla Parhurst. 1987. *Literary France: The Making of a Culture*. Berkeley: University of California Press.

Clinch, Peter. 1990. The Use of Authority: Citational Patterns in the English Courts. *Journal of Documentation* 46(4), 287–317.

Cmiel, Kenneth. 1990. *Democratic Eloquence: The Fight over Popular Speech in Nineteenth-Century America*. New York: Morrow.

Coleridge, Samuel Taylor, 1914. *Lectures and Notes on Shakespeare and Other English Poets*. London: G. Bell & Sons.

Crawford, Robert. 1992. *Devolving English Literature*. Oxford: Oxford University Press.

Crotch, W.J.B. 1967. *The Prologues and Epilogues of William Caxton*. New York: Burt Franklin.

Crowley, Tony. 1989. *Standard English and the Politics of Language*. Chicago: University of Illinois Press.

Dale, Peter Allan. 1989. *In Pursuit of the Scientific Spirit: Science, Art and Society in the Victorian Age*. Madison: University of Wisconsin Press.

Daly, Mary. 1987. *Websters' First Intergalactic Wickedary of the English Language* (with Jane Caputi). London: The Women's Press.

Dante, Alighieri. 1981 (orig. 1577). *Literature in the Vernacular (De Vulgari Eloquentia)*. Trans. Sally Purcell. Manchester, U.K.: Carcanet New Press.

Darwin, Charles. 1993 (orig. 1859, 1871). *The Origin of Species by Means of Natural Selection or the Preservation of Favored Races in the Struggle for Life*, and *the Descent of Man and Selection in Relation to Sex*. New York: Modern Library.

Defoe, Daniel. 1961 (orig. 1702). A Projected English Academy. In Susie Tucker, ed., *English Examined: Two Centuries of Comment on the Mother-Tongue*, pp. 58–60. Cambridge: Cambridge University Press.

DeMaria, Robert. 1989. The Politics of Johnson's Dictionary. *PMLA* 104(1), 64–74.

Derrida, Jacques. 1974. *Of Grammatology*. Trans. Gayatri Chakravorty Spivak. Baltimore: Johns Hopkins University Press.

Dodd, Philip. 1986. Englishness and the National Culture. In Robert Colls and Philip Dobb, eds., *Englishness: Politics and Culture, 1800–1920*, pp. 1–28. London: Croon Helm.

Dodd, W. Stephen. 1989. Lexicomputing and the Dictionary of the Future. In R.K.K. Hartmann, ed., *Lexicographers and Their Works*, pp. 83–93. Exeter, U.K.: University of Exeter.

Dowling, Linda. 1982. Victorian Oxford and the Science of Language. *PMLA* 97(1), 160–178.

Dowling, Linda. 1986. *Language and Decadence in the Victorian Fin de Siècle*. Princeton, N.J.: Princeton University Press.

Dressing Old Words New. 1989, April 1. *The Economist*, p. 79.

Dudek, Louis. 1960. *Literature and the Press: A History of Printing, Printed Media and Their Relation to Literature*. Toronto: Ryerson Press.

Duncan, J. Matthews. 1889. *Clinical Lectures on the Diseases of Women Delivered in Saint Bartholomew's Hospital*. London: J. & A. Churchill.

Eckerman, J. 1984 (Orig. 1836–48). *Conversations with Goethe*. London: Dent.

Eliot, T. S. 1933. *The Use of Poetry and the Use of Criticism*. London: Faber and Faber.

Eliot, T. S. 1963. *A Choice of Kipling's Verse, with an Essay on Rudyard Kipling*. London: Faber & Faber.

Eliot, T. S. 1965. What Dante Means to Me. In *To Criticize the Critic and Other Writings*, pp. 125–135. New York: Farrar, Straus & Giroux.

Emerson, Ralph Waldo. 1912. *Representative Men, English Traits and Other Essays*. London: Ward Lock.

Feather, John. 1988. *A History of British Publishing*. London: Routledge.

Finkenstaedt, Thomas, and Dieter Wolf. 1973. *Order Profusion: Studies in Dictionaries and the English Lexicon*. Heidelberg: Carl Winter.

Fish, Stanley. 1967. *Surprised by Sin: The Reader in Paradise Lost*. Berkeley: University of California Press.

Fisher, John H. 1977. Chancery and the Emergence of Standard Written English in the Fifteenth Century. *Speculum* 52, 870–899.

Foucault, Michel. 1972. *The Archeology of Knowledge and the Discourse on Language.* Trans. A.M.S. Smith. New York: Harper & Row.

Foucault, Michel. 1977. What Is an Author? In Donald Bouchard, ed. and trans., *Language, Counter-Memory, Practice: Selected Essays and Interviews*, pp. 113–138. Ithaca, N.Y.: Cornell University Press.

Fournier, Hannah S., and Delbert W. Russell. 1992. A Study of Sex-Role Stereotyping in the Oxford English Dictionary 2E. *Computers and the Humanities* 26, 13–20.

Freed, Lewis. 1939. The Sources of Johnson's Dictionary. Unpublished dissertation. Ithaca, N.Y.: Cornell University.

Frye, Northrop. 1967. The Problem of Spiritual Authority in the Nineteenth Century. In Richard Levine, ed., *Backgrounds to Victorian Literature*, pp. 120–136. San Francisco: Chandler.

Fumaroli, Marc. 1992, February 14. A Walk in the Desert: The Ghost in the Ruins of the French Literary Tradition. Trans. Robin Buss. *The Times Literary Supplement*, pp. 5–6.

Garber, Marjorie. 1987. *Shakespeare's Ghost Writers: Literature as Uncanny Causality.* New York: Methuen.

Gilbert, Sandra, and Susan Gubar. 1979. *Madwoman in the Attic: The Woman Writer and the Nineteenth-Century Literary Imagination.* New Haven, Conn.: Yale University Press.

Gissing, George. 1985 (orig. 1892). *Born in Exile.* London: Hogarth.

Gray, Jack. 1988. The Shakespeare Citations in the OED and Supplement. Unpublished paper. Waterloo, Ontario: University of Waterloo.

Gray, Jack. 1989. Milton and the *OED* Electronic Database. *Milton Quarterly* 23(2), 66–73.

Gray, Paul. 1989, March 27. A Scholarly Everest Gets Bigger: *The Oxford English Dictionary* Updates and Goes Electronic. *Time*, pp. 64, 68.

Greer, Germaine. 1986. Lady Love Your Cunt. In *The Madwoman's Underclothes: Essays and Occasional Writings, 1968–1985*, pp. 74–77. London: Pan Books.

Gross, John. 1991. *The Rise and Fall of the Man of Letters: English Literary Life since 1800.* Harmondsworth, U.K.: Penguin.

Guillory, John. 1983. *Poetic Authority.* New York: Columbia University Press.

Hake, H. M. 1932. Foreword. In *Catalogue of the National Portrait Gallery.* Oxford: Oxford University Press.

Halsband, R. 1956. *The Life of Lady Mary Wortley Montagu.* Oxford: Oxford University Press.

Harris, Roy. 1981. *The Language Myth.* London: Duckworth.

Harris, Roy. 1982, September 3. The History Men. *The Times Literary Supplement*, pp. 935–936.

Harris, Roy. 1988. Murray, Morre and the Myth. In Roy Harris, ed., *Linguistic Thought in England, 1914–1945*, pp. 1–26. London: Duckworth.

Harrison, Brian. 1982. Press and Pressure Groups in Modern Britain. In Joanne

Shattock and Michael Wolff, eds., *The Victorian Periodical Press: Samplings and Soundings*, pp. 261–296. Toronto: University of Toronto Press.

Harvey, Paul. 1967. *The Oxford Companion to English Literature*. 4th ed. Oxford: Oxford University Press.

Helgerson, Richard. 1992. *Forms of Nationhood: The Elizabethan Writing of England*. Chicago: University of Chicago Press.

Hobsbawm, E. J. 1987. *The Age of Empire, 1875–1914*. London: Weidenfeld & Nicholson.

Hopkins, Gerard Manley. 1956. *Further Letters of Gerard Manley Hopkins Including His Correspondence with Coventry Patmore*. 2d ed. Ed. Claude Colleer Abbot. London: Oxford University Press.

Horne, Donald. 1984. *The Great Museum: The Representation of History*. London: Pluto.

Houghton, Walter E., ed. 1966–1982. *Wellesley Guide to Victorian Literature, 1820–1900*. 4 vols. Toronto: University of Toronto Press.

Houghton, Walter E. 1982. Periodical Literature and the Articulate Classes. In Joanne Shattock and Michael Wolff, eds., *The Victorian Periodical Press: Samplings and Soundings*, pp. 2–28. Toronto: University of Toronto Press.

Howsam, Leslie. 1991. *Cheap Bibles: Nineteenth-Century Publishing and the British and Foreign Bible Society*. Cambridge: Cambridge University Press.

Hughes, Linda K., and Michael Lund. 1991. *The Victorian Serial*. Charlottesville: University Press of Virginia.

Hultin, Neil. 1985. The Web of Significance: Sir James Murray's Theory of Word Development. In *Information in Data*, pp. 41–56. Waterloo, Ontario: University of Waterloo Centre for the New OED.

Huxley, Julian. 1941. *The Uniqueness of Man*. London: Chatto & Windus.

Jansen, Sue Curry. 1991. *Censorship: The Knot that Binds Power and Knowledge*. New York: Oxford University Press.

Jespersen, Otto. 1982 (orig. 1906). *Growth and Structure of the English Language*. 10th ed. Chicago: University of Chicago Press.

Johnson, Samuel. 1968 (orig. 1765). Preface to Shakespeare. In Patrick Cruttwell, ed., *Selected Writings*, pp. 261–288. Harmondsworth, U.K.: Penguin.

Jones, Richard Foster. 1953. *The Triumph of the English Language: A Survey of Opinions Concerning the Vernacular from the Introduction of Printing to the Restoration*. Stanford, Calif.: Stanford University Press.

Kenner, Hugh. 1983. *A Colder Eye: The Modern Irish Writer*. New York: Alfred Knopf.

Kerr, N. R. 1985. The Migration of Manuscripts from the English Medieval Libraries. In *Books, Collectors, and Libraries: Studies in the Medieval Heritage*, pp. 459–470. London: Hambledon.

Kiberd, Declan. 1992, Janurary 3. Bloom the Liberator: The Androgynous Anti-Hero of *Ulysses* as the Embodiment of Joyce's Utopian Hopes. *The Times Literary Supplement*, pp. 3–6.

Koestler, Arthur. 1952. *Arrow in the Blue: An Autobiography*. New York: Macmillan.

Kramarae, Cheris, and Paula A. Treichler. 1985. *A Feminist Dictionary*. Boston: Pandora.

Kushner, Tony. 1989. *The Persistence of Prejudice: Antisemitism in British Society during the Second World War*. Manchester, U.K.: Manchester University Press.

Landau, Sidney I. 1985. The Expressions of Changing Social Values in Dictionaries. *Dictionaries* 7, 261–269.

Landau, Sidney I. 1989. *Dictionaries: The Art and Craft of Lexicography*. Cambridge: Cambridge University Press.

Laski, Marghanita. 1968, January 11. Reading for OED. *The Times Literary Supplement*, pp. 38–39.

Laski, Marghanita. 1972, October 13. Letter. *The Times Literary Supplement*, p. 1226.

Leonard, John. 1990. *Naming in Paradise: Milton and the Language of Adam and Eve*. Oxford: Oxford University Press.

Leonard, Sterling. 1962 (orig. 1929). *The Doctrine of Correctness in English Usage: 1700–1800*. New York: Russell and Russell.

Lipking, Lawrence. 1970. *The Ordering of the Arts in Eighteenth-Century England*. Princeton, N.J.: Princeton University Press.

Locke, John. 1965 (orig. 1689). *An Essay Concerning Human Understanding*. Ed. Maurice Cranston. New York: Collier.

Lowenstein, Joseph. 1988. The Script in the Marketplace. In Stephen Greenblatt, ed., *Representing the English Renaissance*, pp. 265–278. Berkeley: University of California Press.

Lucas, John. 1990. *England and Englishness: Ideas of Nationhood in English Poetry, 1688–1900*. London: Hogarth.

Lukacs, Georg. 1962. *The Historical Novel*. Trans. H. Mitchell and S. Mitchell. London: Merlin.

Lyons, Ponsonby A. 1900. Dictionary. In *The Encyclopædia Britannica*. 9th ed. New York: Werner.

McGann, Jerome J. 1989. *Toward a Literature of Knowledge*. Chicago: University of Chicago Press.

Machan, Tim William. 1991. Editing, Orality, and Late Middle English Texts. In A. N. Doane and Carol Braun Pasternack, eds., *Vox intexta: Orality and Textuality in the Middle Ages*, pp. 229–246. Madison: University of Wisconsin Press.

Mackey, William F. 1991. Language Diversity, Language Policy and the Sovereign State. *History of European Ideas* 13(1/2), 51–61.

McKusick, James C. 1992. "Living Words": Samuel Taylor Coleridge and the Genesis of the OED. *Modern Philology* 90(1), 1–45.

Merryman, John Henry. 1953–1954. The Authority of Authority: What the California Supreme Court Cited in 1950. *Stanford Law Review* 6, 613–673.

Mill, John Stuart. 1940 (orig. 1861). *Representative Government*. London: Everyman.

Mill, John Stuart. 1963 (orig. 1833). Thoughts on Poetry and Its Varieties. In *The Six Great Humanistic Essays of John Stuart Mill*, pp. 3–2. New York: Washington Square.

Miller, Edward. 1973. *That Noble Cabinet: A History of the British Museum*. London: Andre Deutsch.

Mills, Jane. 1989. *Womanwords: A Vocabulary of Culture and Patriarchal Society*. London: Virago.

Montagu, Mary Wortley. 1909 (orig. 1763). Inoculation for the Smallpox. In Henry Cabot Lodge and Francis Halsey, eds., *The Best of the World's Classics*. Vol. 4, pp. 63–65. New York: Funk & Wagnalls.

Morris, Brian, ed. 1981. Introduction. In William Shakespeare, *The Taming of the Shrew*. Ed. Arden. London: Methuen.

Morris, Richard, ed. 1893. *Cursor Mundi (The Cursor O the World): The Northumbrian Poem of the XIVth Century in Four Versions*. Vol. 1. London: Kegan Paul, Trench, Trübner.

Müller, Frederick Max. 1900. Aryan. In *The Encyclopædia Britannica*. 9th ed. New York: Werner.

Müller, Max. 1864. *Lectures on the Science of Language Delivered at the Royal Institution of Great Britain*. London: Longman, Green, Longman, Roberts, & Green.

Murray, James A. H. 1970. *The Evolution of English Lexicography*. The Romanes Lecture 1900. College Park, Md.: McGrath.

Nabokov, Vladimir. 1980. *Lectures on Literature*. Ed. F. Bowes. New York: Harcourt Brace Jovanovich.

Nairn, Thomas. 1977. *The Break-up of Britain*. London: New Left Books.

Ngũgĩ wa Thiong'o. 1981. Literature in Schools. In *Writers in Politics: Essays*, pp. 34–41. London: Heinemann.

Niranjana, Tejaswini. 1992. *Siting Translation: History, Post-Structuralism, and the Colonial Context*. Berkeley: University of California Press.

Olender, Maurice. 1992. *The Language of Paradise: Race, Religion, and Philology in the Nineteenth Century*. Trans. Arthur Goldhammer. Cambridge, Mass.: Harvard University Press.

Orwell, George. 1968. *The Penguin Essays of George Orwell*. Harmondsworth, U.K.: Penguin.

Palmer, D. J. 1965. *The Rise of English Studies: An Account of the Study of English Language and Literature from Its Origins to the Making of the Oxford English School*. Oxford: Oxford University Press.

Partridge, Eric. 1984 (orig. 1937). *A Dictionary of Slang and Unconventional English*. 8th ed. Ed. Paul Beale. New York: Macmillan.

Patterson, Annabel. 1984. *Censorship and Interpretation: The Conditions of Writing and Reading in Early Modern England*. Madison: University of Wisconsin Press.

Phillipps, K. C. 1984. *Language and Class in Victorian England*. Oxford: Basil Blackwell.

Poliakov, Léon. 1974. *The Aryan Myth: A History of Racist and Nationalist Ideas in Europe*. New York: New American Library.

Pope, Alexander, trans. 1870 (orig. 1720). *The Iliad of Homer*. Edinburgh: John Ross.

Pound, Ezra. 1935. *Literary Essays*. Ed. T. S. Eliot. New York: New Directions.

Pound, Ezra. 1950. *The Letters of Ezra Pound, 1907–1941*. Ed. D. D. Paige. New York: Harcourt, Brace & World.

Pound, Ezra. 1956. *The Cantos (1–95)*. New York: New Directions.

Raymond, Darrell R., and Yvonne L. Warburton. 1987. *Computerization of Lexicographical Activity on the New Oxford English Dictionary*. Waterloo, Ontario: University of Waterloo Centre of the New OED.

Reddick, Allen. 1990. *The Making of Johnson's Dictionary, 1746–1773*. Cambridge: Cambridge University Press.

Renan, Ernest. 1990 (orig. 1882). What Is a Nation? Trans. Martin Thom. In Homi K. Bhabha, ed., *Nation and Narration*, pp. 8–22. London: Routledge.

Richardson, Malcolm. 1980. Henry V, English Chancery, and Chancery English. *Speculum* 55(4), 726–750.

Ricks, Christopher. 1988. *T. S. Eliot and Prejudice*. London: Faber & Faber.

Riede, David. 1989. The Church of Literature and Carlyle. In Jerome McGann, ed., *Victorian Connections*, pp. 88–120. Charlottesville: University Press of Virginia.

Robertson, H. Rocke, and J. Wesley Robertson. 1989. *A Collection of Dictionaries and Related Works Illustrating the Development of the English Dictionary*. Vancouver: University of British Columbia Press.

Robinson, Jennifer. 1982. The Dictionary as Witness. *Dictionaries* 4, 110–117.

Rundell, Michael, and Penny Stock. 1992. The Corpus Revolution. *English Today* 8(2), 9–17; 8(3), 21–38; 8(4): 45–51.

Ruskin, John. N.d. *Sesame and Lilies, Etc.* London: Collins.

Ryle, John. 1978, April 28. Good Fad Guide. *The Times Literary Supplement*, p. 464.

Said, Edward. 1978. *Orientalism*. London: Routledge & Kegan Paul.

Said, Edward. 1983. *The World, the Text and the Critic*. Cambridge, Mass.: Harvard University Press.

Sam, Eric. 1992, March 6. Shakespeare and the Oxford Imprint. *The Times Literary Supplement*, p. 13.

Saussure, Ferdinand de. 1959. *Course in General Linguisitics*. Trans. Wade Baskin. New York: McGraw-Hill.

Schäfer, Jürgen. 1980. *Documentation in the O.E.D.: Shakespeare and Nashe as Test Cases*. Oxford: Oxford University Press.

Schäfer, Jürgen. 1987. Early Modern English: OED, New OED, EMED. In Richard W. Bailey, ed., *Dictionaries of English: Prospects for the Record of Our Language*, pp. 66–74. Ann Arbor: University of Michigan Press.

Schäfer, Jürgen. 1989. *Early Modern Lexicography: Additions and Corrections to the OED*. Vol. II. Oxford: Oxford University Press.

Shannon, Richard. 1974. *The Crisis of Imperialism, 1865–1915*. London: Hart-Davis, McGibbon.

Shapiro, Fred R. 1986. Yuppies, Yumpies, Yaps and Computer-Assisted Lexicography. *American Speech* 61, 139–46.

Shapiro, Karl. 1949, March. Prosody as the Meaning. *Poetry*, pp. 336–350.

Shattock, Joanne, and Michael Wolff, eds. 1982. Introduction. *The Victorian Periodical Press: Samplings and Soundings*. Toronto: University of Toronto Press.

Shaw, George Bernard. 1965. *Collected Letters, 1874–1897*. Ed. Dan H. Laurence. London: Max Reinhardt.

Shenker, Israel. 1989, April 3. Annals of Lexicography: The Dictionary Factory. *The New Yorker*, pp. 86–100.

Shevelow, Kathryn. 1989. *Women and Print Culture: The Construction of Femininity in the Early Periodical*. London: Routledge.

Sidney, Philip. 1970 (orig. 1595). *An Apology for Poetry*. Ed. Forrest G. Robinson. Indianapolis: Bobbs-Merrill.

Skeat, W. W. 1873. *Questions for Examination in English Literature: With an Introduction to the Study of English*. Cambridge: Cambridge University Press.

Sloman, Judith. 1985. *Dryden: The Poetics of Translation*. Prepared for publication by Anne McWhir. Toronto: University of Toronto Press.

Small, Ian. 1991. *Conditions for Criticism: Authority, Knowledge, and Literature in the Late Nineteenth Century*. Oxford: Oxford University Press.

Smith, Bromley. 1929. Queen Elizabeth at the Cambridge Disputations. *Quarterly Journal of Speech* 15(4), 495–502.

Smith, Oliva. 1984. *The Politics of Language, 1791–1819*. Oxford: Oxford University Press.

Southey, Robert. 1925. *The Lives and Works of the Uneducated Poets*. Ed. J. S. Childers. London: Humphrey Milford.

Spevack, Marvin. 1988. The Persistence of Shakespeare in Modern Dictionaries. In E. G. Stanley and T. F. Hoad, eds., *Words: For Robert Burchfield's Sixty-Fifth Birthday*, pp. 153–162. Cambridge: D. S. Brewer.

Starnes, DeWitt T. 1963. *Robert Estienne's Influence on Lexicography*. Austin: University of Texas Press.

Steiner, George. 1975. *After Babel: Aspects of Language and Translation*. New York: Oxford University Press.

Sullivan, Zohreh T. 1989. Race, Gender and Imperial Ideology: In the Nineteenth Century. *Nineteenth-Century Contexts* 134(1), 19–30.

Taylor, Gary. 1989. *Reinventing Shakespeare: A Cultural History from the Restoration to the Present*. New York: Oxford University Press.

Taylor, Talbot. 1990. Which Is to Be Master? The Institutionalization of Authority in the Science of Language. In John E. Joseph and Talbot J. Taylor, eds., *Ideologies of Language*, pp. 9–26. London: Routledge.

Teres, Harvey. 1991. Repression, Recovery, Renewal: The Politics of Expanding the Canon. *Modern Philology* 89(1), 63–75.

Tompa, Frank, and Darell Raymond. 1989. *Database Design for a Dynamic Dictionary*. Waterloo, Ontario: University of Waterloo Centre for the New OED.

Trench, Richard Chenevix. 1856 (orig. 1851). *On the Study of Words: Six Lectures, Addressed (Originally) to the Pupils at the Diocesan Training School, Winchester*. 7th ed. London: John Parker. (1892, 22d ed., with questions by Theodore Hunt. New York: Macmillan.)

Trench, Richard Chenevix. 1859. *A Select Glossary of English Words Used Formerly in Senses Different from Their Present*. London: Routledge.

Tricomi, A. H. 1979. *Milton and the Jonsonian Plain Style*. In James D. Simmonds, ed., *Milton Studies XIII*, pp. 129–144. Pittsburgh: University of Pittsburgh Press.

Ulysses and the Golden Rewrite. 1992, February 15. *The Globe & Mail* (reprinted from *The Economist*), p. D2.

Urdang, Lawrence. 1984, December. "To Plagiarize, or To Purloin, or To Borrow . . . ?" A Reply to Robert Burchfield. *Encounter*, pp. 71–73.

Vincent, John. 1992, January 31. Making the Syllabus. *The Times Literary Supplement*, pp. 6–7.

Wallins, Roger P. 1975. Victorian Periodicals and the Emerging Social Conscience. *Victorian Periodical Review* 8(2), 47–59.

Wansbrough, Henry. 1992, December 4. Giving the Plough-Boy the Word. *The Times Literary Supplement*, p. 7

Warburton, Yvonne. 1986. Finding the Right Words: An Account of Research for the Supplements to the Oxford English Dictionary. *Dictionaries* 8, 94–111.

Webb, R. K. 1955. *The British Working Class Reader, 1790–1848: Literacy and Social Tension*. London: George Allen & Unwin.

Weiner, Edmund S. C. 1989. Editing the OED in the Electronic Age. In *Dictionaries in the Electronic Age*, pp. 23–31. Waterloo, Ontario: University of Waterloo Centre for the New OED.

Weiner, Edmund S. C. 1990. The Federation of English. In Christopher Ricks and Leonard Michaels, eds., *The State of the Language*, pp. 492–502. Berkeley: University of California Press.

Wells, H. G. 1910. *The New Machiavelli*. New York: Duffield.

Wells, Ronald A. 1973. *Dictionaries and the Authoritarian Tradition: A Study in English Usage and Lexicography*. The Hague: Mouton.

Williams, Raymond. 1961. *The Long Revolution*. Harmondsworth, U.K.: Penguin.

Williams, Raymond. 1976. *Keywords: A Vocabulary of Culture and Society*. London: Fontana.

Willinsky, John. 1988a. Cutting English on the Bias: Five Lexicographers in Pursuit of the New. *American Speech* 63(1), 44–66.

Willinsky, John 1988b. *The Well-Tempered Tongue: The Politics of Standard English in the High School*. New York: Teachers College Press.

Willinsky, John. 1991. *The Triumph of Literature/The Fate of Literacy: Teaching English in the Secondary School*. New York: Teachers College Press.

Wollstonecraft, Mary. 1975 (orig. 1792). *Vindication of the Rights of Woman*. Harmondsworth, U.K.: Penguin.

Woolf, Virginia. 1929. *A Room of One's Own*. Toronto: McClelland & Stewart.

Woolford, John. 1982. Periodicals and the Practise of Literary Criticism, 1855–1864. In Joanne Shattock and Michael Wolff, eds., *The Victorian Periodical Press: Samplings and Soundings*, pp. 109–142. Toronto: University of Toronto Press.

Wordsworth, William. 1927 (orig. 1800). Observations Prefixed to the Second Edition of the "Lyrical Ballads." In Ernest Rhys, ed., *The Prelude to Poetry: The English Poets in Defence and Praise of Their Own Art*, pp. 168–198. London: Dent.

# Index

Words for which the *OED* definition is discussed in the text are indexed in italics.

and education, 25, 227n.3, 236n.7; national, 23, 201, 228n.12; and *OED*, 8, 13, 39, 44, 46, 56, 59–61, 74–75, 90–91, 95, 119, 185, 196; popular, 135–136, 185; and second edition of *OED*, 168–169, 194; and *Supplement*, 131–132, 147–161
Littré, Maximilien Paul Emile, 35, 50, 236n.1
loan words, 10, 104
Locke, John, 39–40, 226n.4
Longman, 199–200
Lowenstein, Joseph, 227n.4
Lucas, John, 201
Lukacs, Georg, 230n.4
Lund, Michael, 120
Lydgate, John, 96, 230n.1
Lyell, Charles, 37
Lyons, Posonby, A., 28, 226n.6

Macaulay, Thomas B., 24, 47, 119–120, 236n.7
McFadden, Cyra, 169, 172
McGann, Jerome, 150–151
Machan, Tim William, 227n.6
Mackey, William, 12, 236n.1
McKusick, James, 224n.5
*Macquarie Dictionary*, 226n.7
Malone, Edmund, 71
Malprelate, Martin, 181
*Manchester Guardian*, 159
*Manipulus Vocabulorum*, 80
Marquis, Don, 134
Marsh, Nagio, 185
Martineau, Harriet, 87, 185–186, 232n.8
Mayhew, Henry, 92
*Mechanics Magazine*, 181
Melbacke, Brian, 98
Merriam-Webster, 6
Merryman, John, 236n.4
Mill, John Stuart, 24, 36, 60, 68, 228n.10
Miller, Edward, 23
Mills, Jane, 235n.6
Milton, John, 22, 95–96, 101–103, 225n.7
Mitford, Mary Russell, 186
*modesty*, 78–79
Monroe, Harriet, 145–146
Montagu, Mary Wortley, 45, 184–185
Moore, Marianne, 109
More, Henry, 16
Morely, John, 120
Morris, Brian, 78

Morris, Richard, 116
Morris, William, 107
Müller, Friedrick Max, 35–38, 200, 234n.9
Murray, Ada, 42, 54
Murray, Aelfric, 52
Murray, Elisabeth, 33, 42–43, 49–50, 124–125, 225n.3
Murray, James A. H., 3, 7, 34, 35–56, 180–181, 202; career, 8, 38, 49, 51, 53–54, 225n.3, 226n.4; on education, 226n.6; on *OED*, 14, 31–32, 39, 44–48, 51, 62, 72, 77–78, 80, 92, 106, 117, 121, 162, 165, 196, 198, 200; *Evolution of English Lexicography*, 27, 37, 46, 48, 59, 178–179, 183, 207
Murray, John, 33
Murray, Jowett, 38

Nabokov, Vladimir, 233n.3
Nairn, Thomas, 202
Nashe, Thomas, 64, 72, 165
National Portrait Gallery, 23–24
*Nature*, 158
*New Dictionary of the English Language*, 21, 29–30, 62
*New English Dictionary*. See *Oxford English Dictionary*
*New Scientist*, 158
*New Statesman*, 158
Newton, Thomas, 101
*New Yorker*, 158, 173
*New York Times*, 169, 173
New Zealand, 131, 133, 236n.3
*New World of English Words*, 180
Nexis, 167, 199
Ngugi wa Thiong'o, 202–203
Nigeria, 236n.3
Niranjana, Tejaswini, 47, 230n.6
*Nonsense of Common-Sense,*, 184
*Northern Star*, 181

*Observer*, 159
Olender, Maurice, 36, 230n.5
Oliphant, Margaret, 122, 186
O'Neill, Eugene, 168
*On the Aim, Plan, and Completion of Greek Dictionaries*, 225n.8
Onions, Charles T., 49–50, 128
Opie, Iona, 157, 171
Opie, Peter, 157, 171
Orsman, H., 131